Upholding Indigenous Economic Relationships

Shalene Wuttunee Jobin

Upholding Indigenous Economic Relationships

Nehiyawak Narratives

UBCPress · Vancouver · Toronto

© UBC Press 2023

All rights reserved. No part of this publication may be reproduced, stored in a retrieval system, or transmitted, in any form or by any means, without prior written permission of the publisher, or, in Canada, in the case of photocopying or other reprographic copying, a licence from Access Copyright, www.accesscopyright.ca.

Printed in Canada on FSC-certified ancient-forest-free paper (100% post-consumer recycled) that is processed chlorine- and acid-free.

Library and Archives Canada Cataloguing in Publication

Title: Upholding Indigenous economic relationships : nehiyawak narratives/ Shalene Wuttunee Jobin.
Names: Jobin, Shalene Wuttunee, author.
Description: Includes bibliographical references and index.
Identifiers: Canadiana (print) 20220441855 | Canadiana (ebook) 20220442010 | ISBN 9780774865104 (hardcover) | ISBN 9780774865203 (softcover) | ISBN 9780774865258 (PDF) | ISBN 9780774865302 (EPUB)
Subjects: LCSH: Indigenous peoples—Canada—Economic conditions. | LCSH: Economics—Canada—Sociological aspects. | LCSH: Commerce—Social aspects— Canada. | LCSH: Exchange—Social aspects—Canada. | LCSH: Value—Social aspects—Canada. | LCSH: Indigenous peoples—Canada—Social conditions. | LCSH: Canada—Race relations. | LCSH: Canada—Ethnic relations.
Classification: LCC E98.E2 J63 2023 | DDC 330.90089/97071—dc23

Canadä

UBC Press gratefully acknowledges the financial support for our publishing program of the Government of Canada (through the Canada Book Fund), the Canada Council for the Arts, and the British Columbia Arts Council.

This book has been published with the help of a grant from the Canadian Federation for the Humanities and Social Sciences, through the Awards to Scholarly Publications Program, using funds provided by the Social Sciences and Humanities Research Council of Canada.

Printed and bound in Canada by Friesens
Set in Meta Pro, Baskerville 10, and Garamond by Artegraphica Design Co.
Copy editor: Audrey McClellan
Proofreader: Caitlin Gordon-Walker
Indexer: Kel Perro
Cover designer: Gerilee McBride
Cover images: *This Painting is a Mirror,* Christi Belcourt, Collection of the Indigenous Art Centre, Gatineau, Quebec

UBC Press
The University of British Columbia
2029 West Mall
Vancouver, BC V6T 1Z2
www.ubcpress.ca

To five generations of Wuttunee women, including:

My cousins (nîtisânak ᓃᑎᓵᓇᐠ*), Loretta (nikâwiy* ᓂᑳᐏᕀ*), Lillian Marie (nohkom* ᓄᐦᑯᒼ*), Martha (nicâpân* ᓂᒑᐹᐣ*), and Marie (Lillian's nohkom* ᓄᐦᑯᒼ*)*

Contents

List of Figures / ix

List of Cree Syllabics / xi

Preface / xii

Acknowledgments / xiv

1 Grounding Methods / 3

2 Grounding Economic Relationships / 22

3 nehiyawak Peoplehood and Relationality / 41

4 Canada's Genesis Story / 62

5 ᐅᐧᐦᑎᑯ Warnings of Insatiable Greed / 80

6 Indigenous Women's Lands and Bodies / 94

7 Theorizing Cree Economic and Governing Relationships / 108

8 Colonial Dissonance / 136

9 Principles Guiding Cree Economic Relationships / 152

10 Renewed Relationships through Resurgent Practices / 182

11 Upholding Relations / 205

Postscript / 213

Glossary of Cree Terms / 215

Notes / 221

References / 230

Index / 244

Figures

1 Star chart / xi

2 Lillian Wuttunee and her daughters, 1986 / 4

3 One metaphor of Indigenous research / 6

4 A nehiyawak ᗡᵸᐃᐳᐊᐟ peoplehood methodology / 8

5 Map of the territory of the natimîwiyiniwak ᐊᑎᒢᐃᐧᔭᓂᐊᐟ (Upstream People) / 9

6 A metaphor of a livelihood economy / 16

7 nimosôm ᓂᒍᔾᐨ (Grandpa) Gilbert Wuttunee, nimosôm ᓂᒍᔾᐨ (Grand Uncle) Gavin Wuttunee, and nicâpân ᓂᒡᐸᐣ (Great Grandpa) James Wuttunee (n.d.) / 25

8 Plains Cree camp, 1870 / 48

9 Cree flat boat on the Montreal River, Saskatchewan, 1890 / 56

10 Plains sign language for "Exchange" / 58

11 Letter from Alexander Morris, Lieutenant Governor, to George McDougall, Methodist Minister (9 August 1875) / 72

12 Department of Indian Affairs "pass book" for Red Pheasant First Nation, 1918; Business: "Going to Piapot for Horses" / 78

13 *Land / Body*, by Erin Marie Konsmo / 95

14 Al's Facebook post / 96

15 Cree economic and governing relationships / 110

16 Flying Dust Co-operative Garden / 190

17 Beaded okinewâpikonew ᐅᑭᓄᐋᐧᑯᐱᑯᓄᐤ / 206

18 nihtâwihcikewin pîcicíwin: Creation's Round Dance / 211

19 Deer tracks around the perimeter of the Cardinal studio / 212

Cree Syllabics

I WAS TAUGHT SYLLABICS through the cahkipehikanak ᒋᑊᐱᐩᐃᑲᐩᐊᐠ or Star Chart method, encompassing forty-four syllabic symbols and fourteen consonant syllabic symbols.

There is a glossary of terms at the back of the book.

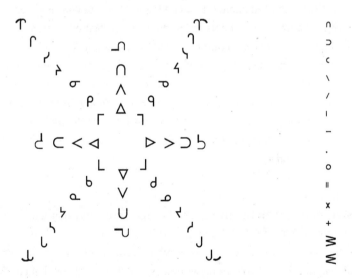

1 cahkipehikanak ᒋᑊᐱᐩᐃᑲᐩᐊᐠ (star chart)

Preface

Cᐧᐤ, Shalene Marie Charlotte Wuttunee Jobin ᓂ∩ᔑᔅᐦᑲᕑᐤ.
ᓂᐦᐃᐧᓯᔅᐦᑲᕑᑲᐃᐧᑲᓇᐃᐧᑯ ᓲᐦᑐᒫ Ȧᐧᐦᐃᐃᐧᐣᐊᐧᐊᐧᐤ. Loretta Wuttunee ᓂᑲᐃᐧᔭ. ᓂᑲᐃᐧᔭ ᐟᐦᐃᓓᐊᐧ ᐅᐦᐨ ᐱᐦᐁᐅᐸᑊᐱᐟᑯᕿ ᐣᐸᐦᐊᐣᑲᓂᐊᐧᐠ ᐊᐦᐃᐧᔓ ᒥᑭᔑ ᐊᐧᐨᐧx. Fred Jobin ᓉᐦᒐᐧᐧᐠᐸᐧᐩ, Ȧᐧᐩ ᐱᐦᐊᐱᐦᒐᐧᐟᔑᐦᓂᐊᐧᐧ ᐅᐦᐨ ᒥᔑᒫᐤᑐᐅᐧ. ᐯᔓᓂᐱᐦᑭᓂᔓ ᐅᐸᐟᑯᐦ ᐃᐣᐅᐦᐦᑲᐦᐸᐃᐧ. Kevin Jobin ᓂᐸᐧᐁᐨ ᐅᐦᐨ ᒍᔑᕐᔓ ᐁᑲᐧ Kingston ᓂᑯᐟᕑᕑᐧᐧᐸᐧᐩ

Welcome, my full name is Shalene Marie Charlotte Wuttunee Jobin. I carry both my grandmothers' middle names. Marie is a name that links at least five generations of Wuttunee women. My mother's maiden name is Loretta Wuttunee. I also carry Wuttunee as a middle name. My mother is Plains Cree and we are both citizens of Red Pheasant Cree First Nation, also known as the Eagle Hills in Treaty Six territory. My late father was Fred Jobin; he was Métis-Cree from Big Prairie in northern Alberta. My husband is Kevin Jobin from Moosomin Cree First Nation, and our son is Kingston.

I AM SITTING IN A VEHICLE driving east through Treaty Six territory. It is opiniyâwewipîsim ᐅᐱᓂᔭᐁᐧᐅᐧᐃᐧᐱᓯᕞᐢ, the leaf budding moon, of 2021. It is warm and sunny and there is new life on the trees, which can also be seen in the newborn animals we pass. It has been a long winter, especially with the global pandemic. I feel both nervous and excited about completing this book. While driving

xii

through the prairies, I reflect on the people who have encouraged me through the years.

When I was still in high school, nikâwîsipan ᓂᐸᐃᕆᐸᓨ (my late "little mom," or aunt) Elsie Wuttunee encouraged me to continue my education with a business degree; she said we needed more Indigenous women in business. I did as I was told. I loved my degree, and in my last year (2000–01), I took two Indigenous studies courses with Métis scholar Chris Andersen that changed the trajectory of my career. Through these two disciplines of business and Indigenous studies, I was introduced to both the benefits and complexities of capitalism. In 2003, I submitted a final paper in my first term of a master's degree in Indigenous governance in which I explored questions of Indigenous economic relationships. I asked whether Indigenous peoples need to be economically independent from the Canadian state to achieve self-determination; I also asked about the implications of this trajectory.

This book is the culmination of two decades of thinking about visions of self-determination and economic relationships through an Indigenous lens that upholds treaties. Against the background of that vision, I acknowledge that I also deal with the dissonance of being grounded in capitalism. I offer this work as a different lens through which to see the economy and to think through the economic dimensions of colonialism. I also offer this work with the words of nohtâwîpan ᓄᐦᑖᐃᐸᓨ (my late father) and nohcâwîs ᓄᐦᒑᐃᐢ (my "little father," or uncle) in my mind. I believe my late father would caution me against being too ideological. I also recall that my uncle Winston Wuttunee once shared with me the fact that he grew up without indoor plumbing, adding that there were many modern-day conveniences he now appreciated. I share this to acknowledge that the current primary economic system we live in has been responsible for many achievements. The story of capitalism's material advantages is one we all know well. This work seeks to add something to the story of capitalism by looking at its intersection with colonialism and examining how Indigenous approaches and understandings of livelihood and economics could help us sketch out a different economic future; a future where all our relations may have miyo-pimâtisiwin ᒥᔪ ᐱᒫᓂᓯᐃᓨ (the good life).

Acknowledgments

KITATAMIHIN ᏢᏟᏟᎱᎱᎾᎪᎢ Thank you to the Cree Elders and knowledge holders from the expanse of Treaty Six territory, who so generously gifted me with their time, guidance, and words. Also, thank you to Dorothy Thunder, for being a mentor to me by her example of how to live nêhiyaw pimâtisiwin ᏆᏦᎪᏀᎾ ᎪᏞᏂᏒᎪᎁ, the Cree life. Dorothy is a knowledge holder and expert in nehiyawewin ᏆᏦᎪᏀᏄᎪᎁ. She reviewed my usage of nehiyawewin ᏆᏦᎪᏀᏄᎪᎁ and copy-edited my standard roman orthography and syllabics spelling (Y dialect). All mistakes are my own. Reuben Quinn taught me Cree syllabics and a way of learning nehiyawewin ᏆᏦᎪᏀᏄᎪᎁ that is grounded in our creation stories, our star stories, and our ways of relating to all living beings. Thank you to colleagues, peer reviewers, graduate students, friends, and family who have read over some or all of this manuscript, in different iterations, and given feedback: Matt Wildcat, Tracy Bear, Rob Innes, Priscilla Settee, Tara Kappo, Loretta (née Wuttunee) Jobin, Avery Letendre, Jade Tootoosis, Javed Sommers, Chris Andersen, Elmer Ghostkeeper, Brock Pitawanakwat, Jeff Corntassel, Johanne Johnson, Mandee McDonald, Naomi McIlwraith, Kirsten Lindquist, Emily Riddle, and Frank Tough.

I started this book project in the fall of 2011. Although the seeds were planted a decade earlier, the formal research and writing began during my interdisciplinary PhD in political science and Indigenous studies (2009–14). I would like to thank my doctoral co-supervisors, Val Napoleon and Isabel Altamirano-Jiménez; my committee members, Robert Nichols and

Dwayne Donald; and my external examiner, Kiera Ladner. Thank you to SSHRC for a doctoral fellowship and now a Canada Research Chair in Indigenous Governance (Tier II).

kitatamihin ᑭᑕᑕᒥᐦᐃᐣ to those Indigenous leaders who carry out the tireless work to hold Indigenous studies space in academia. I have appreciated the support of the Native Studies Writing Group, currently including writers Tasha Hubbard, Nancy Van Styvendale, Crystal Fraser, Sarah Nickels, Nicole Lugosi, and myself. Thank you to Brian Calliou and the beauty of the Banff Centre, including the Banff Centre for Indigenous Leadership and Management, for hosting me through the Fleck fellowship, at the foot of Buffalo Mountain during a month-long residence at the end of the winter in 2018.

My mother and my late father passed on a fierce pride in our peoples. My mother's thirst for knowledge and my father's practical need for action have been tools I rely on in work and in life. My grandparents – Lillian Wuttunee, Gilbert Wuttunee, Helen Chalifoux, and Joseph Jobin – and great-grandparents sacrificed so much for their future generations. Thank you to my brother Don, sister-in-law Trudy, nieces, and the cousins who I grew up with like siblings; to my aunts and uncles who are my little parents; and to ninâpem ᓂᐋᐧᐸᕽ 's family who are now my own – you all inspire me with your lived examples of being Indigenous in the twenty-first century. To my late childhood best friend, Katrina Byer (1978–2020), for always having my back. To the "SLAK" and "SANS" groups of women, your friendships help me navigate the world and remind me to have fun.

Finally, to ninâpem ᓂᐋᐧᐸᕽ Kevin (Moosomin First Nation, Treaty Six), and to nikosisinân ᓂᑯᓯᓯᓈᐣ Kingston: thank you for all you teach me, including grounding me in our own small version of miyo-pimâtisiwin ᒥᐅ ᐱᒫᑎᓯᐃᐧᐣ.

kitatamihin ᑭᑕᑕᒥᐦᐃᐣ thank you, you make me smile.

ACKNOWLEDGMENTS XV

Upholding Indigenous Economic Relationships

1

Grounding Methods

AS I WRITE THESE WORDS, I look out the window of my apartment onto the bend in the North Saskatchewan River. kisiskâciwani-sîpiy ᑭᓯᐢᑲᕐᐊᐧᓂ ᔫᐱᐧ, swift-flowing river, is created from the joining of the North and South Saskatchewan Rivers with its headwaters beginning in the Rocky Mountains (Newton 2009). It is the kisepîsim ᑭᓴᐱᓯᒼ, Great moon month, January in 2016, and the river is frozen, yet still alive. The banks of the river tell an archaeological and geological tale. The river has an ancient history, and yet it is still carving spaces in the present; so, too, are the Cree and other Indigenous peoples. Like my people, this river has witnessed many changes, and yet constants remain. In this work I draw from the time-honoured words of the past that still flow into our collective presents and futures.

The North Saskatchewan River flowed through nohkom's (grandmother's) blood too. I had the good fortune to live with my maternal grandmother as a teenager and as a young adult. My maternal grandmother, Lillian, and grandfather, Gilbert Wuttunee, were born in Red Pheasant Cree First Nation, in Saskatchewan (Treaty Six territory). My grandmother was born in 1914 and my grandfather in 1892. We belong to the sîpîwiyiniwak ᔫᐱᐊᐧᔭᓂᐊᐧᐠ, the River Cree, with the North Saskatchewan River being part of our identity. My mother taped an oral account of Lillian in 1993, and these are my grandmother's own words:

> My father's mother, Marie, first taught me to set snares. She was the younger of the two sisters that my grandfather had for wives before

3

he died in 1904. When the missionaries came to the reserve, he was told he could only keep one wife, and so Marie moved into a separate house. It was behind my parents' home, but when it caught fire and burned down, she moved in with us.

I used to follow behind her as she gathered medicines and listen as she told me what they were used for. I was very young and can only recall her saying, ayîkotâsima (this is frogs' pants) and this is good medicine. She would wrap the different medicines in a little calico cloth and just by smell alone she could tell the names of the different roots and herbs. She also used to dig for Seneca roots, which she would tell me she was going to sell to Chinese people. Having been taught to taste the leaves and barks on the bushes of the berries we picked, I could tell you blindfolded a chokecherry from a raspberry or Saskatoon bush. (L. Wuttunee 1993)

My grandmother, Lillian Wuttunee (Figure 2), chose to record these words, this account, and numerous others for her descendants. She understood the importance of natural medicines, and the knowledge her own ohkomimâw ᐅᐦᑯᒥᒫᐤ (grandmother) carried as a Cree woman. Her stories connect five generations of Cree women, linking my great-great-nohkom Marie's story to my own. I am proud to carry Marie's name as my middle name.[1]

2 Lillian Wuttunee with her daughters in Saskatchewan, 1986. From left to right: Loretta (née Wuttunee) Jobin, Mary Wuttunee, Elsie Wuttunee, Lillian Wuttunee, Amy (née Wuttunee) Eustergerling, and Yvonne Wuttunee.

My grandmother told me stories about trade with non-Cree people, including relationships with animals and other nonhuman beings (for example, plants). Lillian's words bring to the forefront a different form of teaching and learning. These teachings stem from her Cree knowledge, her connection to the land, and her identity as a woman. Lillian's oral history speaks to her resistance to assimilation and the importance of passing down her knowledge to us as a way to reclaim Cree teachings. Her full account conveys the importance of harvesting and hunting, and how these practices were cultivated in her from a young age.

When I was in my twenties, I asked my nohcâwîs ᒧᐦᒑᐏᐢ (my "little father," or uncle),[2] Winston Wuttunee, to explain the concept of self-determination in the Cree language. He explained it as nehiyaw-askiy ᓀᐦᐃᔭᐊᐢᑭᕀ. Cree people are called nehiyawak ᓀᐦᐃᔭᐊᐠ, with the root being newo ᓀᐅᐧ, or the word for "four" in the Cree language. askîy ᐊᐢᑮᕀ is the Cree word for "the land." He explained that we are the four-spirited people of the land, and that self-determination means we are able to live out our roles and the responsibilities that we have to the air, water, earth, and animal kingdom (W. Wuttunee 2003). When I use the term "land" in this study, I am referring to the air, water, earth (including trees, etc.), and animals. In this view, self-determination is intimately linked to our connections to the land. Another aspect of the Cree view of the world is that the land, water, trees, and so on – which I refer to as nonhuman beings – are all considered alive, and that we live in reciprocal relationships not only with people and animals, but also with the landscape and waterscape.[3] These relationships are demonstrated within Cree stories. I explore this through a nehiyawak peoplehood process.

nehiyawak ᓀᐦᐃᔭᐊᐠ Peoplehood Methodology

At every step in this research, the stories I write about bring a different lens to my project. The Indigenous methodology, the archival research, the oral histories, and the interviews, for example, present different interlocking perspectives on my study. As if looking into a river from different vantage points, when I envision Cree economic thought through oral histories, I see an intricate pattern of practices guiding these relationships with all living beings. Stand in another place with the archival research, and the complexities of twentieth- and twenty-first-century lives come into play. Moving to a third vantage point, in the interviews with knowledge holders I see the landscape of resurgence. From these vantage points, I begin to see the ways

3 One metaphor of Indigenous research.

in which individual life stories and community practice, grounded in history and consciousness, evolve from a series of choices – individual and collective choices made against the landscapes and waterscapes of Indigenous territory. Like a river, our picture of Cree economic relationships and their connection to the land shimmers into new focus every time we change the line of sight. Each angle yields an image that seems sharp, detailed, and complete, but there are many such sites on a river, none of which fully registers all the elements of its beauty.

In Figure 3, we see the roots of a tree representing Indigenous world views (ontology).[4] From there we can see the trunk of the tree representing a system of knowledge (epistemology). The methodology, the system of methods used for a study, is represented by the branch system. The leaves represent different methods, which can be seen as flowing all the way from the roots of the tree, and the tree roots are in relationship with other roots in a forest.

My goal is to share with readers the Cree knowledge holders' points of view, which they gifted to me. I explore oral traditions and examine secondary research with the purpose of identifying alternative Indigenous economic relations, relations that are not captured in characteristic understandings of Indigenous economic development. To do this, I use what I call a "nehiyawak peoplehood methodology," drawing on Indigenous methodologies and Indigenous and non-Indigenous methods. A methodology can be seen in general terms as a process for gathering knowledge. The methodology we use answers the question of why we use certain methods and not others. A method could be completing interviews or a survey. I see the nehiyawak peoplehood methodology as one example of an Indigenous resurgent methodology.

Currently, innovative Indigenous research methods are being developed as part of a resurgent paradigm. I call these "resurgent methodologies" and "resurgent methods." These methods focus on Indigenous peoples rebuilding their communities as part of the research process. I am conceptualizing the use of an Indigenous resurgent methodology, which draws from the peoplehood model (Holm, Pearson, and Chavis 2003; Jobin 2013). Cherokee Indigenous studies scholar Jeff Corntassel (2012, 89) explains that a "peoplehood model provides a useful way of thinking about the nature of everyday resurgence practices both personally and collectively. If one thinks of peoplehood as the interlocking features of language, homeland, ceremonial cycles, and sacred living histories, a disruption to any one of these practices threatens all aspects of everyday life." An Indigenous resurgent methodology includes the development of innovative Indigenous research methods, in collaboration with Indigenous communities, that uphold Indigenous languages, Indigenous lands, Indigenous ceremonial cycles, and Indigenous living histories in the research process itself. In this way the process is constitutive of the societies we are rebuilding from a space that upholds those deeply rooted Indigenous knowledges.

I am grounding the peoplehood model in the nehiyawak ᓀᐦᐃᔭᐘᐠ, the Cree, while also using this model as a methodological process. With settler colonialism, the four aspects of the lives of nehiyawak ᓀᐦᐃᔭᐘᐠ – language, territory, ceremonial cycles, and living histories – were disrupted. In the process of conducting research for this project, I interacted with these four aspects as I gathered knowledge.

I developed Figure 4, which displays the different elements within the nehiyawak ᓀᐦᐃᔭᐘᐠ peoplehood methodology, to show the interconnection among the four elements. The overlapping circles and dotted lines illustrate this interconnection. I chose a dotted background to convey further the connections among all spheres. The leaves are discussed more in the conceptual framework (see Figure 6). In the north is nehiyawewin, which is the Cree language. For nehiyawewin, I use both standard roman orthography (SRO) and syllabics in the Plains Y dialect. In SRO the consensus is

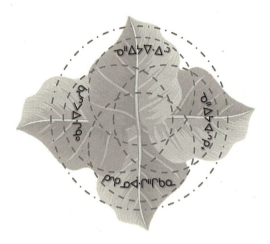

4 A nehiyawak ᓀᐦᐃᔭᐊᐧᐠ peoplehood methodology.

to never capitalize (see Okimāsis and Wolvengrey 2008).[5] In the east is nehiyawaskiy, or Cree territory. The south represents ceremonies, kiskinowâcihcikana. The west is kasispowicikew, meaning "bringing the past to the future." Throughout this project, I drew from these four elements, which formed the foundation of the methodology for my gathering of knowledge.

I focus on paskwâwiyiniw ᐸᐢᑲᐧᐃᐧᔨᓂᐤ (Plains Cree) knowledge, specifically that of the natimîwiyiniwak ᓇᑎᒦᐃᐧᔨᓂᐊᐧᐠ (Upstream People). The Upstream People have nested layers of governance and regional groupings within this larger grouping, including:

- the amiskowacîwiyiniwak ᐊᒥᐢᑯᐊᐧᒌᐃᐧᔨᓂᐊᐧᐠ (Beaver Hills Cree)
- the sîpîwiyiniwak ᓰᐲᐃᐧᔨᓂᐊᐧᐠ (River Cree)
- the paskohkopâwiyiniwak ᐸᐢᑯᐦᑯᐹᐃᐧᔨᓂᐊᐧᐠ (Parklands Cree)
- the wâskahikaniwiyiniwak ᐋᐧᐢᑲᐦᐃᑲᓂᐃᐧᔨᓂᐊᐧᐠ (House Cree).

The paskwâwiyiniw ᐸᐢᑲᐧᐃᐧᔨᓂᐤ (Plains Cree) negotiated Treaty Six, a peace and friendship treaty, in 1876 with the British Crown. Treaty Six also includes the sakâwiyiniwak ᓴᑳᐃᐧᔨᓂᐊᐧᐠ (Northern Plains Cree), Nakoda, Nakawē, Dënesųłįné, and other Indigenous peoples. Within these historical governance systems there are now over forty-five different First Nations' communities party to Treaty Six in central Saskatchewan and Alberta. As one example, Red Pheasant First Nation citizens include people who were

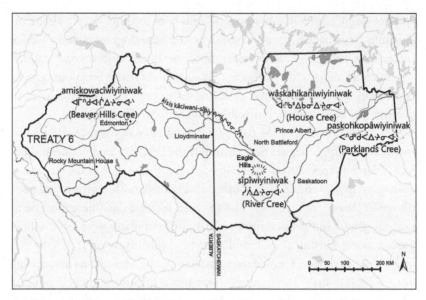

5　Map of the territory of the natimîwiyiniwak ᓇᐦᑏᐃᐧᔨᓂᐊᐧᐠ (Upstream People). | Cartographer Tracy Howlett.

historically from the sîpîwiyiniwak ᓰᐲᐃᐧᔨᓂᐊᐧᐠ (River Cree). I interviewed natimîwiyiniwak ᓇᐦᑏᐃᐧᔨᓂᐊᐧᐠ (Upstream People) throughout Treaty Six in both Alberta and Saskatchewan and I introduce them by their connections to this historic goverenance system.

To locate the Upstream Plains Cree geographically, I have provided a map of the North Saskatchewan River and the Battle River (Figure 5).[6] At the time Treaty Six was negotiated, the Alberta and Saskatchewan borders did not exist. On my mother's side, we belong to the sîpîwiyiniwak ᓰᐲᐃᐧᔨᓂᐊᐧᐠ (River Cree); this connection to kisiskâciwani-sîpiy ᑭᓯᐢᑳᒋᐊᐧᓂ ᓰᐱᕀ (the North Saskatchewan River system) forms part of our identity, as well as our being from the Eagle Hills. I grew up mostly in amiskwacî-wâskahikan ᐊᒥᐢᑲᐧᒌᐋᐧᐢᑲᐦᐃᑲᐣ, Beaver Mountain House (Edmonton), and kisiskâciwani-sîpiy ᑭᓯᐢᑳᒋᐊᐧᓂ ᓰᐱᕀ is what connects me to the places in Treaty Six that formed me.

Grounded Governance

You might ask why I am upholding this historic Plains Cree governance system. Sunney, from the amiskowacîwiyiniwak ᐊᒥᐢᑯᐋᐧᒌᐃᐧᔨᓂᐊᐧᐠ (Beaver Hills Cree), shared with me the concept of mônah-asiskiya ᒨᓇᐦ ᐊᓯᐢᑭᔭ, meaning to dig at the dirt to create that bond or that endearment to one

GROUNDING METHODS 9

another (see Chapter 7). As someone who tries to think deeply about Indigenous governance, I am intrigued by the genealogy of governance for Indigenous peoples – for example, how the First Nations band council system came along with the *Indian Act* system. As this is what our current generation has always known, it is helpful to dig at the ground a bit to uncover our connections, our wâhkohtôwin ᐘᐦᑯᐦᑐᐎᐣ (kinship).

In *Elder Brother and the Law of the People*, Plains Cree scholar Robert Innes convincingly argues that kinship is the best way to describe and define Indigenous peoples on the Plains. Specifically, he shows how we cannot underplay the importance of kinship in Plains band formation and continuation (Innes 2013, 70). He also provides historic documentation demonstrating how Indigenous groups in the northern plains were multi-ethnic groups along kinship lines established in the nehiyaw-pwat ᓀᐦᐃᔭᐅ ᐸᐧᐟ, or Iron Alliance/Iron Confederacy, formed in the early 1800s and lasting until 1870 (60–611). The nehiyaw-pwat was a historic trade and military alliance between the Plains Cree, Assiniboine (Nakoda Sioux), Saulteaux (Nakawē), Métis, and Haudenosaunee who travelled west. Innes demonstrates how wîsahkecâhk ᐄᓴᐦᑫᒑᕽ stories provide teachings around maintaining kinship roles and responsibilities, found within the larger historic legal system to maintain harmony in the family, camp, and community (37). The kinship practices found within Elder Brother stories help to explain how making kin with others, including through adoption and with people outside your own people group, fits within these philosophical principles (42).

Storytelling and Oral Histories

Storytelling as a methodology fits under the oral-history rubric. As Indigenous peoples often come from oral societies, storytelling honours an Indigenous world view and can be a useful decolonization technique that presents a counter-history to Canada's well-documented story:

> Storytelling also taught us about resistance to colonialism – our people have resisted even when legislation attempted to assimilate our children. All stories have something to teach us. What is most important is to learn to listen [to], not simply hear, the words that storytellers have to share. Many stories from First Nations tell a counter-story to that of the documented history of First Nations in Canada. (Robina Thomas 2005, 241)

Beyond providing a counter-history, storytelling can be used as a medium through which to communicate rights and jurisdictional boundaries that have political impact (Robina Thomas 2005, 240). The literature on oral-history research discusses the power embedded within stories that enables communities "to give testimony to their collective 'herstories' and struggles" (L.T. Smith 2005, 89); inherent in stories are ontological teachings and empowering motivators for "transformative praxis" (L.T. Smith 2005, 89). Chamberlin and Vale (2010, para. 8) equate the work of scholars with storytelling: "We [scholars] tell old stories. And we make up new ones. We call the first teaching, and the second research; but whatever we call them, it puts us in an ancient tradition of elders, experts and eccentrics, telling tales and singing songs."

There are different types of stories within Indigenous perspectives. Beyond providing a counter-history, storytelling can be used as a medium by which to decolonize our societies and rebuild them through a "self-conscious traditionalism" (Alfred 2008). As well, oral tradition in general should be seen as a social activity (Cruikshank 1998, 41) that gives us tools for living well today.

Part of my method for exploring Indigenous stories was inspired by the work of Val Napoleon and Hadley Friedland (2016) and their engagement with stories related to Indigenous legal traditions. They explain how they built on the work of Anishinaabe legal scholar John Borrows's approach of retelling Indigenous stories as legal cases and using the case method used in law (Friedland and Napoleon 2015, 22; see Borrows 2002, 16–20). I draw from the understanding that these stories can be useful today, informing such different Indigenous governance practices as legal orders and economic relations. To understand Indigenous legal orders, Napoleon and Friedland (2016) apply an adapted version of a common-law instrument, the case-brief analysis and synthesis, to Indigenous stories. The results have produced a guide for understanding and articulating Indigenous legal orders. Indigenous communities have responded very favourably to engaging with their own legal orders through the knowledge held within their own stories. One way in which my method differs from that of Napoleon and Friedland's is that, instead of using an adapted case-brief analysis, I draw from the principles of grounded theory,[7] such that analytical categories emerge from within the stories. I believe the methods (stories, language, ceremonies, land-based, etc.) we use to gather knowledge are important, and so in this way, I see the nehiyawak peoplehood methodology as resurgent.

Over a six-month period in 2012, I collected and became familiar with over 160 Cree stories that could be characterized as sacred stories, legends, creation stories, historical accounts, and personal stories. I explored these stories in relation to Cree economic relationships, using grounded-theory software to track and code all words and concepts that had a connection to economic relationships. I initially coded these stories in the fall of 2012; then, in the spring and summer of 2013, I repeated this process, recoding the stories in an iterative process. The strength of grounded theory lies in how themes emerge from within the text. For example, the principle of reciprocity was referenced seventeen different times in thirteen stories or interviews. I did not use a scanning function to find these words; I simply read the stories over and over. This meant that, for instance, examples that referred to the concept or idea of reciprocity but did not use the specific word "reciprocity" were included. Another aspect of this process was developing the relationships among the concepts. In some cases I nested up to four levels of topics under one concept. Through a series of iterations, several themes emerged that became the focus of Chapters 7 to 11.

My next step was to take my intuitive understanding and way of theorizing the historical data back to Cree knowledge holders for their feedback and guidance, and as a measure against which to understand their sense of how (and whether) these principles continue to guide Cree economic relationships. I also asked for guidance regarding what cultural or ceremonial knowledge should be shared in this work. A snowball technique was used to gather participants, whose responses and feedback were extremely valuable.[8] I approached knowledge holders in each of the regions of the Upstream Plains Cree (the Beaver Hills Cree, the House Cree, the Parklands Cree, and the River Cree). I interviewed thirteen people, sometimes more than once; eight interviewees identified as women and five as men. Approximately half of the interviews were conducted in various Treaty Six areas of Saskatchewan and half in various Treaty Six areas of Alberta.

Pseudonyms are used to identify those interviewed. This was on the recommendation of two of the Elders interviewed, and with the agreement of all those interviewed. The interview subjects also chose their own pseudonyms. Sunney, one of the knowledge keepers interviewed, told me that he had previously been misrepresented by scholars; as a result, he was very cautious about interviews. Besides using a pseudonym, he and the others interviewed were given the oppourtunity to read through their own interview transcripts and the corresponding chapters to provide feedback. I began each visit by offering protocol to the knowledge holder(s). The interviews I completed for the case study in Chapter 10 were an exception to the general rule of anonymity in this context, as the interview participants wanted to use their own names. They wanted their experiences to be part of the public record. Since the case study is about a specific initiative in a specific community, it would have been difficult to maintain confidentiality. Beyond the general ethics and protocols followed with each participant, I let each person guide me regarding extra steps for protocol, information validation, and reciprocity. Following this synthesis and refinement, I completed literature reviews, and that scholarship is included in the analysis.

During the summer of 2013, my first interview was with a Cree Elder named Paul, his wife, Elder Gail, and their daughter Sharlene. Elder Paul asked me to meet him at an annual Indigenous gathering where his family was camping at manitô sâkahikan ᒪᓂᐋ ᕞᐦᐚᐱᐅ (Creator's Lake or Lake of the Spirit). Having been at this event numerous times before, I knew that there would be thousands of people in attendance from Indigenous communities across Canada. I was concerned about the sound quality of the interview recording so the night before the interview, I went out and bought an expensive audio recorder device and spent a few hours learning how to use it. Once we sat down, I offered protocol and introduced myself, and after a bit of discussion I asked if I could use the recorder. He told me no, not to record the interview or write notes during the interview; gently scolding me, he reminded me that all I have is my mind. He continued by saying that I cannot take the recorder when I go up to the sky (while pointing upwards) and I have to use my mind and my heart. This was an important reminder for me to keep in the forefront of my mind throughout this project. He was asking me to really listen in a different way, not as we are often trained to do in Western academia. The stories he and his family shared were about relationships between humans, nonhuman beings, shapeshifters, and the spirit world.

In this book, I often record the date on which I was originally writing, stating which season it is within the cycle of a year; sometimes the years change within the same chapter, jumping forward in time and then going back. This demonstrates the cyclical nature of time and the cyclical nature of how I approached this study. I include the month I was writing using Cree terms of different moons. Opaskwayak Cree lodge holder and science educator Wilfred Buck (2018, 8) shares that historically many people in this area of the earth "read the passage of time through the lunar cycle, our natural calendar. The lunar cycle consists of 13 full moons, with 28 days separating each full moon."

Working with published stories is always a challenge, and also a potential limitation of this research. In an Indigenous oral-history approach, something is always lost in terms of contextualized and situated knowledge when a story is recorded. Significantly, settler men wrote some of the stories included here, and although they interviewed Cree informants, the researchers often ignored Cree women and did not understand or write about their complex economic relationships. Another issue with the published stories is that most of them are written entirely in English; the richness of the world view found in nehiyawewin ᐅᐟᐃᔭᐯᐧᐁᐃᐧᐣ (Cree language) is lost. Interviewing Cree knowledge holders provided one way to overcome some of these challenges (I am not a fluent Plains Cree speaker, although I am learning and practising). I also tried to use oral stories that were written and published by Cree people themselves.

In Indigenous research, questions of ethics are of paramount importance. Ethical questions arose during all stages of the research process, and a self-reflective ethics is a continual process. How is the sacred honoured within Indigenous research? Ethical considerations regarding what is shared outside of the collective, as in a study, are commonly examined in Indigenous research (Kovach 2005, 31). This is a question I put to Cree knowledge holders. A piece of advice from Sharlene was to talk about the principles of a certain sacred ceremony without talking about some of its specific elements. Elder Gail said that with the changes facilitated by the Internet, the information is available anyway. In struggling through this question, I found the Federation of Sovereign Indigenous Nations' ethical considerations when publishing Cree oral stories informative:[9]

> The legends in this book explain only the significance of the ceremonies to our culture; they do not reveal the various stages and steps that are followed in a ceremony. This knowledge is reserved for men [and women] who have received this right either through a vision or from an elder wishing to pass his knowledge on. (Cuthand, Federation of Saskatchewan Indian Nations, and Deiter-McArthur 1987, xii)

Drawing from this understanding, in this study I share what I have learned regarding the importance of ceremonies, and I will show how this relates to economic relationships. I do not describe the sacred steps followed in the ceremonies. Where possible, I refer to accounts already published and already accessible to the wider public. It is always important to remember that Cree society is complex and dynamic.

> nêhiyawak [Cree] culture is not easily analysed or summarised. As a fluid, ever-changing and evolving set of interconnected relationships and meanings, it cannot be succinctly described or condensed. Even if this were possible, the result would not represent the experiences of all nêhiyawak peoples at any given time, much less through time. That is to say, cultures are complex and multifaceted across both time and space. (Haggarty n.d.)

A Model for Economic Livelihood

In this book, I present Indigenous economic practices that uphold Indigenous economic relationships as envisioned through a livelihood economic model, or pimâcihowin ᐱᒫᒋᐦᐄᐧᐣ. Cree scholar Priscilla Settee is an expert in Indigenous social economies, food sovereignty, and Indigenous livelihoods. She explains how "the community was governed by traditional Cree principles and standards of living known in Cree as *pimatisiwin*, which reflect ancient knowledge for community life, well-being and sharing values" (Settee 2011, 75). The root of pimâtisiwin is pimâtisi, which means "to be alive" (75). In the book *Treaty Elders of Saskatchewan: Our Dream Is That Our Peoples Will One Day Be Clearly Recognized as Nations* (H. Cardinal and Hildebrandt 2000), the Elders explain how the connection to land can be understood through the doctrines of pimâtisiwin, which includes spiritual, physical, and economic realms. This core concept contains many theoretical subsets, including, among other things, the concept of pimâcihowin, which is defined as the ability to make a living.

> When treaty Elders use the word "pimâcihowin" they are describing a holistic concept that includes a spiritual as well as a physical dimension. It is an integral component of traditional First Nations doctrines, laws, principles, values, and teachings regarding the sources of life, the responsibilities associated with them, including those elements seen as necessary for enhancing the spiritual components of life and those associated with making a living. (H. Cardinal and Hildebrant 2000, 43)

6 A metaphor of a livelihood economy.

This concept is intimately connected to askîy ᐊᓯᑲᕀ (the land) as an "important source of life for it provides those things required for the physical, material, and economic survival of the people" (H. Cardinal and Hildebrandt 2000, 43). The Elders then go on to explain different principles of conduct related to livelihood (see Chapter 9).

In a livelihood model, all elements are interconnected and interdependent, and all elements need to be considered and valued. I use the metaphor of a beaded okinewâpikonew ᐅᑭᓀᐚᐱᑯᓀᐤ (rose) that is original to the Plains geography to explain the pimâcihowin livelihood model that grounds this work. I beaded the flower in Figure 6 in 2020 using some of my grandmother Lillian Wuttunee's beads and home-tanned hide made in the Aseniwiche Winewak Nation (AWN); I explain our student-community project of making home-tanned hide in AWN in Chapter 10 (see also Jobin et al. 2021). The act of beading can be seen as grounded governance and as an embodied practice connecting our grandmothers' knowledges into the present (Kappo 2021). Michif artist, author, and activist Christi Belcourt (2007, 61) explains that all aspects of this specific rose can be used medicinally, and it is an excellent source of Vitamin C.[10]

Although my grandmother Lillian was a beader and I watched her bead while I grew up, I am only a beginner. The "mistakes" in the beading I chose to leave as a reminder that the work is messy, and still important. In this model the centre of the flower is the pistil and stamen, which are androgynous in the okinewâpikonew ᐅᕈᑕᐚᐧᐱᑕᐤ, including both the male and female reproductive system of a flower to ensure the continuation of life. The model also draws from the concept of wâhkohtôwin ᐚᐦᑯᐦᑐᐃᐧ (the normative principles guiding relationships) to acknowledge the important principles that stem from being related to all living beings. In the beaded okinewâpikonew, the innermost circle represents spirit beings (âtayohkan ᐋᑕᐧᐦᑲᐤ), the second circle represents all nonhuman beings (land, water, animals, and air beings), the third circle represents a people (for example, nehiyawak), the fourth circle represents other Indigenous peoples, and the fifth circle represents non-Indigenous peoples. When making economic decisions, a livelihood model reminds us of all our interconnected relations and how decisions will affect these relationships.

The five petals of the flower represent each of the different aspects of any society. Elder Elmer Ghostkeeper discusses how every society encompasses four aspects: social, cultural, economic, and political (Jobin and Letendre 2017, 9). For the purpose of this work, I have also included the legal aspect of a society; governance processes are embedded in all five aspects. Currently, Western economic thought can subsume all aspects of society within the economic sphere of capitalism. Figure 6 demonstrates the interconnection of all aspects; paradoxically, Western ways of being can also silo these aspects. In my research, I am interested in interconnections and making visible economic relationships – not to subsume, but to uphold Indigenous social, cultural, political, economic, and legal systems. Each bead represents principles and philosophy that uphold relationality within the nehiyawak world view.

The four leaves around the flower petals link economic relationships to movements toward Indigenous resurgence and self-determination. Sámi scholar Rauna Kuokkanen (2011, 230) explains that the most destructive impacts from the decimation of Indigenous economies are social and cultural. When looking at Indigenous economies today, we also need to include how economic relationships might uphold the elements of the peoplehood model. In Chapter 3 I explore the peoplehood model as an Indigenous studies theoretical paradigm (Corntassel 2012; Holm, Pearson, and Chavis 2003; Robert Thomas 1990). Specifically, it provides Indigenous peoples in settler-colonial contexts with areas to focus on for our continued survival as peoples, as well as suggesting resurgent acts of self-determination. These include continuing our assertion of and relationship with Indigenous territory, reclaiming Indigenous language retention, knowing and transmitting Indigenous living histories, and living out the renewal responsibilities found in Indigenous ceremonial cycles. In this book I explore how an understanding of a livelihood economic model might enable the social, political, economic, legal, and cultural reproduction of our people while upholding our relationships to all living beings.

While I write this (in the ihkopiwi-pîsim ᐃᐦᑯᐱᐄᐧ· ᐱᓯᒼ, frost moon, November 2013), I am enjoying the gift of watching a fast-flowing river while I'm on a writing retreat. Yesterday I watched a bald eagle perched on a branch of a tree beside this river. At one point she swooped down, and I think she found food, as I could see her head grabbing at something. I am reminded of Indian scholar and activist Vandana Shiva's (2005) living economies and the important role of nature's economy within this. Whether we acknowledge it or not, economic relationships are occurring right outside our window. Just where the eagle was yesterday, a small deer has crossed the river, and when I walked to this spot this afternoon, I saw a school of salmon seeking the shallow gravel beds of the river to finish their epic journey. As a Cree Elder told me in one of my interviews, we can learn a fair bit through watching how our nonhuman relations behave. Their teachings can show us how to live in miyo-wîcihitowin ᒥᔪ ᐄᐧᒋᐦᐃᑐᐃᐧᐣ (good relationships).

This research is also a contemporary Cree analysis of "alterNative" and enduring Indigenous economic relations within the Treaty Six geographic space.[11] Uncritical economic development affects Indigenous peoples in very specific ways, often revealing the contradictions and inherent problems within capitalistic systems. As an alternative, I discuss Indigenous economic relations that resist the economic exploitation found in settler-colonial countries such as Canada. When I use the term "enduring," I am referring to the economic relationships that predate capitalism on this land and predate the Canadian state. By reimagining and rearticulating these types of economic relationships, I hope to help us understand exploitation in the economic realm critically and to link Indigenous economic resurgence and self-determination in ways that are useful for Cree society in the twenty-first century. In the following chapters, I delve further into a grounded critique of economic exploitation, and I also explore enduring nehiyawak economic relationships through a nehiyawak peoplehood methodology or process.

The chapters form an interpretive circle. Chapter 2 grounds the book by exploring Indigenous economies as they are described in the literature.

I unpack the concept of economic exploitation and then explore the area of Indigenous political economy and critical Indigenous political economy.

In Chapter 3, I explore Cree ontological relationships through the approaches of oral history and storytelling. I lay the basis for understanding the Cree as a self-determining people who see themselves in terms as valid as (although distinct from) European notions of nationhood, partaking in international trade and foreign affairs. This articulation of Indigenous peoplehood positions Indigenous rights as *sui generis*, flowing from Cree peoplehood as opposed to being granted by the Canadian state or gaining authority only from within (or underneath) the Canadian state (Turner 2006). Articulating Cree peoplehood in this manner raises questions regarding the legitimacy of the "Canadian state's unilateral claim of sovereignty over Aboriginal lands and peoples" (Turner 2006, 7). Historical understandings of Cree inter-nation trade practices provide insight into how to foster Indigenous economic resurgence and contribute to greater governance options for Indigenous peoples.

Chapter 4 provides a genealogy documenting specific examples of exploitation that occurred during the fur-trade era, drawing on archival and academic sources to demonstrate the origin of this relationship. Much of what is now Canadian territory was purchased from the Hudson's Bay Company (HBC) by the Canadian government through an order-in-council in 1870 (Tough 1992). The purchased lands had been stolen by the HBC from the Indigenous people who lived on them. Settler governments then dealt with Indigenous peoples, who continued to inhabit their stolen lands, partly through treaties into which the Indigenous parties entered in good faith, and in Treaty Six, through ceremonial commitments. But as the number of instances of settler governments breaking or disregarding treaty agreements grew, some question whether treaties were seen by settler states as simply international instruments designed to justify colonial pursuits. The "double-forked tongue" of the state, and its exploitation of peoples and territories, formed the foundation of the relationship between Indigenous peoples and Canada that continues to this day.

Indigenous notions of identity through citizenship, and the extent to which these understandings are conditioned by neoliberalism, constitute the focus of Chapter 5. In Indigenous views of citizenship, a reciprocal relationship between economic interactions (relations *to* land) and modes of subjectivity (relations *with* land) is often demonstrated. How we relate to the land has an impact on who we are and the types of responsibilities we claim. In contrast, a neoliberal model can falsely assert that fundamentally altering our relationship to the land will not significantly alter who we are. I argue that negotiating current self-government initiatives that often free or open up Indigenous lands to be exploited by market interests enables one of the logics of settler colonialism: economic exploitation. Similarly, the focus on capitalist exploitation of the land as a way for Indigenous peoples to increase their financial independence from the state, although potentially relieving some bureaucratic control, further embeds this logic. This entrenchment influences identity formation – creating a type of market citizenship (Altamirano-Jiménez 2004, 350) and further subjection to this type of colonial logic. Countering this are Cree notions of identity and how such collective identity is connected to relations with the land.

Chapter 6 examines specific impacts on Indigenous women in resource extraction regions. As principal participants in the subsistence economy, Indigenous women have felt the harmful effects of corporate globalization particularly keenly (Kuokkanen 2008, 217). Indigenous women's bodies are connected to the political, colonial, and neoliberal, as "The body is the first place where women experience exploitation as well as sexual and domestic violence" (Altamirano-Jiménez 2013, 65). In this chapter I look at the history of racism and colonialism linked to missing and murdered Indigenous women, girls, and Two-Spirit + persons ("+" includes 2SLGBTQQIA: Two-Spirit, lesbian, gay, bisexual, transgender, queer, questioning, intersex, and asexual people). A specific type of political culture and discourse emerges in resource extraction provinces, and I link this to the exploitation of lands and bodies.

After Chapters 4, 5, and 6 unpack economic exploitation, the book shifts to examination of an Indigenous world view that upholds relationships to the land. Chapter 7 explores Cree stories and oral histories. In this chapter I uphold, articulate, and theorize Cree economic relationships, principles, and traditions emerging from both recorded and archival stories and interviews with Cree knowledge holders. My intent is to show Cree economic relationships on their own terms, as they provide a guiding framework for Cree resistance to economic exploitation.

Colonial dissonance results from the breaking of wâhkohtôwin ᐅᐦᑯᑐᐃᕀ, which affects the spiritual, physical, emotional, and mental aspects of Cree personhood and peoplehood; it is also the breaking of relationships between Cree people, non-Cree people, nonhuman beings, and spirit beings. Building on Chapter 7, Chapter 8 introduces the notion of colonial dissonance as a way to understand the tensions resulting from not living out wâhkohtôwin ◁·ᐟᒃᑊᑐᐃᐧᐧ. Colonial dissonance theory demonstrates the myriad of impacts of colonialism to all spheres of Indigenous societies: social, cultural, political, legal, and economic.

Chapter 9 discusses normative principles as explicated by interviews with Cree knowledge holders. Here I explore principles found in Cree knowledge systems that speak to Cree economic relationships and resistance to settler-colonial exploitation.

In Chapter 10 I bring the concepts from previous chapters together in order to theorize practices of resurgence. I show the tensions between economic exploitation and self-determination, and the form that resistance takes among the Plains Cree through examples of renewed relationships. This takes us to the specific ways in which the Cree are able to restore wâhkohtôwin ◁·ᐟᒃᑊᑐᐃᐧᐧ through enduring and alternative economic relationships with Cree and non-Cree beings. Chapter 11, the concluding chapter, brings together the different aspects of the book through the lens of upholding relationships.

Just as one can look into a river from different vantage points, so there are different perspectives from which to look at Cree economic relationships. While gazing at the river I see even more how the different perspectives are based on the sets of eyes one has – whether one is an eagle looking for food, a doe not wanting to be swept away by the current, a salmon spawning in a river bed, or a nehiyaw iskwew ᐅᒃᑊᐃᐧᐳ ᐃᐣᖴᐧ (Cree woman) searching for the relationships that connect us all. The art on the cover of this book is from Christi Belcourt's work titled *This Painting is a Mirror*, she explains how it "reflects back to the viewer all the beauty that is already within them. We are not separate from anything, we are born connected to the earth, with the capacity to love, to be kind, to be generous, to be gentle" (Belcourt 2012). My hope is that an understanding of economic and governing relationships in living economies can lead to different approaches to these relationships, and that this could lead to ways in which we can live well with each other and with all of our relations.

2

Grounding Economic Relationships

SIXTY-EIGHT HOURS AGO, on February 9, 2018, a verdict of not guilty of second-degree murder – as well as not guilty of manslaughter – was delivered in the shooting death of twenty-two-year-old Colten Boushie, from Red Pheasant First Nation, by a white man named Gerald Stanley. The fact, not even disputed by Gerald Stanley, is that he shot and killed young Colten, and yet Stanley didn't even get convicted of the lesser charge of manslaughter for the careless use of a firearm. Indigenous peoples felt contradictory feelings at once, both shock and disbelief, but for some the verdict also confirmed the outcome they had dreaded.[1] Within hours, and in the days following, demonstrations and vigils were organized across the country. Thousands upon thousands of people participated in more than twelve cities and communities. The R v. Stanley case represents the intersections of race, colonialism, private property, the criminal justice system, and fractured relationships. This case is also connected to place: the eagle hills of Saskatchewan.

nimosôm ᓂᒧᓯᒼ (my Grandpa) Gilbert Wuttunee (Figure 7), was born on Red Pheasant First Nation in 1892, and he attended the Battleford Industrial (residential) School. Seven years before Gilbert was born, Battleford Industrial School made its students stand outside and watch the hangings of eight Cree warriors involved in the 1885 Frog Lake uprising. My grandpa was at one time a Cree translator in the Battleford courthouse. This is the same courthouse where I sat last week, listening to the legal proceedings of the Gerald Stanley trial and remembering my grandpa's words that my mother transcribed. My grandpa Gilbert wrote these words in 1970 (the italics are mine):

> At that time [with the first settlers], the only village in practically the whole of Western Canada was Battleford, the seat of Government of the NW Territories till in 1905 Saskatchewan and Alberta were made provinces with their own governments and capitals. When the country was opened up for homesteading, people from all over the world came to Battleford, where the land office was situated, to file their claims on land they had chosen. Once a claim was registered, there were certain duties by law to be done. The claimant, or homesteader, had to build a shack or house, live there [at least] 6 months for 3 years, plow and fence 10 acres of land, have some stock horses and cattle and poultry. These completed, the homesteader could go to the land office and claim title to his homestead.
>
> There were several colonies of people who came from England, the Barr Colony, Germans, Russians, Ukrainians, Norwegians, Swedes and many other nationalities, but the English and Germans were the only ones that really stayed together from their arrival in Battleford. From Battleford they went in all directions to search for a homestead ...
>
> The Germans and Ukrainians also formed settlements so they could be together. Such a place was Collenz (Leipsig), the name changed to Wolfe during the First World War. The Ukrainians and Russians also formed a settlement, a village called Cando, about 40 miles south from Battleford. The Germans came very late in the fall. The year was 1905 or 1906. There weren't enough houses in town to accommodate them, so they built a long house like the Iroquois long house, divided into sections for each family. The house was built with pine slabs from the sawmills. There was no way for them to go looking for land but south, into the open prairie.
>
> As soon as spring break-up, they began their search for land and choosing districts to suit them. It must have been terrible for these people to go out into an absolutely uninhabited bald-headed prairie searching for land. Many homesteaded a hundred miles from any bush where they could cut logs for building and wood for fuel. They would drive a day or two to the bush for their winter's fuel. Many got lost and froze to death in the wintertime, losing their way in a blizzard. Many used fresh plowed sod to build their homes and barns. Sod houses

with no lumber for floors, rails and sod for roofs; yet, they stuck to it and became successful farmers. It wasn't very long before the whole country was dotted with sod-and-log shacks and land plowed and fenced.

The people were very friendly and hospitable. A traveller was made welcome day or night, if they happened to be travelling and needed shelter, food for the night. One knew and visited his neighbours for miles around, nothing like the present when you can live in the same building for years with people and yet not know who your neighbours are in the next room or house.

The homesteaders for miles adjacent to an Indian reserve became very friendly with the Indians, sharing in their sports, church and many social affairs, helping one another in building houses, log-houses, barns and fencing land. The Indians were an asset to these immigrants. Many didn't know anything about doing these things for themselves, nor did they have the material to work with. They went to the Indian for help and to be shown how to do these things for themselves.

It's too bad that the friendship that existed between the Indian and immigrant in the early colonization days should have deteriorated to such an extent that an Indian is barred from many public places, hotels, motels, cafes, etc., etc., and looked upon not as a second class citizen, but a nonentity, and [it is] a very rare occasion if an Indian is invited to a social event in a white man's home. The mutual confidence the Indians and whites had for one another has to be rebuilt if the Indian is to progress and become a real asset to the country and society in general.

The white men of today, 1970, haven't the liking and respect for the Indians that they had in the early part of this century.

It is like Grandpa is talking to us today, reminding us of a time when friendship and reciprocity guided the relationship between the Cree and the newcomers in the eagle hills, at a time when a traveller was made welcome day or night.

This book is about unpacking relationships between Plains Cree people and newcomers. Specifically, this book offers an Indigenous perspective on the economic realm. What is the relationship between Canada's "progress" and the exploitation of Indigenous peoples? What gifts are embedded in Indigenous world views to speak to miyo-pimâtisiwin, the good life, and, specifically, good relations related to the economy? In this book I present

7 nimosôm ᓄᒧᐢ (Grandpa) Gilbert Wuttunee, nimosôm ᓄᒧᐢ (Grand Uncle) Gavin Wuttunee, and nicâpân ᓂᒐᐸᐣ (Great Grandpa) James Wuttunee (n.d.).

two main arguments. The first is that economic exploitation was the first and most enduring relationship between newcomers and Indigenous peoples. This set the stage for settler colonialism to take hold. This important characterization has not been analyzed extensively enough. The second argument is that our economic relationships are constitutive; by this I mean that the relationships we have to the land, people, and other beings create and co-create who we are as individuals and as peoples. Indigenous peoples' options for achieving economic self-determination need to be attuned to the constitutive nature of these relationships. I draw from nehiyawak narratives to hold up Indigenous principles related to Cree livelihood that are embedded in our world view. I argue that these enduring principles are still of relevance today. Simply stated, the answer is not trading state colonialism for capitalist colonialism.

A changing economy has fundamentally altered relationships with askîy ᐊᐢᑭᕀ, the land, broadly conceived. This change has different contours. One has to do with a shift from a subsistence and trade economy to capitalism and wage labour. This change has altered our relationships, prioritized waged labour, and changed our relationship from living *with* the land to making a living *off* the land (Ghostkeeper 2007). Tied to this are the particularly destructive aspects of resource extraction. Resource extraction has diminished everyone's ability to live at a subsistence level by decreasing wildlife populations and increasing harmful toxins found in the food system and natural environment. This has left many Indigenous communities without adequate subsistence options. A subsistence livelihood is basic to the economy, but it is also intimately connected with social connections and cultural practices (Kuokkanen 2011). To state it another way, to lose the ability to live with the land has a major impact not only on the economy of a people (historically and currently), but also on its social system. Being able to maintain miyo-wîcêhtowin ᒥᐢ ᐄᐧᓀᐦᑐᐃᐧ᠎ (good relationships) with the land has intrinsic value, even if the land, because of human impact, is no longer able to provide for all the people's subsistence needs.

A common public critique of Indigenous self-determination is that it is not feasible without economic independence from the settler state. This critique and the logics settlers use to try to govern Indigenous peoples serve to push Indigenous communities to look beyond themselves for economic development initiatives that might promise a stronger capital portfolio. This has led to radical transformations for Indigenous peoples, who find themselves increasingly governed from the outside and by the logic of the global market. This story is being told. What has not been fully explored is the Indigenous-nation-specific dissonance that is deeply rooted in settler economic exploitation, and corresponding acts of discord, refusal, and resistance. The duality entailed in revitalizing Indigenous economic relationships, in the context of Indigenous resistance to economic exploitation, has a logic of its own. That logic is the subject of this study. Most non-Indigenous Canadians do not understand this logic underpinning Indigenous resistance. Therefore, this study might be of interest for Canadians to understand an Indigenous world view that underpins Indigenous dissonance and resistance.

The intervention provided by this study is grounded in dual concepts. It is at once a critique of unexamined economic development in a Plains Cree context, and also a narrative that foregrounds accounts of Cree-centred acts of wâhkohtôwin ᐄᐧᐦᑯᐦᑐᐃᐧ᠎, the normative principles guiding relationships, that serve as resistance to these logics. Although this study focuses on one Indigenous people, it is my hope that other Indigenous peoples will see value in the method of drawing from wisdom within their own oral traditions or other resurgent methods (land-based, ceremonial cycle, language, etc.) to revitalize their economic relationships.

Stated in another way: the nehiyawak ᓀᐦᐃᔭᐊᐧᐠ (Cree people), whose knowledge systems I draw upon, have distinctive governing relationships that shape their economic behaviour. In this book, I ask this question: What are the economic relationships that nehiyawak ᓀᐦᐃᔭᐊᐧᐠ hold dear? Drawing on Cree narratives from the past, and those of present-day Plains Cree knowledge holders,[2] this study is a treatise on Indigenous economic relations, practices, and principles. I explore Indigenous economic relationships through both historical and ongoing practices of economic exploitation in settler colonialism, and I bring to light central principles inherent in Indigenous economic relationships. These principles are drawn from historical practices and include oral histories from our archives and current oral narratives. My goal is to bring these integral relationships to the forefront in order to look at economic exploitation and the processes through which the nehiyawak ᓀᐦᐃᔭᐊᐧᐠ renew their relationships in resurgent ways.

As Indigenous societies have strong oral traditions, even under conditions of persistent colonialism, Indigenous peoples find themselves actively and repeatedly reclaiming Indigenous stories, languages, and ways of thinking. These stories represent complex teachings, and speak to the tenuous process of rebuilding Cree economic relationships. Before moving to the antidotes found in Indigenous ontologies, I wish to turn to one of the main concepts used to problematize these relationships: the lens of economic exploitation.

Understanding Economic Exploitation

Colonial domination of Indigenous peoples in settler societies has an insidious impact on the social, political, cultural, legal, and economic lives of Indigenous peoples. Each of these spheres is part of a separate but interrelated system of colonial logics.[3] If we only focus on state domination in settler societies, what I refer to as the first colonial logic, we miss an important part of the larger story – namely, how attempts to resist state domination may further entrench what I call the second colonial logic: economic exploitation. For example, current self-government initiatives are mingled with market forces to exploit Indigenous lands further. Similarly, the focus on capitalist exploitation of the land as a way for Indigenous peoples to gain increased financial independence from the state exemplifies the second type of colonial logic. This entrenchment, enacted over many years, slowly builds layers and layers of subjugation as Indigenous societies are, on the one hand, brought further into the logic guiding colonial policies and practices, while, on the other hand, simultaneously resisting that very logic.

Canadian economic progress has weighed heavily on Indigenous peoples,[4] undermining their collective rights to economic security and self-determination. From the nineteenth to the twenty-first centuries, the Canadian government's initiatives aimed at fostering Indigenous economic development failed repeatedly. They failed both in basic economic terms and in relation to the broad social indicators of the quality of individual and community life. On the whole, looking at costs and benefits, capitalism has come at a great cost to Indigenous peoples.

Capitalist exploitation has especially (negatively) affected Indigenous peoples in settler-colonial states like Canada. A study applying the United Nations Human Development Index explores this paradox (quantifying material standard of living, and a long and healthy life); although Canada ranked number one in 1999, statistics for First Nations people living on reserves show a ranking of seventy-ninth (Beavon and Cooke 2003, 201–9).[5] Canada's socioeconomic "progress" has consistently been at the expense of Indigenous peoples, through a process of economic exploitation. I see capitalism in this land (Canada) predating and creating the environment for settler colonialism to take hold over Cree and other Indigenous peoples.[6] This is evident through the fur-trade era. If capitalism is the investment of money in anticipation of a profit (Fulcher 2004, 2), the birth of capitalism here started with the fur trade, in which, as Innis's staples theory explains, staples (e.g., furs) were taken from Indigenous territories and the profits used to generate wealth in the metropolises of Britain, with Indigenous lands being the hinterland.[7] With settler colonialism, the metropole or core became the Canadian state and, I argue, the hinterland continues to be Indigenous lands, where staples are exploited to increase the wealth of settler Canada. In the staples theory, the trajectory of the hinterland is the perpetual search for new staples (resources) to be exploited by the metropole. In Treaty Six territory the staples are no longer buffalo,[8] beaver, and muskrat but, currently, non-renewable resources (for example, oil and gas). Indigenous peoples are interested in controlling their own economies in their own ways and in modes that also improve their societies – acts of self-determination.

Stated in another way: settler-colonial logic, related to the economy, has taken a two-pronged approach. The first prong is about control – governing control. You can see this through the *Indian Act*, which legislates First Nations people and communities "from cradle to grave" (Crane, Mainville, and Mason 2008, 79). What is often missed is the second prong of colonial logic: colonialism has also centred on disrupting and destroying Indigenous economies – for example, exploitation during the fur trade (when the Hudson's Bay Company unjustly sold 2.9 million square miles of Indigenous lands) or through resource extraction (with oil and gas companies operating on Indigenous lands), and then creating and forcing upon us economic development programs linked to modernization (arguing that Indigenous cultures hinder economic development, and that once we assimilate into white society we will be able to develop economically) (Canada 1996, vol. 2, ch. 5).

There is an ironic aspect to this settler-colonial logic. It trades one master for another. For example, Canada negotiates a Comprehensive Land Claims agreement with a First Nation. This Indigenous nation in a northern part of the prairie region lived a mostly subsistence lifestyle of hunting, fishing, and harvesting for hundreds and hundreds of years, although resource extraction has increasingly infringed on this. The bipartite (with the federal government) or tripartite (with the province included) agreements are made with the uneven power relations of a Canadian government that determines the scope and boundaries of negotiations and seeks to provide certainty (legal and economic) to non-Indigenous interests. This allows, for example, a multinational corporation to start a new oil and gas project in an Indigenous community in Canada, and in exchange the corporation will hire a few community members to operate some of the equipment. Say this community's food security came mainly from living with the land – hunting, fishing, and harvesting. Then the corporation has to build a road, which increases external traffic. The oil and gas project and the new road disrupt and displace the moose, elk, muskrat, and so on that the community hunts for food. With leakages from tailings ponds and unfettered development, the fish in that First Nation's bodies of water now have tumours and are not fit for human consumption, and water from the river is poisoned and no longer potable. The First Nation can no longer be self-sufficient and feed itself. What are the options left for the community? Perhaps an Impact Benefit Agreement is negotiated, and a few members will have training in this new industry. Often, economic exploitation becomes a filter that limits economic choices and viable options for Indigenous communities – it constricts. In this example, self-government, which can often start from an outstanding land claims process, pushes Indigenous societies aggressively into the second colonial logic: economic exploitation through the exposure of Indigenous lands to faster resource development (see Jobin

2020). Gaining more independence from the Canadian government by negotiating self-government or by allowing economic development initiatives that open lands to multinational corporations places Indigenous people more aggressively under the governance of the global capitalist market (Castro-Rea and Altamirano-Jiménez 2008). This is a difficult option for Indigenous communities, because before the negotiations, economic development surrounding the Indigenous territory already had affected their ability to live a subsistence lifestyle.

Currently, economic exploitation can be examined through the lens of neoliberalism. Since the mid-1970s neoliberalism has gained international reach and can be considered a specific mode of capitalism. Three basic aspects of neoliberalism are free trade, the free mobility of capital, and a shift in the role of the state (Bargh 2007, 1). As an ideology, neoliberalism is the belief that sustained economic growth is the way to attain human progress (N. Smith 2007, 597) and that "human well-being can best be advanced by liberating individual entrepreneurial freedoms and skills" (Harvey 2005, 2). Arguably, this has moved the market into all areas of social life (Leitner, Peck, and Sheppard 2006, 28), changing the notion of freedom to market freedom and the "commodification of everything" through privatization (Harvey 2005, 80). Regarding labour, "the figure of the 'disposable worker' emerges as prototypical upon the world stage" (169), where "neoliberalization has transformed the positionality of labour, of women, and of indigenous groups in the social order by emphasizing that labour is a commodity like any other" (171). Neoliberalism as a form of "governmentality" extends the logic of the market into other areas of society. I draw on the concept of governmentality, specifically related to how Plains Cree people have been negatively impacted by the state's practices favouring the interests of the settler population.

Indigenous Political Economy

Connecting interdisciplinary theoretical approaches (in Indigenous studies and political science) is a new and undeveloped area of Indigenous political economy (IPE). Belanger (the first Canadian author I have seen use this term) sees it as beneficial for studying pre-contact North American Indigenous societies as it can "(1) help us discern how the forces of politics and economics influence community development, and (2) inform us how community-based ideologies related to consumption and leadership are structured to help maintain political and ecological balance while ensuring the prosperity of community members" (Belanger 2010, 26). Belanger goes on to define Indigenous political economy as "the study of the environment's influence on Indigenous political institutions and economic ideologies as these respond to prevailing ecological forces and the dynamics associated with Creation. Never forgetting the centrality of the interrelational network, it is imperative that we consider how the actions of individuals in a community influence its overall dynamic and how that one community in turn can affect its neighbours" (26). Belanger provides an important foundation from which to explore IPE, and although his focus on pre-contact Indigenous societies may appear limiting, there are other scholars who also study Indigenous societies and the economy in the present. An IPE approach can enable a multi-scale and broad analysis of Indigenous politics, society, and economy. Although authors do not necessarily define their approach as IPE, there is a fair bit of writing in this area, and in this section I explore works related to Indigenous economies, with a focus on Canada.

There are different ways to conceptualize the history of Indigenous economies in Canada. The Royal Commission on Aboriginal Peoples (RCAP) outlines four periods: the pre-contact period, the fur-trade period, the settler period, and the dependency period. In the Commission's analysis, the pre-contact period is based on living in balance with nature, as opposed to accumulating wealth, and being tied to local means of subsistence that fluctuate seasonally (Canada 1996, 2:755–56). This period is also defined by widespread Indigenous nation-to-nation trade, facilitated by extensive existing Indigenous trade routes. The writers of RCAP argue that during the fur trade, Indigenous peoples were initially able to continue pre-existing economies and that patterns of trade and contact were region- and resource-dependent (2: chap. 5). This era encompasses the impacts of external markets with the volatile boom-and-bust cycle of staple production.

The settler period is marked by Indigenous peoples being "pushed increasingly to the margins" by settlers: newcomers "often simply assumed they had title to these lands and resources" (Canada 1996, 2:758). This is also the period of numbered-treaty making, although it is noted that in many cases Indigenous nations in given areas were missed or not invited to negotiate treaties. This era includes state enforcement of laws, imposition of Western government and governance structures, restrictions on mobility, under-resourcing of treaty obligations, and the beginning of Indigenous peoples participating in the market wage-labour economy, mostly in manual occupations (2: chap. 5). The last era, the dependence period, began sometime between 1930 and 1960, and continues in some form to the present day. This period is defined by Indigenous dislocation and dispossession for the benefit of the settler economy. Resource companies were encouraged by settler governments to establish resource industries (e.g., oil and gas, mining, forestry), devastating territories where Indigenous peoples live and have historical jurisdiction, and where they are trying to continue subsistence-based practices (Canada 1996). RCAP also documents federal and provincial regulations that have harmed Indigenous economies during this period.

The First Nations Development Institute (FNDI) (2004) explores the history of Indigenous economies in North America related to asset eras, in which assets are described broadly as holistic in nature and include financial, physical, natural, institutional, legal, cultural, and political assets as well as human and social capital. In this analysis, the six historical asset periods are stewardship, exchange, theft, extraction, mismanagement, and restriction, with the current era moving toward asset control (FNDI 2009, 52). Asset stewardship, FNDI explains, was a period in which Indigenous societies had control over their assets, with economies based on Indigenous epistemologies in which stewardship "allowed for highly sophisticated and complex economies of asset use and accumulation to occur" (52). Treaty making and negative impacts on Indigenous lands mark the exchange era, in which these lands were no longer under exclusive Indigenous control. The asset theft era focused on the settler state's failure to fulfil the obligations undertaken during the treaty era, and included broad occurrences of theft of land and resources, facilitated by state policies. During the era of asset extraction, natural resources on Indigenous lands were increasingly extracted without significant benefit to Indigenous communities, leaving behind "immeasurable expenses related to environmental pollution, loss of land use and destroyed ecosystems" (52). Asset mismanagement overlaps with the previous era and is described as a time of paternalistic policies giving settler states control, with corresponding mismanagement of the trust funds, leases, and financial assets of Indigenous communities. FNDI argues that these three eras (theft, extraction, and mismanagement) have left Indigenous societies impoverished and in a position of dependency on the state (52). Asset restriction is described as the settler state's usurpation of control over Indigenous assets. FNDI's view is that Indigenous societies need to create asset strategies to move toward asset control, and that this is needed for self-determination (10).

In terms of economic relationships, when did settler colonialism take hold for the Plains Cree? One argument is that this occurred during the fur trade. Historical geographer Frank Tough (2005, 32) explains how commercialization that began during the fur trade provides a lens into Indigenous economic history, in which "aspects of daily life increasingly fall under the influence of exchange value. More and more, needs or wants become satisfied by market-related activities." Furthermore, the privileging of market tendencies is an old colonial logic with "long-standing unequal integration with mercantilism" (31). Mercantilism was an economic system popular in Europe from the sixteenth to eighteenth centuries, and was based on the belief that a nation's wealth and power were best improved by increasing exports. It is significant that this included government regulation of the economy, such that "colonial possessions should serve as markets for exports and as suppliers of raw materials to the mother country. Manufacturing was forbidden in colonies, and all commerce between colony and mother country was held to be a monopoly of the mother country" (Encyclopedia Britannica n.d.-b). Tough (2005, 31) sees the commercial capitalist market as being the first and most enduring institution affecting Indigenous peoples in Canada.

In contrast, historian and poet Walter Hildebrandt (2008, 6) argues that Native societies changed less during the fur-trade era than did European traders, who had to adapt to Native trade practices. For John H. Moore (1993), the main change for Indigenous people was based on an economic conflict that occurred between capitalism and "communal modes of production" (15).[9] Frank Tough (2005, 54), however, argues that on a macroeconomic scale, Indigenous trappers and middlemen did not have real equity and were not partners within the fur-trade system, in which real decision-making power was under European control. Tough also critiques other scholars' denial that economic exploitation preceded political oppression (54). This economic exploitation continued with the reserve system. Sociologist Menno Boldt (1993, 231) argues that the "reserve system was created to clear Indians out of the way of Canadian economic development," removing Indigenous peoples from their full territories to enable capitalist pursuits.

Currently, many scholars advocate for neoliberal conceptions of capital accumulation and corresponding institutions of governance for Indigenous peoples. The main difference among them is how these authors conceive of the "problem" related to "undeveloped" Aboriginal economies. Political scientist Tom Flanagan argues that Native peoples' "problem" rests in a lack of private property and believes that "as quickly as possible, Indian bands should receive full ownership of their reserves, with the right to subdivide, mortgage, sell, and otherwise dispose of their assets, including buildings, lands, and all natural resources" (Flanagan 2013, 50). Similarly, economist Hernando De Soto articulates the need for private property systems in which private property rights are enforced. From this perspective, land can be used as collateral for economic enterprise (De Soto 2000; Woodruff 2001). Opening up land[10] for marketization is in the interests of both the Canadian state and the private sector, but often operates to the detriment of Indigenous peoples (Castro-Rea and Altamirano-Jiménez 2008, 246).

In neoliberalism, citizens are compelled to be self-sufficient and not a burden on the state (Slowey 2008, xv). Calvin Helin, an author from the Tsimshian Nation, argues that dependency is the issue for Indigenous peoples, and that economic development is the solution. He contends that financial dependency, combined with a growing Indigenous population could completely overwhelm Canada's financial capabilities (Helin 2006, 59). To counteract this perceived threat, Helin proposes a development model focused on resource extraction that leverages Indigenous land, cash, and labour (177–90). He suggests Indigenous communities impose "development leverage over traditional territories" by creating procurement agreements (188–90), for example, where companies operating in an Indigenous territory have quotas for how much of their supply chain needs are met by Indigenous businesses. Similarly, in the second volume of the *Report of the Royal Commission on Aboriginal People*, recommendation 2.5.10 states that resource-development corporations operating on Indigenous territories should provide training, employment, and economic "rents" (Canada 1996, 2:857), with a strong correlation between self-government, control over lands, and improved Indigenous economic development.

Self-government and improved self-governance have been strongly correlated to Indigenous economic development. Bureaucratic control has also been seen as the main issue facing Indigenous peoples. Political scientist Gabrielle Slowey (2008, xiv–xv) writes that capitalism is a tool with which First Nations can achieve self-determination through the mimicking of neoliberal principles constituting the "ideal citizen." She elucidates that self-determination is the neoliberal ideal, as "self-determination re-establishes the proper balance between First Nations and the marketplace that was perverted by the welfare state, giving rise to an unhealthy dependency on the state" (17). Business scholar Robert Anderson sees a positive relationship among control of resources, business development, economic development, self-reliance, self-determination, and self-government. In his "First Nations Development Circle" model, improvement in one area is believed to have a positive effect on all other areas (R.B. Anderson 1998, 14). Ineffective and undeveloped governing infrastructures have been correlated to undeveloped Indigenous economies.

The Harvard Project on American Indian Economic Development has largely succeeded in promoting its model of development to Indigenous peoples in Canada and the United States, as well as influencing policymakers at the state/provincial and national levels. Through a national American study, researchers Stephen Cornell and Joseph Kalt (2006, 11) position successful economic development as having everything to do with nation building – focusing on Indigenous nation sovereignty (self-rule), governing institutions, cultural match to these institutions, strategic orientation, and leadership focused on nation building. These authors have done a phenomenal job in making their findings known to Indigenous communities in North America, and many communities and state governments have seen widespread resonance with their findings. Some authors criticize the Harvard Project for not accounting for the complexity of issues in its approach. Specifically, Dowling (2005, 125) writes that the "myopic view of the world" that the Harvard Project suggests "a society must take in order that these conditions take hold (acceptance of the use of natural resources for economic gain, the resulting environmental degradation and stratification of society, to name a few) is not congruent with their [Indigenous] cultures," and further stating that although very successful, the Harvard Project has failed to thoroughly examine or reveal the negative implications and limitations of its approach.

One strain of the Indigenous economic development literature speaks to specific aspects of neoliberal ideology that suggest changes to make the neoliberal paradigm better fit Indigenous communities. Indigenous studies scholar David Newhouse (2004, 38) challenges the tendency to denigrate and displace Indigenous knowledge within the economic development discourse. His answer is to create "people-centred" development theories that enable "an economy that affirms Aboriginal cultural identities and the autonomy of Aboriginal cultures and that sanctions and supports Aboriginal social structures and values" (40). Cree scholar Wanda A. Wuttunee (2004, 12–14) similarly sees a need for a shift in approaches to economic development for Indigenous peoples that would acknowledge spiritual and material relationships to the land. In this approach, neoliberal ideologies are not completely rejected, but they are altered so that the idea of "maximum" short-term profit is replaced with the notion of a reasonable profit that seeks to honour the limits of the planet's resources (7).

Critical Indigenous Political Economy

Discourses promoting Indigenous peoples' success in capital markets have not exhaustively examined the consequences of the hegemonic and individualizing powers of capitalism, but scholars have particularly critiqued the application of neoliberal instruments of capitalism and governance to Indigenous communities (Altamirano-Jiménez 2004; Bargh 2007; Corntassel 2012). In this section I explore the literature that is developing within a theoretical approach I term critical Indigenous political economy (CIPE).[11]

Dene scholar and activist Glen Coulthard draws from political theorists and frames a critical Indigenous political economy approach. Most recognizably using the work of Karl Marx, Coulthard (2014a, 58) maintains that the process of primitive accumulation expropriates the means of production from non-capitalist societies, signalling a defining moment in capitalist extension, the preparation of the sociopolitical and material conditions for the "birth of capitalism" in a territory. Coulthard sees primitive accumulation as not only a moment, but also that which provides an understanding of the ongoing dynamics shaping relations between Indigenous peoples and Canada (56). For Coulthard, Marx's analysis can be better applied to Indigenous peoples in settler colonialism by (1) framing the analysis with a prioritization of colonial domination (59–60); (2) understanding how Indigenous labour in a settler-colonial context becomes increasingly superfluous (61); and (3) understanding "how colonial relations are not primarily exerted through 'brute force' or 'servitude,' but through the asymmetrical exchange of mediated forms of state recognition and accommodation" (62). In this process, Indigenous peoples are increasingly disconnected from land and from their own forms of governance and drawn into capitalist market conditions, and the modes of social organization are reorganized (Coulthard 2014a; Coulthard 2014b).

Māori scholar Maria Bargh (2007, 2) and Sámi scholar Rauna Kuokkanen (2006; 2008) have positioned neoliberalism as the new form of colonization affecting Indigenous peoples. Using New Zealand as a case study, social scientist Wendy Larner (2000, 18) states that the Māori struggle to self-administer their social services in culturally appropriate ways has neoliberals and some Māori finding "themselves in unexpected agreement on a key theme: namely, the dangers of continued dependency on the state." Therefore, this path can be seen as "part of the discursive construction and reconstruction associated with welfare state restructuring" (18). This is the exact predicament many Indigenous peoples in Canada face. The Indigenous goal of self-government has constructed the movement along a neoliberal trajectory, directly affecting collective ideologies and Indigenous relationships with human and nonhuman beings. Along this economic-development path, Indigenous peoples can achieve self-government to lessen state control and simply exchange it for hegemonic forms of market control. Zapotec political scientist Isabel Altamirano-Jiménez (2013, 75) sees Indigenous land dispossession occurring under the "liberalization of nature," and then a "double dispossession" occurring with neoliberalism, "through the recognition of a reified version of indigeneity and through a bundle of rights based on the alienation of Indigenous peoples' relations and responsibilities to place." She explains that this "rescripting of indigeneity is embedded in notions of entrepreneurialism, the self, and the economy" (75). Neoliberalism as colonization charts a connection between colonial and neoliberal practices (Bargh 2007, 1).

Indigenous peoples striving for meaningful self-determination are being pushed into a version of citizenship based on the values of the market. Altamirano-Jiménez (2004, 349) argues that neoliberal governmental practices regarding Indigenous demands serve to disconnect self-government from Indigenous territory. The marketization of Indigenous citizenship is tantamount to "the fulfilment of Indigenous demands through market integration and the rhetoric of cultural recognition" (350). In a neoliberal framework, then, Indigenous rights and citizenship are commodified in a way that is profitable for the Canadian state. I draw from Altamirano-Jiménez's connections between place-based understandings of Indigenous peoples and the specific impacts of neoliberalism.

Providing an analysis of settler colonialism in the United States, Kul Wicasa scholar Nick Estes (2019, 123) reminds readers how Indigenous resistance has been and continues to be about fighting against settler colonialism and fighting for Indigenous life and just relationships with humans and nonhumans, including the land. His work also demonstrates the transformative power that occurs during resistance (Estes 2017, 119), even in situations of extreme power imbalance. Political theorist Robert Nichols (2020) unpacks the process and structural conditions of dispossession in

Anglo settler colonial contexts through two processes: transforming an Indigenous worldview of land relations into proprietary terms, and systematically transferring the title of this property (into settler hands); he writes, "dispossession merges commodification ... and theft into one moment" (8). Through making property, Nichols writes, an abstraction occurs, one that anchors a certain type of settler "relations, rights, and ultimately, power" (31). In this way, Anglo settler colonialism always includes a transformation in how humans relate to land (34). This is a genesis moment of economic exploitation for Indigenous peoples. Tsimshian and Nuu-chah-nulth scholar Clifford Atleo (2015, 49) asks if capitalism can be Indigenized; his analysis shows "not without radical changes to either capitalism or Indigenous worldviews that might render either unrecognizable." In *Land Back*, critical theorist Shiri Pasternak and Anishinaabe scholar Hayden King (2019, 48) provide meticulous examples of the techniques of dispossession that have occurred in Canada against Indigenous peoples as well as different forms of Indigenous-led strategies of reclamation to "restoring Indigenous land and life." Their grounded analysis shows gaps in federal and provincial policies, the resulting implications to Indigenous peoples, as well as potential for transformation in these structural relations of dispossession.

Critical Indigenous political economy (CIPE) can facilitate a multi-scale analysis in which a research question can be explored in a broad context – settler colonialism, impacts of unfettered capitalism through a nation-state and an international lens, etc. – while also situating analysis, as one example, in Plains Cree specificity. CIPE provides an approach through which to examine not only the ways in which Indigenous peoples have been affected by all of these settler-colonial processes, but also Indigenous peoples' challenges to these forces that try to reconstitute them or attempt to make them disappear legally, socially, or politically.

Being Indigenous is a form of resistance in and of itself, but putting into practice a certain set of normative customs, grounded in an Indigenous-specific peoplehood, adds another layer to this resistance. For my work, I focus on the specific ways in which Plains Cree people are in relationship with the land;[12] the specific ways economic development affects the relationships of Cree people with each other, the land, and other human and non-human beings; Cree practices of resistance against economic exploitation; and acts of resurgence. New literary works are beginning to theorize alternatives for Indigenous peoples. In contrast to neoliberal approaches, and outside the confines of capitalism, Kuokkanen (2007) explores the gift paradigm in Indigenous societies. In this view, the gift illustrates more than just an economic function; it is applicable to "all my relations" (23). In many Indigenous world views, "giving entails an active relationship between the human and natural worlds, one characterized by reciprocity, a sense of collective responsibility, and reverence toward the gifts of the land" (23). Kuokkanen (2011, 232) also writes about the need to reorient Indigenous self-governance around the notion of social economy, which "recognizes the ways in which in indigenous economic systems, economy is embedded in social relations." Although this new discourse is dynamic, there is still space to include further analysis from diverse perspectives by inviting more voices and Indigenous knowledges connected to place. Further research is needed into Indigenous economic relations that uphold the complexities and beauty embedded in Indigenous knowledges.

For the purpose of my work, I am interested in understanding economy in a broad sense, not one confined to the dominant capitalist economic system. I agree that there is "the tendency to constitute 'the economy' as a singular capitalist system or space rather than as a zone of cohabitation and contestation among multiple economic forms" (Gibson-Graham 2006). There are authors, such as Vandana Shiva, who see three economies at work: the dominant capitalist economy; nature's economy, based on "the production of goods and services by nature" (Shiva 2005, 16); and the sustenance economy, which "includes all spheres in which humans produce in balance with nature and reproduce society through partnerships, mutuality, and reciprocity" (16). Seeing economic relations through nehiyâwiwin ᓀᐦᐃᔭᐄᐧᐃᐧᐣ ("Creeness") broadens the discussion on the economy to include nature's economy and the sustenance economy based on relations to human and nonhuman beings.

> **CONTENT WARNING:**
> **THE FOLLOWING CONTAINS A DESCRIPTION OF A SHOOTING.**

Returning to young Colten Boushie. In the Gerald Stanley trial, the defence used the argument of Indigenous bodies intruding on settler private property. Cree scholars Gina Starblanket and Dallas Hunt (2020, 87) invert this logic and demonstrate that this is actually a continued structure of settler intrusion on Indigenous lands and how this settler violence is in contrast to the ongoing acts of generosity to share the land through treaty. Returning to my grandpa's telling of a time when settlers relied on Indigenous peoples, how "many [immigrants] didn't know anything about doing these things for themselves, nor did they have the material to work with. They went to the Indian for help and to be shown how to do these things for themselves." Grandpa also said, "The people were very friendly and hospitable. A traveller was made welcome day or night, if they happened to be travelling and needed shelter, food for the night."

Driving home after swimming one afternoon, a group of young Indigenous friends and family had a flat tire and drove onto a settler's farm. After a series of unfortunate events, Gerald Stanley made the unreasonable decision to fire his gun; his gun went off while pointed at the back of Colten Boushie's head. Young Colten died, and Gerald Stanley walked away.

Gina Starblanket and Dallas Hunt (2020, 51) explain that settler colonialism operates through a logic of elimination where the "driving motivation is land" – land that is seen through a settler lens as private property. In this example, the logic of protecting private property is a valuing of private property over life. Colten Boushie had relations, human and other living beings. While the Stanley family sat in their house and drank coffee while Colten's body lay in the dirt on their driveway,[13] I believe the askîy ᐊᐢᑮᕀ was providing healing and helping him in his transition to the next world. The beauty of natural law is that it happens whether we acknowledge it or not. We are in relations to all other living beings, whether we acknowledge it or not.

I see the transformative potential embedded in Indigenous world view, Indigenous bodies, and relationality with human beings, the landscape, and waterscape to shape-shift Canadian colonialism and Canadian institutions. Inferring from my grandpa's words, that Canadian society would come to Indigenous knowledge holders collectively, in humbleness, to seek ways to live in miyo-pimâtisiwin ᒥᔪ ᐱᒫᑎᓯᐃ·ᐣ, the good life. That Indigenous peoples would one day be free or unshackled from the ongoing acts of settler colonial violence and would continue to live in self-determining ways, demonstrating acts of renewal in wâhkohtôwin ᐋ·ᐦᑰᐦᑐᐃ·ᐣ and miyo-wîcihitowin ᒥᔪ ᐄ·ᒋᐦᐃᑐᐃ·ᐣ (good relations) with Indigenous and non-Indigenous peoples, animals, and other beings.

3

nehiyawak Peoplehood and Relationality

The first treaty we entered into was with the trees. Humans breathe in oxygen and breathe out carbon dioxide; symbiotically, trees take in carbon dioxide and release oxygen. This first treaty cannot be broken; our survival depends on it.

– Laura Calmwind

NISIKOS ᓂᐢᑯᐢ, MY AUNT, Laura Calmwind,[1] shared this teaching with me in the fall of 2012. This teaching came back to my mind two months ago, on December 18, 2017, when I woke up from a dream. As it was a very meaningful dream to me, I wrote the following at 6:45 that morning: "I just woke up from a dream. Actually, to be more precise, I woke up *in* my dream, and now I have woken up *from* that dream. I have never dreamed in a dream before, my dream's dream state, I will call this my double-dream." In this dream, there were many of us sleeping in a concrete building that had large cut-outs in the walls instead of windows. We were all on the lookout, as it was a dangerous time. There was no furniture to be found. I was with my partner. I let him know that I would be back and then started walking through the building. There were also others, nonhuman living beings, in this building. I had noticed them before, and it was striking, but this one morning was the first time I had an interaction. I bumped into a human-tree. I call it a human-tree as she held "person-hood" but resembled a tree. The closest comparison I can make is to the character Groot in Marvel comics, as well as in the movie *Guardians of the Galaxy*. In my double-dream, I accidentally opened a door and bumped her limb with my arm. I bumped her where she had an open sore. Some of the pus transferred to my arm, and I remember feeling nervous that I might now be infected with her ailment.

I woke up from this dream, and the next day, in the double-dream, I saw my friend and colleague, Cree scholar Tracy Bear. I told Tracy about my dream. I said it was transformative for me. I could talk theoretically about being in relationships with nonhuman living beings, but actually having an interaction with a humanlike tree created a different sort of attachment; mistik ᒥᐢᑎᐠ (the tree) allowed me to see her through different eyes, a shared humanity. In my dream, I told Tracy that now that I had a relationship with mistik, it affected how I interacted within the environment. In our shared *human*-ity, or unity, our small interaction created a relationship in which I didn't other her, but saw her through a new perspective. We were both seeking refuge and would need to work together for our common survival.

This double-dream provided many teachings, which I will unpack in later chapters. For now, I would like to state that many Indigenous people and peoples have very real relationships with other living beings. My aunt's teaching of our first treaty is an example of this. Another example is drawn from a Treaty Six Confederacy workshop, at which Bob Smallboy (2012) shared how his uncle introduced him, at the edge of a creek, to a bird. The uncle called the bird, and the bird flew over and landed on the man's shoulder to meet his nephew. My own dream expresses a subconscious longing for deeper relationality with other living beings. My dream is a reminder that people or peoples who want to be in closer relationships with living beings can begin to do this, and it can and will be constitutive. Even an Indigenous person living off a reserve or settlement can do this. The practices will be different for each person, as they are contextual; I share contemporary examples of these resurgent acts in Chapters 10 and 11.

In this chapter I explore Plains Cree peoplehood through the lens of relationality. I turn to archival research and historical evidence regarding Plains Cree peoplehood, diplomacy, and trade.[2] The historical data creates a narrative that weaves together Indigenous territorial jurisdiction, economic trade, and diplomacy that guides relationality. One way to explore relationality is through the concept of "all my relations." Cree Elder George Brertton explains, "We are all related, not only by blood. All things are alive.

All things that were created are related – trees, grass and rocks. We are related to everything" (BearPaw Media and Education 2016). We are related to everything in nihtâwihcikewin Ꭴᐢᐨᐊᐧᐦᐸᐧᐃᑫᐧᐃᐧ (creation); this includes humans, animals, plants, land, etc.

In this section I provide a primer on the Plains Cree through the lens of peoplehood. While you are reading this, I hope you will attune yourself to Indigenous peoples' relationships to other living beings and to spiritual beings – our ontological relationships. Peoplehood is a way to conceive of Indigenous nationhood by applying the interlocking components of language, living histories, ceremonial cycle, and territory. In the Cree language, these are nehiyawewin Ꭴᐢᐊᐯᐧᐃᐧᐃᐧ, kasispowicikew ᑲᐢᐯᐅᐧᐃᒋᑫᐧ, kiskinowâcihcikana ᑭᐢᑭᓄᐋᐧᒋᐦᒋᑲᓇ, and nehiyawaskiy Ꭴᐢᐊᐯᐊᐧᐢᑭᐩ. As a helpful theoretical lens, I do not see these four aspects of peoplehood as fully encompassing all of an Indigenous people's nationhood. For example, governance can be seen in all of these aspects but it can also be seen in the nation as a whole.

When negotiating space for Indigenous peoples within colonial contexts, terminology, which is associated with rights, is often contested. In Western political thought, there has been a guiding hierarchical evolutionary hypothesis that positions bands as the most primitive social group, then tribes, then chiefdoms, with nation-states as the most highly civilized form of sociopolitical organization (Holm, Pearson, and Chavis 2003, 15–16). The positioning of nation-states, as defined in Western thought, above all other forms of governance provided the rationale for Western countries to intrude on Indigenous lands. The Peoplehood Matrix, a theoretical paradigm developed for and within the discipline of Indigenous studies, moves beyond the hegemonic construction of nation-states as the only political form deserving of self-determination (Corntassel 2012; Holm, Pearson, and Chavis 2003; Robert Thomas 1990). Significantly, for Indigenous peoples in settler-colonial contexts, peoplehood also provides four foundational areas to focus on in terms of our own people's resurgence: Indigenous language, Indigenous living history, Indigenous ceremonial cycle, and Indigenous territory.

An important distinction that I make in terms of peoplehood is how citizenship is constructed. The *Indian Act* system has crushed complex kinship and wâhkohtôwin ᐋᐧᐦᑯᐦᑐᐃᐧ norms. For the Plains Cree people, adoption, even of adults, was a common practice. I see peoplehood as one way to move beyond race-based classifications that flatten complex Indigenous kinship systems (see Innes 2013). Although I refer to the Plains Cree as Cree,

I want to acknowledge that this distinction is not limited to blood quantum, as alliances and adoption were (and are) custom practice.[3] Similar to other nations, with the Plains Cree, a strict definition on blood quantum does not always determine citizenship. The Cree people's language, living history, territory, and ceremonial cycle provide one way to understand the inherent self-determination of an Indigenous people.

nehiyawewin ᓀᐦᐃᔭᐍᐏᐣ is the Cree language. nehiyawewin ᓀᐦᐃᔭᐍᐏᐣ provides the lens through which nehiyawak or iyiniwak ᓀᐦᐃᔭᐘᐠ or ᐃᔨᓂᐘᐠ (Cree people) see themselves and through which they understand the world around them. One Cree Elder explains how the Cree language provides a world view and directions on how to live:

> We are called *Iyiniwak*. That is the foundation of who we are, our identity. We are supposed to heal ourselves and others and *iyiniwaskamkaw*, that is, our relationship to our land, our connection here. *Nehiyaw* [a First Nations person] is the four directions, *newoyak*. There are four parts and those are our four directions and that is, in our language. Additionally, *newoyak ehoci pikisweyan,* I speak from the four directions, so you are always honouring your four directions. That is the philosophy of it. The four directions are, we have to be caring, sharing, we have to be honest and we have to pray daily for our strength. Continued strength of our people and our land – our very existence. (Makokis 2001, 90)

nehiyawewin ᓀᐦᐃᔭᐍᐏᐣ (the Cree language) provides a framework for understanding the world based on the four-directions teachings – these are considered central teachings that guide the Cree in daily living. The language itself demonstrates relationships and is based on the animacy of the world around us. The act of speaking and transferring knowledge through the language can be thought of as one act of self-determination, enacting a key component of peoplehood.

The Cree language is often referred to as an oral language as opposed to a written language. One controversy is around the origin of the later written form of the language; many say that missionaries who came to Cree societies developed the Cree syllabics writing system. Fine Day, of the Plains Cree, was over eighty years old when he relayed this account in the mid-1930s, disputing the origin of Cree syllabics:

"Mestanuskwe-u," or Badger Call, once died and then became alive again. While he was dead he was given the characters of the syllabic and was told that out of them he would write Cree. He was of the "Sakawiyiniwok," or Bush Cree. Strike-Him-On-the-Back learned how to write syllabic from Badger Call. He made a feast and announced that he would teach it to anybody who wanted to learn it without pay. That is how I learned it. The missionaries got the writing from Badger Call, who taught it to them. When Badger Call was given the characters he was told, "They will change the writing and will believe that the writing belongs to them, but only those who know Cree will be able to read it." So it is that no one can read the syllabic writing unless he knows Cree, and so the writing does not belong to the whites. (Fine Day 1973a, 58)

Corroborating this, Cree professor Clifford Cardinal presents important information from a letter in his possession from Calling Badger to a minister named Evans. In the letter, Calling Badger strongly criticizes Evans for misinforming the public about the origin of Cree syllabics, accusing Evans of gathering the information and then plagiarizing it (C. Cardinal 2014). Cree syllabics pictorially illustrate aspects of the four directions teachings that are of such importance to the Cree people. nehiyawewin ᓄᐦᐃᔭᐍᐏᐣ is an important aspect of Cree peoplehood and has been used to communicate Cree history over the ages.

Indigenous living histories provide citizens with knowledge of their roots, as well as a set of principles encompassing roles and responsibilities within the community. Drawing on the foundational work of Robert K. Thomas, Tom Holm et al. (2003, 14) explain that "sacred history" also details kinship structures while conveying "its own distinct culture, customs, and political economy." Joseph Dion (1888–1960), a Cree who published extensively about Cree society, wrote that "the power and wisdom that the Cree Native possessed was derived from two distinct sources, namely Magic rites and Nature's own laws ... Prophecy from dreams has been in existence among all peoples since the beginning of man. Certain men and women among the Cree have been known for their wonderful power in foretelling events and their ability to interpret dreams correctly" (Dion 1958, 51). Many Indigenous peoples see dreams as a form of communication with the subconscious and with those with whom they share metaphysical relationships.

The retelling of historical accounts is one way to pass on these living histories to the next generation of Cree.

Growing up, I heard ᐄᐧᓴᑲᒉᐦᒃ stories; I was excited to find these same stories in numerous published accounts. The stories of ᐄᐧᓴᑲᒉᐦᒃ explain the Cree creation account as well as numerous adventures, all of which provide important lessons and knowledge and are an important part of the sacred history of the Cree. ᐄᐧᓴᑲᒉᐦᒃ stories are accounts of the Cree trickster and detail important norms and valuable information on cosmic order, medicinal plants, and the roles of animals. Amelia Paget, one of the few women authors of Indigenous histories in the early twentieth century (and also one of the few with Indigenous ancestry), wrote in 1909: "He (ᐄᐧᓴᑲᒉᐦᒃ) has been treated as a creator, a defender, a teacher and at the same time a conqueror, a robber, a deceiver" (Paget 2004, 57). ᐄᐧᓴᑲᒉᐦᒃ stories are told in pipon ᐱᐳᐣ (winter).[4] Paget explains that ᐄᐧᓴᑲᒉᐦᒃ has a most wonderful personage, "claiming to have created the earth after the flood and to have been the means of saving all the birds of the air and beasts of the field by his wisdom. He is also claimed to have understood and conversed with all the animals, birds, fishes and insects, and also with all manner of plants" (Paget 2004, 57). It is said that ᐄᐧᓴᑲᒉᐦᒃ was last seen on earth on the southern side of the Sweetgrass First Nation in Saskatchewan; there is a hill with a slope there called "we-sa-ka-chak's Slide" (B. Ahenakew, Hardlotte, and Jensen 1973, 1:9). At the end of this chapter I will expand on this introduction of ᐄᐧᓴᑲᒉᐦᒃ as the stories provide a substantive analysis of economic relationships found within Cree philosophy.

ᐄᐧᓴᑲᒉᐦᒃ provides teachings about the responsibilities of Cree to all other living beings. Another aspect of sacred living histories is providing teachings on the meaning of ceremonies. Indigenous spirituality is often based on the connection of ceremonies to land, language, and living histories. Cree people have a complex ceremonial cycle. Ceremonies teach of the importance of renewal; instead of looking through time as a linear concept, Indigenous renewal ceremonies orient us to the cycles that are the basis of many Indigenous world views. These ceremonies also form part of Cree governance through the groups known as societies that often hold the ceremonies. Joseph Dion (1958, 42–53) talked about the extensiveness of ceremonies that include the Prairie Chicken Society, Buffalo Dance, Horse Dance, witigo Dance, Wapiti Society, Bear Dance, Ghost Dance, Give Away Dance, Calumet Dance, Smoke Feast, and Tea Dance. He also discussed the importance of the Medicine Lodge, the Shaking Tent ceremony, the Skunk Dance, the Bee Dance, the Great Dogs, the Rattlers Society, and the Kit Foxes (Dion n.d.). These renewal practices are still of great importance today.

The Sun Dance or Thirst Dance is often considered the most important ceremony for the Cree. nipâhkwesimowin ᓂᐸᕽᐃᐧᓯᒧᐃᐧᐣ (the Sun Dance) is described as "dancing through a day and night without quenching one's thirst" (Paget 2004, 5). Planning starts the year before, and the ceremony itself, which is generally performed in late spring to early summer, usually lasts three to four days. This ceremony is described as a thanks offering to the Great Spirit, a time for making braves (a rite of passage), making specific petitions, and mourning loved ones who have died (Dion n.d.). The Sun Dance provides an important example of a ceremony that is at the heart of Cree peoplehood. The complex organization found at these Indigenous annual gatherings, I would argue, provides essential information about Indigenous governance. Many different tribes meet together during big events like this.

Figure 8 shows a Cree camp in the spring of 1870 as drawn by the Cree leader Fine Day. Among the Upstream Cree were the bands of the River People, the Beaver Hills People (West People), the House People, and the Parklands People (Prairie People) (Milloy 1990, 73). At this encampment there were 500 tipis for the River People, 300 for the Prairie People, 600 for the West People, and 200 for the House People. At these large encampments each tipi had a specific location, based on the band, the society to which a person belonged, and rank. As there were thousands of people at these gatherings, every society within Cree peoplehood fulfilled a different function. For example, the Rattlers Society of the River People was composed of warriors, and during large encampments the Warriors' lodge was erected at the centre of the camp circle (Mandelbaum 2001, 113–15). As Cree informants explain, "When several bands were camped together, each Warrior lodge was pitched near the center of the camp circle, opposite that segment of the circle occupied by its band. The tipi of the band chief stood between the Warrior lodge and the arc of the camp circle. The tipi of the Warrior Chief was placed directly behind that of the Band Chief" (Mandelbaum 2001, 117). Joseph Dion (1996, 17) explains that during a Sun Dance, the Prairie Chicken Dance Society took over, and one of their many duties was to ensure order was kept in camp. As recorded by the late Cree leader Dr. Harold Cardinal, Elders continue to speak emphatically of the importance of the Sun Dance, stating "through the Sundance ceremonies, First Nations

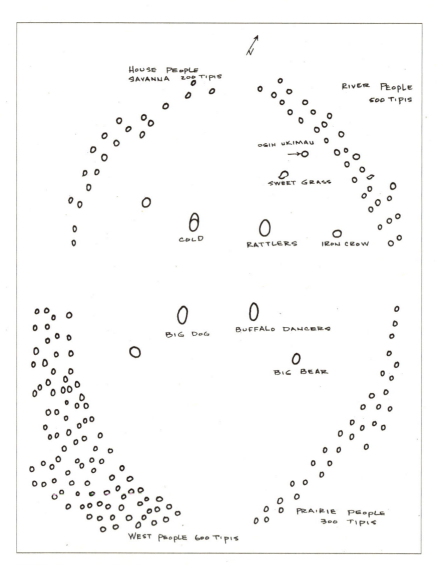

8 Plains Cree camp, 1870. | *From David Goodman Mandelbaum,* The Plains Cree: An Ethnographic, Historical and Comparative Study *(Regina, SK: Canadian Plains Research Center, 2001), 371.*

continually reaffirm and renew the sovereignty aspect of the relationships given to them by their Creator. They symbolize and represent the existence of a living, sovereign First Nations circle" (H. Cardinal and Hildebrandt 2000, 41). Ceremonies are an integral part of Cree peoplehood, connecting living histories with the language and the significance of the land encompassing Cree territory. Colonialism severs relationships, but we should distinguish how it does so in relation to land and spirituality, while still understanding how these two fronts are also constitutive of each other.

Indigenous people are often characterized through their connection to the land and environment. As explored throughout this study, self-determination for the Cree is intimately connected to the land, and to relations with and reciprocal responsibilities to the earth, air, water, and other living creatures. The territory of the Plains Cree before the disappearance of the buffalo is described as extending across the present provinces of Saskatchewan and Alberta, from the region "where the Qu'Appelle River crosses the Manitoba line to the vicinity of Edmonton. The various bands of Plains Cree centred in the river basins included in this area and the tribal range may be defined in terms of the valleys of the Qu'Appelle, the lower North Saskatchewan, the lower South Saskatchewan, and the lower Battle rivers" (Mandelbaum 2001, 7).

Before European colonialism in North America, Indigenous people lived in complex and symbiotic relationships with the land. There were normative principles and practices guiding these relationships. Plains Indigenous lives revolved around the buffalo – the hunt, the spiritual ceremony around a kill, and social and political structures – with daily needs being met by what the buffalo provided: food, shelter, clothes, and many other necessities of life. Bison (pasqua-mostos) were part of the social, political, economic, and spiritual lives of Plains people. One of the most fundamental aspects of colonialism was felt when the land and its abundance were exploited and Indigenous peoples were no longer able to live off the land. This changed a people who enjoyed food sovereignty to a people dependent on colonial systems for their livelihood. The bison, and the loss of these herds, shaped the land and the people.

When Indigenous peoples describe territory within their histories, "quite often creation and migration stories specify certain landmarks as being especially holy. Ancestors are buried in particular places. Shrines are erected and certain parts of the immediate environment – plants, water, earth, animal parts – are often utilized in religious ceremonies" (Holm, Pearson, and Chavis 2003, 14). There are over one million tipi rings still visible in Alberta alone. Forms known as effigies are also located across the Plains; for example, a bison effigy is located in Big Beaver, Saskatchewan (Bryan 2005, 66–82). mistasiniy ᒥᐢᑕᓯᓂᕀ (Big Rock) was a large rock in the Qu'Appelle Valley in the shape of a bison. The Cree revered it as a sacred site where, a legend states, a Cree boy was turned into a bison and then into the rock

(B. Ahenakew, Hardlotte, and Jensen 1973, 2:61). The rock measured 79 feet (24 metres) around the base and 46 feet (14 metres) from one side to the other (Soagie n.d.). In the 1960s, the sacred site was detonated in preparation for the construction of two dams, which flooded the location. A memorial featuring a part of the rock is located in Elbow. It is said that Cree men also took remnants of the rock and placed them on Chief Poundmaker's grave (Soagie n.d.).

The components of the Peoplehood Matrix are considered inseparable, and land cannot be understood outside of ceremony, language, or history. The Cree have a strong connection to all these aspects of peoplehood. They saw and see themselves, and were seen by others, as a people. This distinction was not based on blood quantum but on Indigenous forms of citizenship guided by normative principles like wâhkohtôwin. Indigenous jurisdiction over territory is not simply a right granted by a nation-state; many see it as a responsibility and gift given by the Great Spirit. Historian John Milloy (1990, 70) wrote that although early trade systems and geography created the regional divisions among the Cree, they should still be considered one nation. I agree.

As a self-determining people, the Cree undertook diplomatic relations with foreigners; inter-nation trade within the Plains region was one important aspect of a Cree political economy. The following section considers the diplomatic relations among the Plains Cree. Through the lens of historical data, I show the external economic relations of the Cree. I have chosen to focus on inter-nation trade, trade networks, transportation, and trade language.

Diplomacy

Diplomatic relations with other governments, citizens, and other living relations are important to ensure that the objectives of a people are met. As a self-determining people, the Cree embark upon formal alliances and treaties. In the eighteenth century, the Cree were regarded as a strong "nation of the plains" (Milloy 1990, 2). The Cree and their Anishinaabe and Nakota relations (called "Ojibwa" and "Assiniboine" in the records quoted here) were collectively considered the most powerful group in western Canada: "By the 1860's, the Cree-Ojibwa-Assiniboine group was by far the largest alliance in Canada. Their domain, generally speaking, spread from Quebec to the Rocky Mountains and from the northern tree line to the Missouri River" (Light 1987, 25). Despite linguistic barriers, the Cree and Assiniboine were considered each other's closest allies. Many Assiniboine spoke Cree and vice versa, and by the mid-seventeenth century there was a firm alliance between the two nations, and with other Algonquin-speaking confederates (Mandelbaum 2001). The nehiyaw-pwat ᐅᐱᐊᐣᐅ ᐸᐧᐟ, or Iron Alliance, was a strong confederacy between the Plains Cree, Woods Cree, Saulteaux, Nakoda (Nakota), and Métis (Barkwell 2018). The Cree also established a trading alliance with the Arapaho and the Mandan to the south during the period of the Horse Wars (Hildebrandt 2008). Besides alliances, the Cree also participated in formal treaties.

Before European settlement in North America, Indigenous peoples entered into various kinds of treaties – for example, the treaty between humans and trees explained at the beginning of this chapter. The Cree and Blackfoot entered into a treaty titled wîtaskewin ᐄᐧᑕᐢᑫᐃᐧᐣ, meaning "to live in peace together" in the Cree language. This peace treaty was created to end the hostilities between the two peoples (H. Cardinal and Hildebrandt 2000, 53). Archival, archaeological, and oral-history research provides key insights into Cree international trade practices. In my research I found an abundant assortment of traded goods from across Turtle Island (an Indigenous term for North America) and beyond. Trade required a complex transportation infrastructure, with numerous trail systems running from Canada to Mexico. These trail systems provide further evidence of the importance and frequency of international trade to pre-contact Indigenous peoples.

Inter-nation Trade on the Plains

As introduced in Chapter 1, pimâcihowin ᐱᒫᒋᐦᐅᐃᐧᐣ is about livelihood, making a living. Elders in Saskatchewan explain how the word and underlying principles derive from life itself. They explain it this way:

> This connection to the land, as described by the Elders, consists of at least the following elements: spiritual, physical, and economic. This connection is rooted in the Cree concept and doctrines related to pimâtisiwin (life). It is a concept that contains many theoretical subsets including, among other things, a concept called "pimâcihowin" (the ability to make a living). Land (askiy) is an important source of life, for it provides those things required for the physical, material, and economic survival of the people. When treaty Elders use the word "pimâcihowin" they are describing a holistic concept that includes a

spiritual as well as a physical dimension. (H. Cardinal and Hildebrandt 2000, 43)

The principles embedded in pimâcihowin are about how to have miyo-pimâtisiwin, the good life. Chapters 7, 8, and 9 delve into this more fully. Trade, facilitated through good relations among different peoples, is one way to exchange physical and spiritual elements for the good life. One important function of a self-determining people is to engage in external trade to diversify a local and regional economy. For the Cree, food, ornamental goods, livestock, raw goods, processed goods, medicines, and ceremonies were key commodities for import and export. In this section, examples of trade practices are explored, with a focus on goods traded, trading networks, and ceremonial practices regarding trade.

Trading often revolves around exchanging goods available in abundance in an area for desirable items that are rare or difficult to obtain in the same area. Before European settlement, bison, other game, fish, fowl, vegetal foods, and berries were found in abundance on the plains, but it is recorded that the Cree made an annual journey to the southwest to obtain corn. Trade with those living by salt water provided mussel shells used for utensils and jewellery (Mandelbaum 2001, 24, 91, 84). A trade relationship also occurred in which "agricultural producers living in what is now southern Ontario and the St. Lawrence valley supplied corn and other products ... exchanging them for fish or furs" (Canada 1996, vol. 2, ch. 5). The Kootenay people used red ochre pigment for trade after they processed it into red oxide; this was taken from the area called "Usna Waki-Cagubi" (Lakusta 2007, 85). The Cree also traded ceremonies with other Indigenous peoples.[5] The Buffalo Dance was obtained from the Dakota in exchange for clothing and horses, and was preceded by a transfer ceremony. Similarly, the Stoney bought the right to perform the Rattlers' Dance from the Cree (Mandelbaum 2001, 111–12).[6]

Archaeological discoveries provide an account of trade items. Bones and shells from the west coast have been found by the South Saskatchewan River. Native copper mined outside what is now Thunder Bay over eight thousand years ago was manufactured into different items and is found across the Plains. Significantly, shell gorget was recovered on the Plains from a clamshell only available in the Gulf of Mexico (Bryan 2005). In Edmonton, a piece of pottery, up to a thousand years old, was uncovered (Goyette 2004, 11). Oral accounts, written records, and archaeological evidence all point to a diverse market of goods that were part of an international trade network throughout Turtle Island.

All across North America runs an extensive Indigenous trail system predating European contact. As mentioned above, these trails provided migration routes, supported trade networks, led to locations of warfare, and were used for various travel purposes. These trade routes extended across numerous Indigenous nations' territories and provided the infrastructure on which the fur-trade and settler road systems were built. The Old North Trail is one of the most extensive and best known. It is also referred to as the Wolf Tracks and the Blackfoot Tracks. The Wolf Tracks is not a single trail but a network of north–south trails running from Edmonton to Mexico. Within the Rossdale Flats area of Edmonton, a pêhonân Vᵗᴰȯ᾽ (gathering place) (Goyette 2004, 20) was located: "Situated on the old Indian trail called Wolf's Track, was long ago an ancient meeting place of Plains people – a place of trade, celebration and ceremony" (Coutu 2004, 105). Evidence shows this was a site for many activities, including intertribal trade among the Cree, Chipewyan, Beaver, Nakoda, and Blackfoot (Goyette 2004, 22). This trail went south from the Rossdale Flats, basically following the route on which Highway 2 (Queen Elizabeth II Highway) lies today (Petty 1962, 2). At present-day Wetaskiwin, the trail forked (7), with the western branch following the foothills region parallel to the Rocky Mountains. Brings-Down-The-Sun, one of the most respected Piikani spiritual leaders, shared this enlightening account with Walter McClintock in 1905:

> There is a well-known trail we call the Old North Trail. It runs north and south along the Rocky Mountains. No one knows how long it has been used by the Indians. My father told me it originated in the migration of a great tribe of Indians from the distant north to the south, and all the tribes have, ever since, continued to follow their tracks ... The main trail ran south along the eastern side of the Rockies, at a uniform distance from the mountains, keeping clear of the forest, and outside of the foothills. It ran close to where the City of Helena [Montana] now stands, and extended south into the country, in-habited by a people with dark skins, and long hair falling over their faces [Mexico]. In former times, when the Indian tribes were at war, there was constant fighting along the North Trail. In those days, Indians who wanted to travel in peace avoided it and took to the forest. My father once told me of an expedition from the Blackfeet, that went

south by the Old Trail, to visit the people with dark skins. Elk Tongue and his wife Natoya were of this expedition, also Arrow Top and Pemmican, who was a boy of twelve at the time. He died only a few years ago at the age of ninety-five. They were absent four years. It took them twelve moons of steady travelling to reach the country of the dark-skinned people, and eighteen moons to come north again. They returned by a longer route through the "High Trees" or Bitter Root country, where they could travel without danger of being seen. They feared going along the North Trail because it was frequented by their enemies, the Crows, Sioux and Cheyennes. Elk Tongue brought back the Dancing Pipe. (Reeves 1990, 4–5)

This informative account provides insights into the age of the Old North Trail, the uses of the trail, length of travel time, and ceremonial trade with Indigenous peoples in Mexico. It is well-documented that fur traders often used Indigenous trail systems; later, settlers used these same trails for their carts, and our current highways and railways were often laid along large portions of the same transportation networks.

There was also an extensive east–west trail system connecting Hudson Bay to the Rocky Mountains. One part of this trail system has been referred to as the Carlton Trail, which was "the main highway into the Saskatchewan country from the Red River Settlement" (Russell 1840, 1), further connecting to Fort Carlton, Fort Pitt, and Edmonton (Russell 1955, 2). This has been described as the only overland route between Upper Fort Garry and Fort Edmonton (Hall 1969). Before the Carlton Trail was used in the fur trade, it was used as an Indigenous trail, part of a migration path established six thousand years ago when Lake Agassiz glacier retreated (Hall 1969). South-west of the junction of the north and south branches of the Saskatchewan River is one location where the Cree and Blackfoot traded (Milloy 1990, 17). At important points along this ancient trail, by lakes and on high ground, many artifacts have been found from large encampments "at such places as Upper Fort Garry, Deer Lodge, Whitehorse Plain, Portage la Prairie, Neepawa, Minnedosa, Shoal Lake, and Fort Ellice – all on the Carlton Trail" (Milloy 1990, 17). The pêhonân ᐁᐧᐃᐅᐢ (gathering place) mentioned above was only one of many Indigenous gathering places on this route. These centres were seen as locations of trade and "the heart of the cultural and spiritual life of the First Peoples" (Coutu 2004, 64). The spiritual, trading, and cultural significance of these repeated-use seasonal encampments led David Meyer from the University of Saskatchewan to research six of these sites:

> These campsites were often located approximately 80 kilometres apart along the North and South Saskatchewan Rivers ... from east to west the location of these gathering places, and their Cree meanings, are as follows: Grand Rapids, "Mitipawitik, a large rapid"; Cedar Lake, "Cimawawin, a seining place"; The Pas, "Opasskweaw, the narrowing between woods"; "Paskwattinow" near the Pasqua Hills, the original location of Fort St. Louis; Nipawin, Nipowiwwinihk, "a standing place"; and finally Fort de la Corne, known as "pehonan, the waiting place." (Coutu 2004, 64–65)

Research at the University of Saskatchewan has found a strong correlation between these ancient gathering places and the later positioning of fur-trade posts by the Hudson's Bay Company and the Northwest Company (Coutu 2004). Different sources also point to complex networks existing in other areas, including a trade network from the west coast to the interior of what is currently Canada (Canada 1996, vol. 2 ch. 5). Similarly, there are accounts of an Oolichan Trail (named for the oolichan or eulachon, also known as candlefish, from which oil is made) that crossed the Rocky Mountains. Historian and journalist Olive Dickason (2002, 3:60) stated that oolichan oil, which had ceremonial and medicinal functions, "was extensively traded from the Pacific coast into the interior along established routes"; this trade goes back to at least 4000 BC. It is apparent that Indigenous trail systems were expansive and well-developed before European contact.

Travelling over extended distances required an infrastructure of trails, modes of transportation, diplomacy, and systems of governance that enabled an efficient process for moving camp. For land travel, before the introduction of the horse, the dog travois was used in the summer, and a dog with cariole was used in the winter (Brown 1927). The Saskatchewan River was another significant part of this east–west trail system. Archaeological evidence has confirmed that boats have been used on the Prairies for over thirteen thousand years (Goyette 2004, 8), and various types of boats were used for water travel. Figure 9 displays Cree men on a Cree flat boat on the Montreal River in Saskatchewan.

9 Cree boatmen on a Cree flat boat on the Montreal River, Saskatchewan, 1890. |
Saskatchewan Archives Board (Database ID 26030), online: Our Legacy http//scaa.sk.ca/ourlegacy/permalink/26030.

This extensive infrastructure of trails and transportation devices indicates a robust trading system stretching throughout Turtle Island. To engage in successful inter-nation trade requires the establishment of accepted norms and practices that become part of a diplomatic function, regardless of whether a nation-state or other model of nation is engaged in the activity. It is clear that Indigenous peoples in historic North America were thus engaged.

There was an accepted protocol among Plains peoples before trade commenced, with the type of protocol or ceremony depending on the material being traded. For example, Mandelbaum (2001, 38) was told by his informants that when the Buffalo Dance was brought from Dakota (see Chapter 7), there was a "ceremony of adoption and an exchange of property [among] the Assiniboine and the Cree and the Mandan." Mandelbaum's informants also stated that many Cree medicines originally came from the Saulteaux (Plains Ojibway). maskwa[7] (Bear) spoke of a Plains Cree who travelled to the east to receive medicines from the Saulteaux. He presented to them two horses loaded with well-made clothes. In exchange, the Saulteaux took him into their mitewin lodge and taught him about many plants that could be used for medicinal purposes (165).

Traditionally, a Chief had to give freely of his possessions and "usually set the pace for ceremonial giving"; gift-giving was considered one dispute-resolution mechanism (Mandelbaum 2001, 106–7). The Giveaway Dance was one institutional mechanism that any person could start if he "happened to have something he wished to give some friend of his" (Paget 2004, 14). I discuss giveaways and gift-giving more extensively in Chapters 7, 8, and 9.

Fur traders also adopted Indigenous trading protocols. Norbert Welsh, a Métis born at Red River in 1845, was a buffalo hunter and trader; he describes how, before trading, he would invite the Chief – for example, Chief Starblanket – and present him with a pound of tea, a few pounds of sugar, and tobacco. He told Starblanket "to divide these among his men, and to let them have a good drink of tea, and a good smoke, then we would trade" (Welsh as told to Weekes 1994, 100). Today, tariffs are accepted measures imposed on foreigners doing business in another country. Similar to this practice, Welsh recounts another story in which Pish-e-quat (Blackguard), speaking on behalf of his Chief, Shash-apew, requested a duty or tariff for any bison hunted by settlers on his nation's territory, stating that the "headmen of his band believed that the Indians were more entitled to the buffalo than the white men" (51). This story is informative in further substantiating how the Cree exerted jurisdiction over a defined territory and how they expected payment for use of the resources of their land.

The extent of international trade conducted in the Americas before European contact is further substantiated by the spread of languages, which facilitated diplomatic relations such as trade. It was quite common for Indigenous peoples to speak more than one language as an aid to foreign relations. Similarly, in certain areas of North America, hybrid languages developed, described as trade languages (Dickason 2002, 3:60). A sign language was also known among the different peoples living on the Plains of North America. Figure 10 displays the way to sign the term "exchange": "both hands, palms facing each other, forefingers extended, crossed right above left before the breast" (Mallery n.d.). There are hundreds of hand signs in this system, including those for "trade," "barter," "buy," "exchange,"

10 Plains sign language for "Exchange." | *From Garrick Mallery, "Hand Talk: American Indian Sign Language," http://sunsite.utk.edu/pisl/illustrations.html.*

and "pay." Of the Plains Cree, it is written that the amiskowacîwiyiniwak ᐊᒥᐢᑿᒌᐃᐧᔨᓂᐊᐧᐠ (Beaver Hills People) seemed to use this sign language the most frequently (Mandelbaum 2001, 361). In 1930, the American Department of the Interior held a conference in Browning, Montana, at which thirteen different First Nations from across the Plains met to communicate and document the sign language; this was filmed and can be viewed online (Scott 1930). Flashing mirrors in the sun was another method used to communicate over a distance (Mandelbaum 2001, 361). Diplomatic functions, such as trade, were facilitated by the use of trade languages like the Plains Indigenous sign language.

The international trade practices of the Plains Cree, including the plethora of goods traded, the complex trading infrastructure, and established protocols, demonstrate the extensive function of international trade within Cree society and the making of Cree peoplehood. This system of international trade was one key aspect of a larger diplomatic relations function for Cree people. A historical understanding of Cree international trade practices can provide insights into fostering Indigenous economic resurgence and aiding in greater governance options for Indigenous peoples. Re-engaging Indigenous trade systems is another aspect of reclaiming Indigenous self-determination.

In this chapter I have attempted to provide a deeper understanding of Plains Cree peoplehood, and how its reach expands through diplomacy and trade. Indigenous trade alliances expose a plethora of economic avenues based on Cree peoples' own understandings of the land, allowing the Cree to realize the aspirations of their ancestors: to have miyo-pimâtisiwin ᒥᔪ ᐱᒫᑎᓯᐏᐣ, the good life.

As introduced earlier in this chapter, ᐑᓵᐦᑫᒑᕽ stories share teachings about ways of being relationally in the world, ways of interacting with other humans and animals, and ways of being in relationship with the land, including with mistikwak ᒥᐢᑎᑿᐠ (trees). Drawing back to my dream I recounted at the beginning of this chapter, this ᐑᓵᐦᑫᒑᕽ legend grounds us back into the importance of upholding our relationships – including to the mistikwak – our first treaty. My grandmother's nohkom (grandmother) shared ᐑᓵᐦᑫᒑᕽ stories with her, like nohkom (my grandmother) shared with us. These legends explore gifts provided by living beings, and in this account the relationship with a tree, mistik, whom ᐑᓵᐦᑫᒑᕽ endearingly calls his brother. The following is a ᐑᓵᐦᑫᒑᕽ story from nohkom ᓄᐦᑯᐹᐣ (my grandmother) Lillian Wuttunee, passed on to her by her nohkom ᓄᐦᑯ. nikâwiy ᓂᑳᐏᕀ (my mother) audiotaped nohkom ᓄᐦ sharing this story on February 27, 1993, and then transcribed her words.[8] The rest of this chapter is a ᐑᓵᐦᑫᒑᕽ story; there are teachings that these stories should be shared when there is snow on the ground. I leave it to you to observe these teachings. Lillian Wuttunee's words:

> My grandmother always wore black. A black skirt and blouse, moccasins, and a black handkerchief tied around her head. She spoke only Cree. She still had good eyesight, for I remember she could spot an insect from across the room.
>
> "nohkom," I'd tell her, "you are so beautiful."
>
> "kayâsês nôsisim," she'd answer. "Long ago, granddaughter, I used to be a beautiful young woman."
>
> "You're still beautiful, nohkom," I'd reply and ask her to tell me a

story, which she would do only in the winter, for she said it was bad luck to tell them in the summer.

"Okay," she'd answer, "but first sit there until I finish smoking."

I would watch as she filled her little clay pipe with tobacco and stare as she took each puff, waiting patiently for her to finish so that she could tell me a story. Finally she'd begin:

wîsahkecâhk was walking in the woods when he heard some laughter. Being inquisitive by nature, he followed the sounds until he came across a flock of little birds.

"Why are you laughing, brothers?" he asked them.

"We have headaches," they answered, "and so we are throwing our eyeballs up into the trees."

"What happens then?" wîsahkecâhk asked his feathered friends.

"We have only to shake the trees and our little eyeballs fall back into our heads, and so we cure our headaches," they answered him, for everything had to answer wîsahkecâhk when he talked to them.

"I have a headache too," wîsahkecâhk said.

"Oh, you must not say that just for the fun of it," the birds chirped. "Or something bad will happen to you," they added.

"I understand," wîsahkecâhk said, before adding, "but I do have a headache."

The little birds did not believe him and so said, "We're warning you. You must not do this for nothing."

wîsahkecâhk did not listen to the birds' advice. Instead, he threw his eyeballs up into the trees. Just then a fox was walking by and when wîsahkecâhk shook the tree to get his eyeballs back, the fox caught them in his mouth and ran away. wîsahkecâhk didn't really have a headache and now found himself without eyes. Being blind now, he stumbled to the different trees and touched their bark.

"Brother," he asked, "what kind of tree are you?" Each of the trees he touched identified themselves and told wîsahkecâhk what kind of medicinal powers their bark, leaves, and roots were good for. Finally, wîsahkecâhk reached a spruce tree and, after feeling its bark, asked, "What kind of tree are you, my brother?"

"minahik," the tree answered.

"You are just the tree I need," wîsahkecâhk cried out in happiness. He climbed into its branches until he found its resin. He put it into his mouth and began to chew it until it finally became soft. From that he rolled out first one and then another eyeball and placed them into his empty sockets. He thanked the tree for giving him its medicine so that he could see once more.

Commenting on this legend, my grandmother Lillian said, "Now, it wasn't until I reached my seventies that I finally understood what that story was all about." The story is indeed full of layered meanings. It speaks to proper (and improper) relations with other living things. It also speaks to Indigenous knowledge of the natural world and the medicines that are abundantly available. Lillian realized later in life the specific medicinal teachings that this legend speaks, based on the relationship to and medicinal properties of spruce tree resin. Lillian went on to say:

My grandmother never explained the curing part to me, for I was just a child. Instead, she told it to me like a story. The next night I would say to her again, "âcimow nohkom" [Tell me a story, grandmother]. "cêskwa" [Wait a minute], she'd answer, and she would go through the same ritual of smoking her pipe before beginning.

4
Canada's Genesis Story

Great Father, – I shake hands with you, and bid you welcome. We heard our lands were sold and we did not like it; we don't want to sell our lands; it is our property, and no one has a right to sell them.

– Chief Sweetgrass et al. (1871)

THE LETTER EXCERPTED above is from three nehiyawak (Plains Cree) Chiefs and was sent to Governor Archibald, the colonial representative on the Plains, in 1871 (the full letter is provided later in this chapter). In this letter Chief Sweetgrass calls himself the "Chief of the country." I surmise Chief Sweetgrass is using a powerful rhetorical device in this letter. He is writing in terms that can be understood by the settler-colonial state. Drawing on this letter as inspiration, I write this chapter showing the unjustness of Canada's genesis story through the lens of economic exploitation within capitalism. I draw heavily on archival sources to demonstrate the unjustness even from within a settler logic. Canadians and others around the world often exalt Canada for its democratic principles and good governance, but the often-withheld truth is that most of Canada's lands became Canada through an order-in-council unjustly buying stolen Indigenous territories from a corporation (the Hudson's Bay Company) to create a country (Tough 1992). Specifically, in 1870 before Treaty Six was negotiated, 3.89 million square kilometres, approximately 63.5 percent of present-day Canada's total land mass, was incorporated into the Dominion of Canada (Tough 2018, 2). This genesis story of Canada is a key example of the exploitation of Indigenous peoples and territories; this is the foundation of the relationship between Indigenous peoples and Canada to this day. In this chapter, I provide specific examples of exploitation that occurred during the fur trade, drawing on archival and academic sources to demonstrate the origin of this relationship. Indigenous peoples have complex normative principles related to other nations' use or misuse of traditional territories. Property is only one way to view land that collapses the myriad of relationships found in a concept like nehiyawaskiy ᗷᐦᐊᔭᐧ·ᐣᕈᐩ. The creation of a property regime that supplanted Indigenous legal orders on this land is a violence. This expropriation is exploitation. Within this initial violence there is also the further exploitation that occurs even within the internal logic of capitalism. This chapter unpacks the economic exploitation that is at the heart of Canada's creation.

As introduced in Chapter 2, the social, political, legal, cultural, and economic lives of Indigenous peoples have been and continue to be negatively affected by exploitation that occurs. Each of those spheres are part of an interrelated system of colonial logics. In movement toward self-determination we often focus on state domination, what I refer to as the first colonial logic. However, we miss an important part of the larger story: namely, how exploitation of Indigenous lands and bodies – economic exploitation – is a key component of the Canadian story. Through an economic analysis of colonialism we can examine how state economic interests, policies, and practices negatively affect Indigenous peoples – which then negatively impacts all aspects of Cree peoplehood. All are related. As colonial logics are intimately connected, so are the practices of principled self-determination; for example, renewing economic relationships ethically has positive implications for social and political realms too. Understanding the logics in settler colonialism can help us develop strategies and practices to unravel them.

Settler Colonialism

Settler colonialism is a specific type of colonialism, like that of British-established settler states in Canada, the United States, Australia, and New Zealand. The act of settler colonization – traced back to the thirteenth and twelfth centuries BC – is described as settlement patterns on newly possessed lands, already occupied by others, where those settling (or their home country rulers) provide "mechanisms of spatial expansion and often powerful instruments ... for establishing and enforcing control over the newly settled territories" (Lloyd and Metzer 2012, 5). The late Australian historian Patrick

Wolfe (1999, 2) states that settler colonies are based on eliminating Indigenous societies: when "the colonizers come to stay – invasion is a structure, not an event." Settler colonialism can be seen as a structure that enacts events (or practices) to self-perpetuate its legitimacy and reach continually. Isabel Altamirano-Jiménez (2013, 32–33) sees British colonialism as centred on separating Indigenous peoples from land, and on other elements that devalue unimproved nature and separate it from society while simultaneously building an economy where those who can transform nature can have exclusive control with the seemingly unlimited ability to accumulate it.

Related to North America specifically, scholars' broad analyses explore settler colonialism's impacts on Indigenous economies. Economists Christopher Lloyd and Jacob Metzer (2012, xvii) explain that the characteristics of a settler economy include 1) settlers wanting to become permanent residents; 2) settlers wanting to exploit natural resources; and 3) settlers and their offspring wanting to dominate the society, the economy, and the culture of the area. In North America, settler colonization was driven by settlers' desire for land (10). Lloyd and Metzer explain that one feature of British settler colonialism in North America, Australia, New Zealand, and southern Africa "was that their land regime, initially one of an imperial or company 'grab,' became by the 19th century largely based on the emerging concept of private property rights within a market economy" (14). I have learned that it is important to understand how economic exploitation preceded bureaucratic control in what became Canada. I see economic exploitation on this land creating the environment for settler colonialism to take hold over Indigenous peoples through the fur trade.[1]

The Genesis of Economic Exploitation on Indigenous Lands

As mentioned in earlier chapters, Indigenous peoples hold diverse legal and political concepts regarding relationships to land. The fact that the concept of private property was foreign to Cree peoples before settlers' contact does not mean that Indigenous peoples do not have complex understandings of and legal orders for the jurisdiction and use of land. Cree Elders explain wîtaskewin Ꭺ·ᑕᐣᑫᐊᐧ as one concept that relates to jurisdiction:

> witaskêwin is a Cree word meaning "living together on the land." It is a word that has multiple applications and multidimensional meanings. It can include or refer to individuals or nations who are strangers to one another, agreeing to either live on or share for some specific

purpose a land area with each other, or it can be applied to land-sharing arrangements between individual members of the nation. (H. Cardinal and Hildebrandt 2000, 40)

In the last chapter, I gave the example of Chief Shash-apew, during the fur-trade era, requesting a tariff on any bison hunted on his people's territory. This example demonstrates normative practices around territory. Although Cree people did not subscribe to the idea of private property, as the British did at the time, this does not mean that the Hudson's Bay Company had any right to sell Indigenous peoples' lands. In 1670 the Hudson's Bay Company (HBC) became the first corporation in the world, establishing monopoly trading on Indigenous lands. The Royal Charter of 1670, establishing the HBC, was completed without treaty with the Indigenous peoples on whose land the HBC operated. I see the Royal Charter of 1670 as the genesis moment of economic exploitation of Indigenous peoples and Indigenous lands.

In 1763, King George III issued the Royal Proclamation to claim extensive areas of North America as British territory, although the proclamation acknowledges "Indian" title to land existed and continues to exist. Legal and constitutional scholar Brian Slattery (2015, 22) writes of how in the proclamation the Crown "tacitly acknowledges the autonomy of the 'Nations or Tribes of Indians' as distinct political entities with their own political structures and laws." (As an aside, as someone who sees the legitimacy of Indigenous peoples at that time, I am incredulous that a man born in London, albeit a king, could make declarations and take possession of land, and – at least regarding Treaty Six territory – do so before negotiating with Indigenous societies on the lands in question.) Slattery states that in the Royal Proclamation of 1763, the Crown asserts sovereignty over extensive regions of the American territory, and yet it also "recognizes that these territories are actually in the possession of numerous Indigenous nations, which are described as 'connected' with the Crown and living under its 'Protection'" (22).

Often, the fur trade is seen as symbolically important to, and positive for, both Indigenous peoples and Canadians. Many academics have pointed out that Indigenous societies changed less during the fur trade than did the European traders, who had to adapt to Indigenous trade practices (Rotstein in Hildebrandt 2008, 6). Indigenous peoples were able to draw on thousands of years of trade practices and trade networks throughout Turtle Island. I am not disagreeing with this, but I want to focus specifically on the exploitation of Indigenous people that occurred during the fur trade. As this was a defining moment in our collective history, this genesis story is still relevant today. In the next section I will discuss how the fur trade introduced capitalism to Indigenous peoples. Then I will analyze how Indigenous peoples were exploited through this capitalistic mode of production, exploring different elements of exploitation that laid the foundation for settler colonialism to take hold.

Exploitation within a New Economic System

With the fur trade, a fundamental tension developed for Indigenous peoples, taking the form of an economic conflict between capitalism and communal modes of production (Moore 1993, 15). As introduced in Chapter 2, Frank Tough (2005, 32) writes that the commercialization that began during the fur trade provides a lens through which to understand Indigenous economic history under settler colonialism, in which "aspects of daily life increasingly fall under the influence of exchange value. More and more needs or wants become satisfied by market related activities." Tough sees the commercial capitalist market as being the first and most enduring institution affecting Indigenous peoples in Canada (31). Furthermore, he critiques other scholars' denial that economic exploitation preceded political oppression (54). The exploitation of capital and labour in the fur trade is what I will focus on next.

An important aspect of understanding the fur trade relates to an analysis of power. Tough (2005, 54) states that on a macroeconomic scale, Indigenous trappers and middlemen did not have real equity and were not partners in the fur-trade system; real decision-making power was under European control. While Indigenous people received material trade items (e.g., blankets, tea, flour) in exchange for furs, Europeans and settlers were able to invest the money received through the sale of furs to create more wealth in the capitalist system. Even within a capitalist logic, Indigenous peoples were structurally positioned to remain financially stagnant, unable to wield governing influence or control (at the HBC management level) over the economic decisions affecting them, or to invest capital to generate wealth within the capitalist system. This had a disastrous impact on them, as the reproductions of economic exploitation were amplified by 1) capitalism's infiltration of Indigenous peoples' economic systems; 2) Indigenous peoples' growing dependence on trade items, which meant dependence on settlers; and

3) the gradual demise of subsistence-based livelihood options that were the core of Indigenous economies. The fur trade exploited Indigenous labour and lands to gain money that was then invested for the benefit of fur-trade shareholders, the British economy (through the HBC) and then the Canadian state, and non-Indigenous Canadian society. No matter how great the input in increased Indigenous labour or the output in furs, Indigenous peoples were never, and would never be, shareholders or decision-makers in the fur-trade system. Therefore, Indigenous labour and lands were exploited, and Indigenous peoples were also exploited in financial terms. Given the institutional constraints imposed on them, Indigenous people would never be in a position to profit from their lands and labour as much as companies like the HBC. This exploitation logic embedded in capitalism continues for Indigenous peoples today.

The fur-trade era also saw the dwindling access to land and land-based subsistence practices through the decimation of the bison, an essential component of the life and diet of the Plains peoples.

Canada as Corporate Creation

The transferring of 63.5 percent of what is currently Canada's land mass from the HBC to the Dominion of Canada was completed through an order-in-council,[2] without Indigenous involvement, in 1870. Métis scholar Adam Gaudry (2016, 16) explains that Canada's "fantasy of sovereignty" was not based on sound legal logic; he states, "Since the Company's claim was itself founded on the fantasy of discovery, Canada was in effect purchasing a fantastical claim to this already-peopled territory." Frank Tough's 1992, 228) assessment is that "we do not know exactly why and how the HBC ended up with one-twentieth of the surveyed lands of the Prairies. An examination of the terms might cause one to ponder the legal implications of the Crown granting lands to the HBC prior to treaty making between the Canadian state and the Indians."

A double exploitation occurred here. First, the Dominion of Canada bought stolen Indigenous lands. The HBC sold 2.9 million square miles for £300,000, along with 50,000 acres of land around fur-trade posts and a selection of one-twentieth of the lands surveyed in the fertile belt (Tough 1992, 238). The HBC was also relieved of the duty of dealing with Indian claims, leaving that to the Dominion of Canada. The second exploitation is the large amount of land the HBC had received from the Crown compared to what Indigenous peoples received. Tough writes,

In the case of Manitoba, the Department of the Interior calculated that by 1930, some 559,301 acres had been set aside for Indians (2.6 percent of the land that had passed from the Crown), but 1,279,965 acres had been granted to the HBC (6.1 percent of the land that had passed from the Crown). The outcome of these very different claims was not equitable. (245)

A corporation with questionable jurisdiction over Indigenous lands, let alone claim to ownership, was able not only to sell this land for a profit, but also to receive more lands back in compensation than the Indigenous peoples from whom they stole it. This is economic exploitation.

The following is a response from Cree leaders to the problematic 1870 sale of Indigenous lands. In 1871 a letter from Cree Chiefs, excerpted in the epigraph at the beginning of this chapter, was sent to Governor Archibald, the colonial representative at Fort Garry, Red River Settlement:

1   The Chief Sweet Grass, The Chief of the country.

GREAT FATHER, – I shake hands with you, and bid you welcome. We heard our lands were sold and we did not like it; we don't want to sell our lands; it is our property, and no one has a right to sell them.

Our country is getting ruined of fur-bearing animals, hitherto our sole support, and now we are poor and want help – we want you to pity us. We want cattle, tools, agricultural implements, and assistance in everything when we come to settle – our country is no longer able to support us.

Make provision for us against years of starvation. We have had great starvation the past winter, and the small-pox took away many of our people, the old, young, and children.

We want you to stop the Americans from coming to trade on our lands, and giving firewater, ammunition and arms to our enemies the Blackfeet.

We made a peace this winter with the Blackfeet. Our young men are foolish, it may not last long.

We invite you to come and see us and to speak with us. If you can't come yourself, send some one in your place.

We send these words by our Master, Mr. Christie, in whom we have every confidence. – That is all.

2 Ki-he-win, The Eagle.

GREAT FATHER, – Let us be friendly. We never shed any white man's blood, and have always been friendly with the whites, and want workmen, carpenters and farmers to assist us when we settle. I want all my brother, Sweet Grass, asks. That is all.

3 The Little Hunter.

You, my brother, the Great Chief in Red River, treat me as a brother, that is, as a Great Chief.

4 Kis-ki-on, or Short Tail.

My brother, that is coming close, I look upon you, as if I saw you; I want you to pity me, and I want help to cultivate the ground for myself and descendants. Come and see us. (Chief Sweetgrass et al. 1871)

This letter is significant for several reasons. Chief Sweetgrass calls himself and is recognized as the Plains Cree Chief of the country; nested layers of governance are indicated in this letter. Plains Cree nested layers of governance are also illustrated in Figure 8 (Chapter 3). Secondly, the Cree declare their possession of their land and indicate that they are not interested in selling it. Finally, it is clear that the Cree understand the land is changing (for example, they note the disappearance of the bison) and want to prepare for a new livelihood. It is very important to understand that the Cree saw themselves as a nation and that they were also recognized as such by others. Alexander Morris (1880, chap. 9), lieutenant-governor of the Northwest Territories in the 1870s, states, "The great region covered by them [the Cree], abutting on the areas included in Treaties numbers Three and Four, embracing an area of approximately 120,000 square miles, contains a vast extent of fertile territory and is the home of the *Cree nation*" (emphasis added).

Treaty Six

Before European settlement in North America, Indigenous peoples entered into treaties. The Cree and Blackfoot, as noted earlier, entered into a treaty whose name in the Cree language meant "to live in peace together" (H. Cardinal and Hildebrandt 2000, 53). Indigenous languages have their own words and terms to describe different treaty relationships. Cree Elders have used the term iteyimikosiwiyecikewina ᐃᐅᕐᑯᕁᐅᐧᐧᑊᕆᖁᐅ·ᐆ as one way to refer to the treaties signed with the British. This term can be translated as "treaties inspired by our Creator" (H. Cardinal and Hildebrandt 2000). These treaties are based in Cree teachings and beliefs, and as such their arrangements are described in the Cree language: "They are grounded in the laws of miyo-wicehtowin governing the manner in which relationships are to be conducted internally among the members of the Cree Nation and externally with other peoples" (53). okimâw miyo-wîcihitowiyicikewin ᐅᑭᒫᐤ ᒥᔪ ᐑᒋᐦᐃᑐᐃᐧᔨᒋᑫᐃᐧᐣ is another common phrase used by Cree Elders to describe treaties such as Treaty Six; the translation is "agreements or arrangements establishing and organizing good relations or relations of friendship between sovereigns" (53). tipahamitowin ᑎᐸᐦᐊᒥᑐᐃᐧᐣ means "treating each other commensurately," and is understood as an act that involves reciprocal responsibilities that must be fulfilled (54). The Cree language and the terms used to describe treaties entered into with Europeans substantiate Cree understanding and assertion of their jurisdiction over their people and territory.

With the encroachment of an increasing number of settlers on Cree lands, the dubious sale of HBC lands, and the disappearance of bison herds on the prairies (resulting in famine), there was a push by the Plains peoples to negotiate a treaty with the British colony to ensure they would be able to survive as distinct nations or sovereign peoples. On March 9, 1876, Father Albert Lacombe wrote a letter to the Department of the Interior, Indian Affairs branch, requesting a law be passed to ensure bison would be preserved for the First Nations and Métis on the Plains. He wrote, "With the experience of twenty-five years, passed in the midst of the Indians of that Country, I am troubled to tell the Government ... that unless they have a law enacted to protect the Buffalo, before ten years those great herds will have disappeared" (Lacombe 1876).

Although the Cree requested treaty negotiations in 1871, it took a while to gather the attention of the colonial government authorities in Upper Canada. W.J. Christie, retired HBC employee and Treaty Commissioner, emphatically wrote to Richard Hardisty, chief factor of the Upper Saskatchewan District, in July 1875:

> I have done all I could the past winter to press the Government to send up and make a Treaty with the Saskatchewan Crees and Indians, but they are in no hurry, and say what you like you can't get them to see the thing in the same light as we do, there are people at Ottawa who seem to think that they know a great deal more about Indians and the

Country, than we do. I have told the Government that the longer they delay the Treaty, the harder it will be to make, and the more exacting will be the Indians, and their advisers. The Government may delay too long. I have said and written enough about Saskatchewan and the Indians that I am tired of the subjects. Nothing can be done this year as we are too late in beginning. (Christie 1875)

Christie had an understanding of the Cree from his years working for the HBC. His frustration stemmed from the inactivity of the government in Ottawa in pursuing treaty negotiations with the Cree. Finally, under the hand and seal of Alexander Morris, lieutenant-governor of the Northwest Territories (see Figure 11), dated August 1875, came instructions to the Reverend George McDougall to inform the Cree of upcoming treaty negotiations:

I have to request you to proceed to the Saskatchewan Region, as a messenger from me, and inform the Cree Indians of the Saskatchewan, that the Government of the Queen will send Her commissioners to make Treaties with them next summer at Fort Carlton and Fort Pitt, towards the end of July or beginning of August next. The Queen is mindful of all her Indian children, and has not forgotten the Crees. In the meantime, I ask the Cree to live at peace with other Indians and the Whites, and not to interfere ... The Queen has always dealt justly with her Indian children and has their good at heart. This letter will be your authority for delivering the message I send by you, and you may show it to any Chief you meet. (Morris 1875)

On August 18, 1876, the official proceedings for negotiating Treaty Six began. Following the protocol of the Plains people, a sacred pipe ceremony ensured that this treaty would be blessed by the Great Spirit and bound on earth and in the spiritual realm. Strike-Him-On-The-Back used the sacred Medicine Pipe Stem, praying in the four directions (Light 1987, 30). Lieutenant-Governor Morris (1880, chap. 9) recounts the opening ceremony:

On my arrival I found that the ground had been most judiciously chosen, being elevated, with abundance of trees, hay marshes and

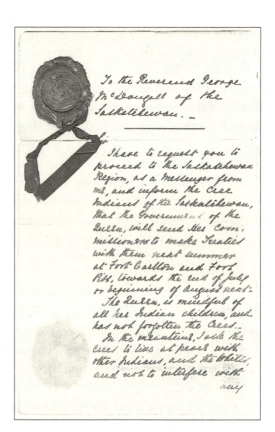

11 Letter from Alexander Morris, lieutenant-governor, to George McDougall, Methodist minister, August 9, 1875. | Series 1-a, M-729-2a, George and John McDougall Family fonds, Glenbow Archives, Calgary, AB.

small lakes ... The view was very beautiful: the hills and the trees in the distance, and in the foreground, the meadow land being dotted with clumps of wood, with the Indian tents clustered here and there to the number of two hundred ... In about half an hour they were ready to advance and meet me. This they did in a semicircle, having men on horseback galloping in circles, shouting, singing and discharging fire-arms ... They then performed the dance of the "pipe stem," the stem was elevated to the north, south, west and east, a ceremonial dance was then performed by the Chiefs and head men, the Indian men and women shouting the while.

They then slowly advanced, the horsemen again preceding them on their approach to my tent. I advanced to meet them, accompanied by Messrs. Christie and McKay, when the pipe was presented to us and stroked by our hands. After the stroking had been completed, the Indians sat down in front of the council tent, satisfied that in accordance with their custom we had accepted the friendship of the *Cree nation.* (emphasis added)

Morris and his contemporaries saw the Cree as a nation with agency; the active participation of the negotiators in the pipe ceremony conveys acceptance of Cree peoplehood as distinct yet legitimate. Morris and his colleagues' writings about the Cree as a nation display their regard for the Cree as a self-determining people. For the Cree, Treaty Six, with both parties participating in its spiritual ceremonies, "expanded the First Nations sovereign circle, bringing in and embracing the British Crown within their sovereign circle" (H. Cardinal and Hildebrandt 2000, 41). It is an arrangement between nations, acknowledging the "sovereign character of each of the treaty parties, within the context of rights conferred by the Creator to the Indian nations" (41).

The archival documents show this treaty negotiation to be the most expansive of the numbered treaties, offering the most provisions to that date (Talbot 2009, 94). The initial terms presented, however, were basically the same as those offered in Treaty Four (97). Once the initial terms were presented, Mistawasis, as one of the head Chiefs, responded by shaking Morris's hand and stating, "We have heard all he had told us, but I want to tell him how it is with us as well; when a thing is thought of quietly, probably that is the best way. I ask this much from him this day and that we go and think of his words" (Morris 1880, chap. 9). The Cree went into council and returned to negotiations on August 22, 1876. Interestingly, it is written that the negotiations were both oral and written. Morris's published text, recounting the proceedings from the perspective of the different government participants, states:

> Eventually the Commissioners made them an offer. They [the Indigenous leaders] asked this to be reduced to writing, which was done, and they asked time to consider it, which was of course granted. When the conference resumed, they presented a written counterproposal. This the Commissioners considered, and gave full and definite answers of acceptance or refusal to each demand, which replies were carefully interpreted, two of the Commissioners, Messrs. Christie and McKay, being familiar with the Cree tongue, watching how the answers were rendered, and correcting when necessary. (Morris 1880, chap. 9)

The Cree had enough foresight to anticipate the "double-forked tongue" of the government, and tried to mitigate this by requesting that the terms of the negotiations be written. Cree knowledge holder and scholar Sharon Venne (1998, 193) writes that Elders have shared how the original treaty was written on the back of a bison hide.

nehiyaw knowledge holder, scholar, lawyer, and activist Sylvia McAdam (saysewahum) explains the role of the okihcitâwiskwêwak lodge as an integral part of nehiyawak governance. This role was filled by women who were the "law keepers as well as knowledge keepers of the principles and customs of their people" (McAdam 2015, 54). Sylvia explains that during treaty making, "the *okihcitâwiskwêwak* would have been consulted regarding the land, because authority and jurisdiction to speak about land resides with the women" (55). She further explains:

> It was in the lodge called *okihcitâwiskwêwikamik* (clan mother/warrior woman lodge) that a ceremony was conducted during the treaty making process. The *okihcitâwiskwêwak* knew that the land was going to change and that their decisions would affect generations to come. The men informed the *okihcitâwiskwêwak* of the negotiations and what decisions must be made. A ceremony was conducted for four days and four nights asking the âtayôhkanak (spirit keepers) what must be done ... An understanding was made and taken to the men (56).

In Morris's account, he states that on August 23, 1876, the Indigenous peoples' counter-offer was presented to the negotiators:

> One ox and cow for each family. Four hoes, two spades, two scythes and a whetstone for each family. Two axes, two hay forks, two reaping hooks, one plough and one harrow for every three families. To each Chief one chest of tools as proposed. Seed of every kind in full to every one actually cultivating the soil. To make some provision for the poor, unfortunate, blind and lame. To supply us with a minister and school teacher of whatever denomination we belong to. To prevent fire-water being sold in the whole [of] Saskatchewan. As the tribe advances in civilization, all agricultural implements to be supplied in proportion.
>
> When timber becomes scarcer on the reserves we select for ourselves, we want to be free to take it anywhere on the common. If our choice

of a reserve does not please us before it is surveyed we want to be allowed to select another. We want to be at liberty to hunt on any place as usual. If it should happen that a Government bridge or scow is built on the Saskatchewan at any place, we want passage free. One boar, two sows, one horse, harness and wagon for each Chief. One cooking stove for each Chief. That we be supplied with medicines free of cost. That a hand-mill be given to each band. Lastly in case of war occurring in the country, we do not want to be liable to serve in it.

When we look back to the past we do not see where the Cree nation has ever watered the ground with the white man's blood, he has always been our friend and we his; trusting to the Giver of all good, to the generosity of the Queen, and to the Governor and his councillors, we hope you will grant us this request. (Morris 1880, chap. 9)

I believe it is instructive to include the text of this counter-offer here, as it shows the astuteness of the Indigenous leaders in understanding their changing way of life and wanting to negotiate a fair treaty that would enable them to continue and prosper as the Cree nation. I must note that these are the Crown negotiator's words that he chose to record himself; these are not even the words or understandings of the Indigenous leaders or from their perspective. This demonstrates how they took this process to be a negotiation between two nations. Although Morris arrived at Fort Carlton with the terms of Treaty Six already written, this account displays the significant negotiations undertaken. The final agreement contained three new concessions compared to previous treaties: 1) added provisions for agriculture; 2) the provision of a medicine chest; and 3) the provision of assistance during famine (Hildebrandt 2008, 16).

One of the foundational components of this negotiation was the question of jurisdiction within each nation's sphere of influence. Chief Big Bear[3] spoke of mwâc esakapayikini ᒫ ᐁᓴᐠᐸᔨᑭᓂ. Indigenous politics scholar Kiera Ladner (2003b) has effectively argued that the colonial negotiators misunderstood the meaning of this request, thinking Big Bear wanted immunity from being hanged. Ladner contends that the correct translation refers to Big Bear wanting not to be led by a rope around his neck:

Big Bear's request demonstrates his reluctance to allow the government to interfere in the lives of his people, and thus, the importance that he placed on remaining sovereign. Furthermore, it seems to be

CANADA'S GENESIS STORY 75

> suggestive of Big Bear's unwillingness to be limited to a *skunkun* or a small "roped off" piece of land called a reserve, and his desire to retain Cree sovereignty and authority over all of the traditional territory, even that which is being shared with the white settlers. (Ladner 2003b, 177)

This is a significant difference in meaning. Morris also discussed jurisdiction during negotiations, explaining a type of divided authority and control. He stated that the Crown "would not interfere with Indians' daily life except to assist them in farming" (Ladner 2003b, 177; Morris 1880, chap. 9). The Chiefs at the Treaty Six negotiations understood that they had "agreed to share the land in return for annuities, education, medical and famine assistance, as well as a commitment to establish ranching and farm economies" (Hildebrandt 2008, 17). The Cree people understood from the negotiators that they would still be able to hunt and fish freely without being restricted to the boundaries of the reserve. Morris stated, "Understand me, I do not want to interfere with your hunting and fishing. I want you to pursue it through the country, as you have heretofore done; but I would like your children to be able to find food for themselves and their children that come after them" (Morris 1880, chap. 9). It is apparent from the first-hand accounts of Morris and others that the sovereignty of the Cree people over their society, their sustenance, and their land, and their shared jurisdiction over communal lands, were mutually understood and agreed upon.

There is consensus among Cree Elders, substantiated by numerous oral accounts and published sources, that the terms of Treaty Six did not include subsurface land rights.

> At the time of treaty signing, it was understood through verbal agreement that the land which was opened to the white settlers was only to the extent of the depth a plough would furrow. This was indicated by a gesture of a closed fist with thumb extended. "The rest" was to be retained by the Indian people. Thus, the birds of the air, fish in the sea, the trees, the rivers, the minerals were not given up. (Saskatchewan Indian Cultural College 1976, 27)

A separate published account records Elder Gordon Oakes stating: "As I was saying about the depth of the plough, the Treaty Commissioner [Alexander Morris] also advised that some day he will be mining valuable minerals and at the time I will come back and negotiate with you again on it" (H. Cardinal and Hildebrandt 2000, 42). An edited volume gives an oral account from Lazarus Roan, born in the Smallboy Camp in 1904; his father and two uncles were at the Fort Carlton negotiations and signing. The account always relayed to Roan was that the chief negotiator

> would indicate with his hands approximately one foot in depth: [stating] "That is the depth requested from you, that is what the deal is, nothing below the surface, that will always belong to you. Only land where agriculture can be viable; other areas where nothing can grow, that will always belong to you. You will always be the owner of that land." (Price 1987, 155)

It is significant that there is consensus in accounts across provinces and over different time periods on the matter of negotiations being restricted to settlers' ability to till the land. From an Indigenous perspective, subsurface rights, as well as animals, trees, etc., are still within the jurisdiction of Indigenous peoples, at least in principle. There is still the potential for the Canadian state once again to acknowledge Indigenous jurisdiction or co-management over shared lands – even lands within the historic numbered treaties, those outside the modern-day treaty process.

Indian Act

In 1876 the Parliament of Canada first passed the *Indian Act*. The *Indian Act* does not make reference to treaties. The Royal Commission on Aboriginal Peoples writes that "it is almost as if Canada deliberately allowed itself to forget the principal constitutional mechanism by which the nation status of Indian communities is recognized in domestic law" (Canada 1996, 1: 255). The *General Enfranchisement Act* of 1869, a precursor to the *Indian Act*, had two main purposes: to assimilate First Nations until they qualified for enfranchisement,[4] and to force an exclusively male, British-style municipal-type government onto First Nations (Milloy 2008, 7). Under Sir John A. Macdonald, the notion of Indian nationhood, which even from a Crown perspective was founded in the Royal Proclamation and affirmed in treaties, was changed to a view of domination and subordination in which Indians were absorbed into the colonial project as wards of the state. In the House of Commons in 1867 it was stated that "Indians were like children; they were like 'persons underage, incapable of the management of their own affairs' and, therefore, the government had to assume the 'onerous duty of ... guardianship'" (Milloy 2008, 7). Economic exploitation continued with the reserve system, which, Boldt (1993, 231) argues, "was created to clear Indians out of the way of Canadian economic development," removing Indigenous peoples from their full territories to enable capitalist pursuits by settlers.

In her book *Lost Harvests,* Sarah Carter (1993) meticulously documents how during the time of numbered treaties, Plains Indigenous peoples had an early and sustained interest in agriculture; it was Canadian government policies that continually attempted to thwart this. Another example of economic exploitation can be found in the pass system. While I was researching at the Glenbow Archives in Calgary, Alberta, I found archival records from my own First Nation, Red Pheasant. I was able to go through some of the original Red Pheasant passbooks, seeing the names of some of my late relatives and how they had to apply for a pass from an Indian agent to be allowed to leave the reserve (Figure 12). The Indian agent could choose to grant or disallow the request. If granted, the First Nation person would have to carry the pass at all times. It is said that the passes of South Africa's apartheid system were based on Canada's pass system. Carter (1993) provides meticulous evidence of settlers (for example, settler farmers) pressuring politicians to thwart the economic competition posed by First Nation success at farming

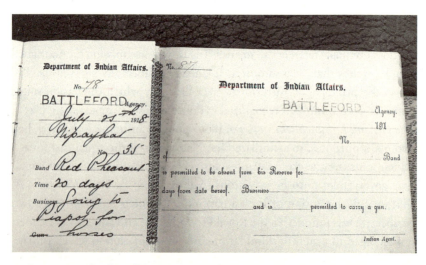

12 Department of Indian Affairs "Pass Book" for Red Pheasant First Nation, July 25, 1918. Under "Business," the reason given for leaving the reserve is "Going to Piapot for Horses." | *M1781.0.S.17, Battleford Indian Agency Papers, 1884–1944, vols. 21–26, Glenbow Archives, Calgary, AB.*

78   UPHOLDING INDIGENOUS ECONOMIC RELATIONSHIPS

and selling agriculture produce. Policies like the pass system negatively affected Indigenous social, political, legal, and economic realms, and made it impossible to live out the treaty.

There is little debate that the pass system, a policy put in place in the 1880s and continuing till the 1940s (Carter 1999, 163–64), deeply alienated the Plains Cree and damaged their economic and governance systems,[5] challenging and dissolving relationships beyond the band level. Implementation of the *Indian Act* disrupted the fabric of Cree relationships with the land, water, air, plants, and animals, among others, and Cree connections to the expanse of Cree territory that lies beyond reserve boundaries. The pass system also served to alienate relationships between Cree and non-Cree people.

This genesis story of Canada is a key example of the extent of the exploitation of Indigenous peoples and territories. Understanding Canada's creation story is imperative to understanding the current relationship between Indigenous peoples and Canada. This chapter provided the genesis story of the exploitation that occurred during the fur trade and the limited self-determination opportunities that were made available to Indigenous peoples. Understanding Canada's creation story allows the Cree to honour the sacrifices made and realize the aspirations of their forefathers. Even after Treaty Six was signed and reserve life began, the Cree still understood themselves as a nation. For instance, my ancestor Red Pheasant,[6] signatory to Treaty Six, wrote a letter to Canadian authorities in which he raised the hopes for a powerful Cree nation. In 1881, Chief Red Pheasant dictated the following as part of his letter to Edgar Dewdney, Indian Commissioner and lieutenant-governor of the Northwest Territories:

> I wish that nothing may bother me, that the law may rest in peace; in the first treaty [Treaty Six] the hand of the good fellowship was lifted up to put law and order in this land; this I still hold onto, oh that the Cree nation may be raised up ... (Chief Red Pheasant 1881)

5

ᐃᐧᐦᑎᑯ
Warnings of Insatiable Greed

The Weendigo gorged itself and glutted its belly as if it would never eat
again. But a remarkable thing always occurred. As the Weendigo ate,
it grew, and as it grew so did its hunger, so that no matter how much it
ate, its hunger always remained in proportion to its size. The Weendigo
could never requite either its unnatural lust for human flesh or its
unnatural appetite. It could never stop as animals do when bloated,
unable to ingest another morsel, or sense as humans sense that
enough is enough for the present. For the unfortunate Weendigo,
the more it ate, the bigger it grew, the more it wanted and needed.

– Basil Johnston (1995)

THERE ARE ACCOUNTS in nehiyawak and annishnawbek societies of the
wihtikow or weendigo. The above words are from Anishinaabe scholar and
esteemed storyteller Basil Johnston. ᐃᐧᐦᑎᑯ stories can be historical accounts, or they can be legends. These stories are also teaching tools.

There are many ways to describe the wihtikow; one translation the
maskwacîs Dictionary (2009) provides is simply "a greedy person." Other
translations or accounts refer to a superhuman figure that is a man-eater, a
person who goes crazy, a giant, or someone who turns to eating flesh. I use

---

A note to the reader: wihtikow ᐃᐧᐦᑎᑯ is mentioned on the first and last two pages of this
chapter. (There are teachings to talk about this during certain times of the year.)

80

the Plains Cree syllabic spelling of ᐄᐧᐦᑎᑯᐧ and the annishnawbek spelling of weendigo in this chapter. Legal scholar Hadley Friedland (2018, 17) sees the ᐄᐧᐦᑎᑯᐧ as an Indigenous legal concept that provides legal principles, obligations, and processes about how to protect, recognize, and respond to those close to us who may cause harm. ᐄᐧᐦᑎᑯᐧ teachings can also be helpful for understanding the harmful aspects of capitalism. In this chapter, I present two main arguments: one is that capitalism is a constituting force, and Indigenous peoples are not innately immune to its pressures; the second is how Indigenous legal concepts, like that of the ᐄᐧᐦᑎᑯᐧ, provide strong warnings against the harms caused by insatiable greed.

The first question I ask is whether the approach to self-determination that Indigenous peoples are taking – pursuing economic autonomy to lessen state control – is leading us to be increasingly subjected to constitutive, hegemonic, and individualizing forms of being, thus challenging notions of communal Indigenous identity and relations to the land. Inherent in this question is this query: What are the implications for the Cree in trying to be economically independent from the state by moving toward neoliberal economics? What do I mean by a neoliberal trajectory? What do I mean by neoliberalism? In Chapter 2 I explored this concept. In summary, instead of the social, political, legal, cultural, and economic spheres of society interacting in balance, neoliberalism embeds all spheres in, and under, the economic sphere, and everything is seen primarily through that lens. The economy bleeds into all areas of life and takes primary focus. At an extreme, it can be seen as an insatiable greed, one that is never satisfied.

With the federal recognition of the inherent right to self-government for Aboriginal peoples *within* the *Constitution Act, 1982,*[1] many Indigenous peoples have pursued state-defined arrangements for self-government and economic self-sufficiency. One of the logics of settler colonialism in Canada is that state-defined self-government is the only way to achieve self-determination. However, more time needs to be spent focusing on what the constitutive effects are of seeking economic self-sufficiency through economic development. A common argument is that Indigenous peoples need to be economically autonomous from the state to have "true" self-determination. In the service of this belief, settler-colonial governing systems and economic forces are making an effort to reconstitute Indigeneity, altering social relations, governing practices, and economic patterns. Canada's economic exploitation of Indigenous lands and bodies restricts and constricts the options Indigenous peoples have for economic self-sufficiency, forcing them further into neoliberal economies. If the land and animals are decimated, subsistence is no longer an option.

The other question I ask relates to how the values of being in reciprocal relationships with physical and metaphysical beings shape notions of Cree citizenship and challenge the values surrounding market citizenship. How are Indigenous notions of identity and citizenship challenged within the context of capitalism? Indigenous identities are continually struggling against colonial and economic forces. Colonial domination of Indigenous peoples in settler societies has taken a two-pronged approach: state domination (e.g., bureaucratic control) and economic exploitation (e.g., resource extraction, "development" programs, etc.). If we focus on just the state domination aspect of settler society, we miss how Indigenous attempts to resist this first colonial logic may further entrench the second.

In the last chapter, I examined economic exploitation of Indigenous peoples. A reasonable response to this is that Indigenous peoples must have economic opportunities that are comparable to those enjoyed by Canadians. The argument goes that if Indigenous peoples have equal economic development opportunities, then economic exploitation will be negated. In this chapter, I complicate that logic by demonstrating how Indigenous peoples' relationship to the land is more expansive than simply an economic question. I examine ideas of citizenship and identity through analysis of Cree peoples' conceptions of citizenship, and I compare this with market notions of citizenship embedded in capitalism. I begin with a discussion of Indigeneity and Indigenous nations' own naming practices, and how this relates to Indigenous perspectives on citizenship. After that, I analyze market citizenship and how it affects Indigenous perspectives on the land. Then I explore collective reflexivity through Elmer Ghostkeeper's revitalization model. I end this chapter with reflections from Basil Johnston on the Δ·ᵸᑎdᵒ.

Indigeneity

Indigeneity is a contested concept, steeped in colonial history, with very real political implications. At one level, it is fundamentally about inclusion and exclusion. At another level, it is intimately linked to who is doing the naming. The concept of Indigeneity will be explored here through the work of academics and Indigenous communities. Indigeneity is based on (1) the definition of who is Indigenous and (2) the politics surrounding that identity (Bennett 2005, 72). Depending on who is doing the naming and when the naming was done, Indigeneity in Canada can include or exclude the following identities: Aboriginal, First Nation, Métis, Native, Indian, Status Indian, Non-Status Indian, Treaty Indian, Non-Treaty Status Indian, Inuit, and Indigenous. Each of these terms takes on a specific political meaning, which can be framed by the corresponding legal rights it obtains from the state. These "identities" do not even include the naming of the forty to sixty Indigenous nations (Abele 2001, 141) that are distinct, "meaning peoples in the usually accepted international sense of a group with a common cultural and historical antecedence" (Chartrand 1999, 104).

The term "Indigeneity" – derived, although different, from the term *Indigenous* – relates to the contestation of how the dominant state chooses to accommodate the cultural, social, and political distinctiveness of Indigenous peoples (Bennett 2005, 73). Indigeneity is not conceived outside of the "politicized context of contemporary colonialism" (Alfred and Corntassel 2005, 597). For legal scholar Mark Bennett (2005, 73), the "principle of 'self-determination' is the best liberal justification for the significance of Indigeneity, and best fits how Indigenous peoples view their claims and rights." Furthermore, he states that his appeal to self-determination is based on the "historical fact of Indigenous self-determination – the fact that Indigenous peoples lived by their own laws, traditions and customs before they encountered colonizing powers – [and that this can be used] as a crucial basis for a return to that historic status in the present" (74). Mohawk political anthropologist Audra Simpson and Teme-Augama Anishnabai political scientist Dale Turner (2008, 18) argue that, although Indigeneity characterizes distinctiveness that occurs in part because of Indigenous peoples' "unique political and historical experiences with European settlers," Indigenous relationships with the homeland "constitute the main moral and political force of their legal and political distinctiveness."

Another way to understand Indigeneity is through Indigenous concepts. As mentioned in the preface, nehiyaw ᓀᐦᐃᔭᐤ means a Cree person (and nehiyawak ᓀᐦᐃᔭᐊᐧᐠ are Cree people) and is derived from the word newo ᓀᐅᐧ, which means four. The number four has special significance for responsibilities and relationships with the environment (living beings). It can also relate to the four-direction teachings of physical, spiritual, intellectual, and emotional well-being. When Cree scholar Leona Makokis (2001, 90) asks a Cree Elder about world view, the Elder states that nehiyaw "is the four directions, newoyak. There are four parts and those are our four directions and that is, in our language." The Elder goes on to explain, "We are called Iyiniwak. That is the foundation of who we are, our identity. We are supposed to heal ourselves and others and iyiniwaskamkaw, that is, our relationship to our land, our connection here." Nehiyawewin ᐅᑊᐃᐱᔦᐁᐧᐃᐧᓂᐤ, the Cree language, provides a framework for understanding the world based on the four directions teachings – these are considered central teachings that guide the Cree in daily living. The language itself demonstrates relationships and is based on the animacy of the world around us. Through this perspective our relationship to land is constitutive. Therefore, our economic relationships are constitutive; by this I mean that the relationships we have to the land, people, and other beings create and co-create who we are as individuals and as peoples. When I invoke the term "Indigeneity," I am referring to our own nations' conceptions and normative principles of being human; I also include our conflicted relationships occurring from settler colonialism. In this work I am specifically exploring the tension that derives from the constitutive nature of changing relationships to land and to non-human beings.

Citizenship

In one of the dominant versions of the Western liberal framework, citizenship can take on a procedural focus through rationales for voting, paying taxes, joining organizations, or standing for office.

> Citizenship refers to the status of being a citizen, usually enshrined in law. Citizenship may entail rights and responsibilities or result as a consequence of being part of a polity or a community. Participation entails a legal membership of a polity premised upon universal suffrage. Citizenship is a relationship between the state and the individual that comprises a series of rights and responsibilities. It may be defined objectively, as a legal status, or subjectively, as comprising a sense of belonging and identity. (Savigny 2007, 82)

Citizenship is said to establish a regime of inclusion and exclusion, defining both national and internal (to the nation) boundaries, those citizens with complete rights and those with limited rights – "second-class citizens" (Jenson and Phillips 1996, 114). Indigenous peoples have historically been excluded from many rights associated with Canadian citizenship.[2] Institutional instruments like constitutions can shape notions of citizenship in ways different from Indigenous obligations regarding reciprocal roles and responsibilities. Western liberal democracy and Indigenous normative commitments to reciprocity point to different roles for "citizens."

Different governance eras have had different ideas of the ideal citizen – the imperial subject, social citizen, entrepreneurial citizen, and the world citizen (Brodie 2002, 2003) – with differing immigration and multiculturalism policies (Stasiulis and Abu Laban 2003). Articles and texts on identity and citizenship tend to provide typologies of difference. Differentiated citizenship has been grouped based on self-government rights, accommodation rights, and special representation rights (Kymlicka 2014, 26). A long debate relates to the division between group rights and individual rights; group rights are further divided between internal restrictions and external protections, and some authors argue that the former is inconsistent with liberal-democratic values (Kymlicka 2014, 36; Trudeau 1994, 84–90). These scholars are concerned that internal restrictions can lead to intragroup oppression, and that differentiated citizenship amounts to disunity and potentially the dissolution of the country (in this case, Canada) (Kymlicka 2014, 37–39).

The settler state has always had a differentiated "citizenship" for First Nations.[3] Their perspective is also concerned with societies' perceived devaluation of the unifying force of national citizenship (Kaplan 1992). What are the identity and citizenship conceptions for different Indigenous peoples, such as the Cree? These separate ontological understandings of the world provide distinct reciprocal responsibilities and roles that could provide a fuller understanding of citizenship. What are the negative implications for Indigenous peoples' self-determination of having federal citizenship?[4] Reviewing early throne speeches, political scientist Janine Brodie (2003) writes about a shift: "Indians" were originally seen as autonomous and competent. After the *Indian Act* (1876) became law, First Nations moved from subjects to objects "needing to be civilized" (Brodie 2003, 22). She writes how First Nations have not moved toward the "promise of social rights to social inclusion" (Brodie 2002, 53). Canada's liberal individual rights have also been challenged based on Indigenous nationalism (Jenson 1999, 42). Audra Simpson (2014, 188) sees a distinction between First Nations membership and citizenship, where Indigenous citizenship can be seen as "a complex of social belonging, of family, of intracommunity recognition and responsibility."

Citizenship in the Cree world view has not historically related to rights and responsibilities to a nation-state, but has had more to do with a way of being in the world as a human being. I conceptualize Indigenous citizenship in a very broad and non-state-oriented fashion. Citizenship, in fact, might not be the accurate term to use in Indigenous languages. For example, îyinewiwin ᐃᔨᓀᐅᐃᐧ means simply "being human" in Cree, and can be related to certain responsibilities, such as that of developing good relations with others. This view of citizenship, or pimâtisiwin ᐱᒫᑎᓯᐃᐧ (the act of living), is related to roles and responsibilities not only to other humans, but also to other living things; in Chapter 1, I explain Winston Wuttunee's (2003) description of relationships and responsibilities to nonhuman beings on the land. And in one of the interviews I conducted, I was told about a Cree person's responsibilities and need for reciprocal relationships with the earth, air, fire, and water (Walter 2014b). Harold Cardinal and Walter Hildebrandt (2000, 39) describe Elders' views of Cree citizenship:

> In each of their languages, the Elders described the collectivity of their citizenry in the following terms: Elder Jacob Bill describes the Cree as "Nehiyawak," a Cree term meaning "people of the four directions." Elder Peter Waskahat uses another term: "Iyiniwak," a Cree term meaning "people made healthy by the land."

These readings of Cree world views reveal that citizenship entails specific roles and responsibilities to all other living beings through relations with the land. The land needs to be healthy if we are to be a people made healthy by the land. We hold responsibilities to the land. Cree education scholar Margaret Kovach (2009, 63) explains the importance of reciprocity and a relational way of being through the concept of miyo-wicihitowin ᒥᔪ ᐃᐧᒋᐦᐃᑐᐃᐧ (good relationships), which is referred to as the "heartbeat of Plains Cree culture," including "sharing and generosity, respecting the earth and all inhabitants, working hard, and caring for other people." Chapters 7 to 10 will draw out further Cree knowledge found in oral accounts and interviews.

In these Cree views of citizenship, there is a reciprocal relationship between economic interactions (relations to land) and modes of subjectivity (relations with land). How we relate to the land affects who we are and the responsibilities we claim. In contrast to this Cree perspective, a liberal economic model can (falsely) claim that fundamentally altering a relationship to the land will not significantly alter who we are. The state pushes citizens to make land productive based on market interests. Indigenous citizenship, in Cree world view, is not simply a negative right; it includes responsibilities to the earth itself.

Market Citizenship

Indigenous peoples striving for meaningful self-determination are being pushed into a liberal version of citizenship based on market values. Indigenous peoples' goal of self-government has constructed the movement for autonomy along a neoliberal trajectory, directly affecting communal ideologies and relationships with the land. As already introduced, Zapotec scholar Isabel Altamirano-Jiménez (2004, 349) notes that government practices regarding Indigenous demands are based on neoliberalism, which disconnects self-government from Indigenous territory. Indigenous scholars identify neo-liberalism as a new form of colonization affecting Indigenous peoples (Kuokkanen 2006, 2008; Bargh 2007). The marketization of Indigenous citizenship is "the fulfillment of Indigenous demands through market integration and the rhetoric of cultural recognition" (Bargh 2007, 350).

Citizenship through a neoliberal lens is often connected with "Indigenous communities entering the market through a resource extraction model of development, and with a commitment to human rights" (Altamirano-Jiménez 2009, 132). This type of citizenship model is challenging Indigenous identity and connections to the land, creating an environment in which Indigenous rights are settled through state negotiations, and land is therefore free to be exploited by market interests. There have been numerous federal and provincial policies that have demonstrated this logic.[5] There is a significant gap in analysis regarding the corresponding negative impacts on communities, on subsistence practices, on relations with the land, and on the nonhuman kin on these territories. For example, the *Federal Framework for Aboriginal Economic Development* report suggests that the federal government will work with those "opportunity-ready Aboriginal communities that have stable, efficient and predictable investment climates attractive to business and investors" (Canada 2009, 20). This "opportunity-ready" caveat refers to those communities that have adopted Western liberal institutional forms and are federally determined to be a good "fit" for market citizenship. The framework's strategies are about making Indigenous communities "ready" for economic development and corporate partnerships, and especially for resource development on their lands. Through policies such as these, government changes the idea of citizens receiving public goods to that of individualized subjects being held responsible for their choices, and being conceived of and constituted as market citizens (Schild 2000, 305).

In Canadian state policy there is an increasing market-citizenship push to have First Nations further generate their own source revenues in order to decrease state financial obligations[6] – financial obligations that remain through the treaty relationship. This disciplines First Nations to be self-reliant and able to compete in the marketplace (Slowey 2008). The Canadian government's market-citizenship model is increasingly forcing Indigenous nations into neoliberal citizenry, where Indigenous rights are primarily mediated through the economic sphere of Canada's interests. This can stand in direct contradiction to Indigenous understandings of their relations with the land.

Shifting Landscapes

Cree epistemology is embedded in relationships with the land. Treaty Six Elders see the core normative principle of pimâtisiwin ∧ᒥᐣᕫᐊ·ᐟ (the act of living) including pimâcihowin ∧ᒥᒥᐦᐅᐊ·ᐟ (the ability to make a good living), which is intimately connected to the askîy ᐊᐣᐅᐧ (the land), which is described as "an important source of life, for it provides those things required for the physical, material, and economic survival of the people" (H. Cardinal and Hildebrandt 2000, 43). From this perspective, Cree economy is intimately tied to relations with the land, encompassing laws, principles, values, teachings, and responsibilities regarding these relationships, including responsibilities to the land and other living beings.

In the book *Spirit Gifting: The Concept of Spiritual Exchange*, Elder Elmer Ghostkeeper (2007) explores the importance of living in relationship with the land to the Indigenous world view: "The eastern sky at sunrise is usually a brilliant yellow in my region. When I arise in the morning I face the east and say a prayer asking for a strong mind and giving thanks for my source of fire, heat, light and energy" (1). Ghostkeeper positions himself within his writing by stating that his father's teachings regarding the Indigenous world view and the living universe were all in the Cree language. Ghostkeeper says that this "might indicate that he had more of a Cree cultural perspective on life than my mother, whose lessons were mostly in the English language" (6). Ghostkeeper describes himself as having a Metis world view.[7] I see his perspective regarding the shift from Indigenous relations with land to relations with land based on market-citizenship principles as also instructive to Cree interactions with market citizenship.

How does the value of being in reciprocal relationships with physical and metaphysical beings shape notions of Cree citizenship and challenge market citizenship? I address this question in the rest of this chapter, and in the rest of this book. Ghostkeeper describes an Indigenous world view regarding sustenance:

> Food to sustain life is created by The Great Spirit. It comes in the form of a gift (*mekiwin*), or something that is freely exchanged and shared between a donor and recipient through the relations of giving and receiving ... It is the gathering and harvesting of plants and animals in order to make a living with the land. In this livelihood, a ritual is considered to be a decision made through the recital of a prayer by a gatherer or harvester. The person requests permission from The Great Spirit, Mother Earth, and the aspects of the spirit, mind, and emotion of a plant or animal to sacrifice its body for human sustenance. The spirits of the donor and recipient are thought to be equal. This request is in exchange for an offering in the form of a gift of a pinch of tobacco or food, and it signals spiritual equality. (Ghostkeeper 2007, 11–12)

Ghostkeeper sees this type of subsistence-based philosophy as a sacred relationship: living *with* the land. According to Ghostkeeper, through changes in subsistence patterns a shift occurred to a secular world view: living *off* the land.

In his book, Ghostkeeper documents his own shift, from the patterns of subsistence-based living in his community to the wage economy, encompassing the construction of a natural gas field and the beginning of grain farming on his community's land. In analyzing these changes, Ghostkeeper examines the technical and social relationships involved, in which the "land, equipment, and labour, or forces of production, are more or less under the control of individuals from the community; [while] the relationships, or means of production, are under the control of forces outside the community" (4–5).

Ghostkeeper explains that his community has historically seen itself as part of the land with all other living beings, and that one process in these relationships includes the exchanging of *aspects* of the mind, body, and spirit thought to "provide life for the body through the activities of ceremony, ritual, and sacrifice" (4). He explains this as Spirit Gifting, "when one makes a living with the land, using the gifts of plants and animals for food and medicinal purposes" (4). He says that this relationship with the land changed when he was awarded an oil-field contract by the company in Calgary that was completing the natural gas development of land in his community. The move into mechanical grain farming also affected his people's spiritual world view.

In the change to these two modes of production, land was viewed as a commodity and treated as an inanimate object as opposed to a gift that was part of a reciprocal relationship. This new view resulted in emotional and spiritual detachment among the people (Ghostkeeper 2007, 68–69). In this new economic and social system, community contractors did not have time to "gather and harvest wild plants and animals for food and did not have the time to enter into a relationship with the land" (74). The result, for Ghostkeeper, was dissatisfaction so intense that it motivated him to revitalize his repressed traditional world view.

The "group revitalization" model developed by Anthony Wallace (1970, 188) outlines this process. Wallace begins by noting that there is a "period of increased individual stress" during which the sociocultural system is increasingly pushed out of balance through disease, conquest, or internal decay, resulting in a "period of cultural distortion," in which community members try to restore individual equilibrium through self-medicating strategies such as gambling and alcoholism to such an extent that these coping mechanisms get institutionalized in the "system" (quoted in Ghostkeeper 2007, 76). Wallace explains that at this point the population will die off, separate into "splinter" groups, or be assimilated into another, more stable society unless the culture is revitalized.

Ghostkeeper's community, and numerous others, are in transition, with Indigenous peoples hopeful that expanded self-governing powers and partnership agreements providing new economic resources will revitalize the community. However, an unknown number of people like Ghostkeeper have pinpointed their growing dissatisfaction with the negative impacts these new market "relationships" bring. These agreements may actually push his community further into sociocultural market rationalities. Although Ghostkeeper found a way to revitalize his Indigenous world view and sustain it within the current global neoliberal economic system, it is important to understand the complexities of the changing relationships with land.

Collective Reflexivity

Increasingly, Indigenous scholars are critiquing the application of neoliberal instruments of capitalism and governance to Indigenous communities

(Bargh 2007; Altamirano-Jiménez 2009; Kuokkanen 2006; Corntassel and Witmer 2008). Māori scholar Maria Bargh (2007, 2) equates neoliberalism with a new form of colonization of Indigenous peoples. Within the market-citizenship regime there is a widening gap between rich and poor. Historically, Cree communities imposed norms preventing this sort of stratification. For example, in Cree society, the Giveaway Ceremony, still occurring today, is a way to express thankfulness for the gifts of sustenance throughout the year and also a means of wealth redistribution. During this ceremony, people bring gifts to share with others. Part of the purpose of this ceremony is to provide the "necessities to live a prosperous life, with enough food to carry families through each winter" (Makokis 2001, 107). I explore the Giveaway Ceremony more extensively in Chapters 7, 8, and 9.

Elmer Ghostkeeper (2007, 44) writes that when his community lives in relationship with the land, the norm of sharing is principal, with hunters distributing and sharing what they harvested, "beginning with the elders, the next of kin, the most in need, and finally others that had shared with them in the past." When he started to live *off* the land, Ghostkeeper "viewed the land as a commodity instead of a gift." That shift from seeing the land as a gift changes Indigenous perceptions regarding sharing such gifts with others.

Ghostkeeper describes how his disconnection from the land translated to an unbearable dissatisfaction with life, motivating him to reflect on the Indigenous knowledge he had been repressing, and to develop his own revitalization model to explain his personal revitalization process (81). As mentioned earlier, this model is informed by Anthony Wallace's (1970, 188) group revitalization theory and adapted to fit an Indigenous context. Within this rediscovery, Ghostkeeper (2007, 80) reflected on the normative and behavioural ideals of an Indigenous world view, acknowledging the diversity within:

> During the process of self-appraisal, using the concept of the ideal self (what I really wanted to be), I rediscovered a repressed code from my traditional knowledge, the concept of spiritual exchange, which I now refer to as "Spirit Gifting." I revitalized this concept as a part of my way of knowing to form a new code which blends both traditional and Western scientific knowledge in a way that had been impossible for me before.

Ghostkeeper decided to live *with* the land once again. However, for him this did not mean a complete rejection of Western scientific knowledge or

Western economic practices. The ethic does require a continual critical and reflective approach, thoroughly examining how decisions and actions will affect the roles and responsibilities that Indigenous peoples hold as central to their identities. It also requires collective deliberations on how a people (for example, the Cree) will apply their collective revitalization. This issue is explored further in Chapters 7 to 10.

For Ghostkeeper and other Indigenous leaders, this process is not about trying to protect themselves and their communities from outside influences at all costs. It is, however, about critically examining detrimental governmental and market forces.[8] It is crucial to understand fully the two-pronged approach of settler colonialism: state domination and economic exploitation. Self-determination is not achieved by replacing one colonial logic with the other. The process of Indigenous collective reflexivity should guide community visioning and decision-making. Ghostkeeper's personal narrative shows how market citizenship can be incompatible with Indigenous world views regarding reciprocal relationships, especially surrounding resource development endeavours. Relations with the land shape Indigenous identity.

I am drawn back to teachings from Δ·ⁿ∩dº stories and the words of the late Basil Johnston (1995, 227). He said that "a human being could become a Weendigo by his or her own excesses. This was the usual way. But one human being could also transform another into a Weendigo." This makes me think of Hadley Friedland's (2018, 64–65) analysis in which she points to examples of people becoming Δ·ⁿ∩dº in times of great distress, including those of mental and/or physical suffering. Economic exploitation constricts and often eliminates Indigenous peoples' abilities to live *with* the land via subsistence practices, and forces people into market relations guided by unfettered capitalist logics. In this way, settler exploitation can attempt to transform Indigenous peoples, providing the conditions for going Δ·ⁿ∩dº.

Basil Johnston (1995, 223) makes this connection as well, and states it with extreme clarity. He states that the old people warned, "'Not too much, think of tomorrow, next winter, and the need to think of others'" – how "we must have balance, moderation, and self-control." Johnston ends his book, *The Manitous*, by making the connection between weendigoes and economic exploitation. May these Δ·ⁿ∩dº warnings be heeded:

> Actually, the Weendigoes did not die out or disappear; they have only been assimilated and reincarnated as corporations, conglomerates, and multinationals. They've even taken on new names, acquired polished

manners, and renounced their cravings for raw human flesh in return for more refined viands. But their cupidity is no less insatiable than that of their ancestors.

One breed subsists entirely on forests. When this particular breed beheld forests, its collective cupidity was bestirred as it looked on an endless, boundless sea of green. These modern Weendigoes looked into the future and saw money – cash, bank accounts, interest from investments, profits, in short, wealth beyond belief. Never again would they be in need ...

Yet, as fast as they cut and as much as they hewed, it was never enough; quantities always fell short of the demands of the Weendigoes ...

Still, the Weendigoes wanted more ... it didn't matter to them that their modus operandi resulted in the permanent defilement of hillside and mountainside by erosion. They are indifferent to the carnage inflicted on bears, wolves, rabbits, and warblers. Who cares if they are displaced? What possible harm has been done? Nor does it seem as if these modern Weendigoes have any regards for the rights of future generations to the yield of Mother Earth.

Profit, wealth, and power are the ends of business. Anything that detracts from or diminishes the anticipated return, whether it is taking pains not to violate the rights of others or taking measure to ensure that the land remain fertile and productive for future generations, must, it seems, be circumvented ...

These new Weendigoes are no different from their forebearers. In fact, they are even more omnivorous than their old ancestors. The only difference is that the modern Weendigoes wear elegant clothes and comport themselves with an air of cultured and dignified respectability. But still the Weendigoes bring disaster, fuelled by the unquenchable greed inherent in human nature. (B. Johnston 1995, 235–37)

6

Indigenous Women's Lands and Bodies

I AM WRITING THIS CHAPTER in niskipîsim ᓂᐢᑭᐲᓯᒼ, the goose moon of 2020. The news of #WetsuwetenStrong has been in the media, on our minds, and in many hearts. This has been a very divisive time. It has been an interesting moment, again, to consider Indigenous social movements, connections to Indigenous lands, and the economy. It has also been interesting to live in what is now western Canada, and specifically Alberta, to see the specificity of the political culture around oil, the economy, and Indigenous lands and bodies.

In the fall of 2015, I tried online dating. This was a new experience for me, and a bit of a traumatic one at times. My intellectual reflections on that moment in my life revolve around connection to patriarchy, extractive resources, and Indigenous women's bodies. For a holiday gift exchange in 2015 I was given this print by Métis artist Erin Marie Konsmo (Figure 13); for me, the print is a visual representation of this chapter. I started dating an Indigenous fellow at this time – let's call him Al. Al worked in a fly-in camp that was part of the resource extraction industry. He grew up hunting and fishing in his community, and continues to do so. His waged job pays very well and requires a certain skill set and expertise; he is proud of what he has accomplished. When he is at camp, his life revolves around work and sleep; when he is not at work, he has a few weeks off. One of the interesting reflections from my short time dating Al was that he expected, and was expected by others, to support his family and community members financially.

13 *Land / Body,* by Erin Marie Konsmo.

This was something he felt proud of, but he also shared that he sometimes felt used. His wage was redistributed to the collective.

While dating Al, I suddenly found myself acting as an untrained counsellor one day when a woman called me and asked me to leave her boyfriend Al alone. Al had not shared with me that he was in a relationship with another woman. I broke up with Al, but he and the alleged ex-girlfriend hounded me for a while. I made it clear to both of them that I wanted to be left alone. Both of them continued to call me – Al asking me to return to him, and his girlfriend begging me not to take her man away. I somehow ended up providing a few hours of listening and relationship advice to this woman. One evening Al would not stop calling and asking to see me, and, in a moment of desperation, I told him that if he left me alone for a month, he could then contact me. This worked, and he stopped hounding me – or so I thought. What was interesting is what he posted on his Facebook page right after our phone call (Figure 14).

The end of our relationship had nothing to do with his job in the oilfield, but for him it became an easy way to justify his behaviour. What became solidified in my mind and body that evening, after looking at this meme, were the intimate connections between extractive resources, the exploitation of land and bodies, and violence. The man kicking the woman

14 Al's Facebook post.

off the cliff in the image affected me viscerally. The political culture in places dominated by resource extraction, where a segment of the population believes it is justifiable to have beliefs like those implied in the meme, is an aspect of the political culture of western Canada (and other locations) that we seldom discuss.

Indigenous women's bodies are affected by the society in which they live, including its political and overarching colonial systems and practices, as "the body is the first place where women experience exploitation" (Altamirano-Jiménez 2013, 65). Resource extraction affects Indigenous women in specific ways, having an impact on Indigenous rights and framing discrimination based on the intersections of sex, race, and class (Altamirano-Jiménez 2009; Kuokkanen 2008, 2019; Green 2001). This chapter weaves prairie discourses into the specificity of the political culture of resource extraction; I then tie this to the ongoing exploitation of Indigenous lands and bodies.

One of the concepts examined by critical race scholars is the idea of structural determinism (see Gillies 2021). Cree scholar Verna St. Denis introduced me to this concept in 2017. The general idea is that colonizers needed stereotypes of Indigenous peoples (for example, beliefs that Indigenous peoples are savages, less than human, drunks, addicts, sexually promiscuous, etc.) to justify discriminatory laws, policies, practices, and processes. Powerful examples of these laws, policies, practices, and processes are the *Indian Act* (see Chapter 4) or the Indian residential school system. These discriminatory laws, policies, etc., led to negative social, cultural, political, and economic outcomes for Indigenous peoples.[1] The resulting statistics (e.g., number of incarcerated Indigenous peoples, number of Indigenous children in the child welfare system, etc.) serve to normalize settler-colonial society's (and governments') discriminatory discourse – that is, public discussion or debate – and views of Indigenous peoples. This continues as a vicious cycle – one in which we are still stuck. A knock-on effect of this is that sometimes we as Indigenous peoples also internalize these beliefs (see Jobin 2016).

Resource Extraction and Political Culture

For my purposes here, I would define political culture as "broad patterns of individual values and attitudes toward political objects" (Jackson and Jackson 2006, 63). Political culture can be viewed as constitutive; that is, it has the power to create things. This means that it can be linked to behaviour (Welch 2013, 213). Although political culture is only one aspect of the culture of a region or society, "it serves many purposes: it draws individuals together; supports judgment and action; helps to constitute the character and personality of a community; differentiates one community from another; and encourages its members to seek common objectives" (213). I see the prairies, and specifically areas where resource extraction is prominent, as having created a political culture around resource extraction.

A resource extraction political culture can be defined as one in which collective values and attitudes produce judgments about and seek common objectives around, for example, the oil and gas industry. Esteem for and pride in association with oil and gas may be displayed through popular media, regional or nationalistic emblems, and popular culture. The hockey team I have cheered for ever since I was a young child is called the Edmonton Oilers. On May 7, 2017, I attended an Oilers hockey game. At the beginning of the event, as the national anthem was being sung, a Canadian flag the length of the ice was unrolled over people's heads on one side of the arena. Simultaneously, on the other side, a flag of equal size was unrolled that said LOILTY. In this display of patriotism, loyalty to oil was given the same level of importance as the Canadian flag to Canadian nationalism sentiments. This is one illustration of how political culture manifests itself in a resource extraction centre.

This book explores how our relations with the land are constitutive; they create and co-create who we are as individuals and who we are as peoples. In this chapter, I argue that when we change our relationship to Mother Earth, we can also constitute a different way of relating to our other relations, including women, girls, and Two-Spirit + persons ("+" includes 2SLGBTQQIA: Two-Spirit, lesbian, gay, bisexual, transgender, queer, questioning, intersex, and asexual people). This different constitution of relationships to land can be exploitative, and exploitation can be violent. This is why it is important to explore the history of economic exploitation. Resource extraction is only one factor to examine, and without resource extraction, there would still be violence. However, there is a specificity to the relationships created in resource extraction areas that needs to be examined further.

Harold Innis was a founding scholar in the area of Canadian political economy. His work illustrates how different "staples" (like fur in the fur trade, or oil and gas) led to different regional economies and societies within the Canadian state, as well as elsewhere. Some of my favourite learnings from Innis relate to the dependency that a staples economy creates. In Chapter 2, I discussed how colonialism in Canada started with economic exploitation that began in the fur trade, and how Indigenous lands and bodies were exploited through the trading of furs to companies like the Hudson's Bay Company.[2]

During the fur trade, much wealth was created for Great Britain. Innis calls Britain the "heartland," and Indigenous territories (now called Canada) the "hinterland." The heartland, via British colonists, searches for and exploits staples in the hinterland, which gives the heartland increased economic and political power. In Innis's theory, once one staple, such as furs, has been successfully exploited, the hinterland economy will be on a perpetual search for new staples to exploit – for example, oil. In Spring 2022, I went to an Oilers round-one playoff game. As I was looking at the Oilers' flag waving, with fans on their feet in the midst of the playoff excitement, I thought that in five years we might have to change our name to the

"Hydrogen-ers," as Alberta is now exploring hydrogen as the next main staple. On one scale, central Canada can be seen as the core (or heartland) of Canada, and the prairies as hinterlands built on staple economies. In another sense, we can see specifically how Indigenous lands are exploited for different staples mainly for the benefit of non-Indigenous governments and corporations, which increase their economic and political power thereby.

Structural determinism, political culture, and staples theory combine to form an environment in which both lands and bodies are exploited. Racist and discriminatory views of Indigenous peoples traditionally provided justification for exploiting Indigenous lands and bodies. Certain practices, like Canada's pass system, ensured Indigenous peoples became economically dependent on the state (see Sarah Carter's [1993] linkage of agriculture, economic dependency, and the pass system). Similar portrayals of Indigenous people as "less than" or "Other" continue to provide justification for policies and practices that contribute to the ongoing exploitation of Indigenous lands and bodies. In the Indigenous world view I am grounding this work in, all animate beings (people, animals, plants, etc.) have spirit, innate worth, and agency. There is a connection between the exploitation of Indigenous lands and bodies (including bodies of water, women's bodies, etc.); it is part of the same logic. In many Indigenous societies, including that of the Cree, the Earth is considered our collective Mother. Elmer Ghostkeeper (2007, 61) reframes the concept of ownership from an Indigenous perspective; he says that, in the Cree language, tipêyihcikêwin ᒋᐸᔅᒥᕐᑫᐅᐧᐁᐧ "is viewed as a gift of collective stewardship for Mother Earth, a living being, from The Great Spirit (*Kechi Manitow*)." In his book *Spirit Gifting*, Ghostkeeper (2007, 79) explains how adopting technology to engage in resource extraction made it faster and relatively easier to "destroy and rearrange ecosystems during the construction of a natural gas field." He then explains that during the period in his life when he engaged in resource extraction labour for his community, there was a change in his world view; he says, "I did not have time to evaluate my beliefs and practices involving the *rape* and *exploitation* of the gifts of Mother Earth" (79) (emphasis added). Ghostkeeper makes this important link – exploiting the gifts of Mother Earth shifted his world view. I see this shift enabling a specificity of violence that also occurs against Indigenous women's bodies. Resource extraction creates conditions in which exploitation of lands and bodies becomes part of the same overall logic. Instead of seeing Indigenous women as beings to be honoured, we are seen as beings to be exploited. There is not only a logic of exploitation but also one of disposal, in which, like oil and gas, Indigenous women+ bodies are resources to be used for gain, for profit, for pleasure. When that "resource" is used up, then the body, like the land, becomes disposable, junk – worthless.[3] Our behaviour toward land creates and co-creates who we are. The public discourses we engage in create and co-create who we are. Discriminatory views of Indigenous peoples continue to justify logics of exploitation and disposal.

The next section of this chapter examines the issue of Murdered and Missing Indigenous Women, Girls, and Two-Spirit + persons.

MMIWG+

In her testimony to the National Inquiry into Missing and Murdered Indigenous Women and Girls (MMIWG), Connie Greyeyes, a member of the Bigstone Cree Nation and a community activist, said:

> And, you know, being a front-line, kind of, grassroots person, I have often talked to women who have experienced violence the previous night from somebody that they met that is just in town working. And, more often than not, it has often – almost always been, "I didn't know them, but they were here working for so-and-so." ... And, when you have that dynamic of all of that money, all of that pressure working, and then they get to blow off some steam and come into ... [town] and party? It is a bad mixture for the women and girls of the communities (National Inquiry into MMIWG 2019, 1a: 584–85).

Murdered and Missing Indigenous women, girls, and Two-Spirit + persons are a part of the colonial project in Canada. This tragedy has a history. Grassroots Indigenous movements (K. Anderson, Campbell, and Belcourt 2018), international pressure, and recommendations from the Truth and Reconciliation Committee pressured the government of Canada to create a National Inquiry into Missing and Murdered Indigenous Women and Girls, which released its final report and Calls for Justice in 2019. In this report the commissioners wrote:

> The National Inquiry heard testimony and examined evidence that suggested that resource extraction projects can exacerbate the problem of violence against Indigenous women and girls. Expert Witnesses, institutional witnesses, and Knowledge Keepers told the National

Inquiry that resource extraction projects can drive violence against Indigenous women in several ways, including issues related to transient workers, harassment and assault in the workplace, rotational shift work, substance abuse and addictions, and economic insecurity. They argued that resource extraction projects can lead to increased violence against Indigenous women at the hands of non-Indigenous men, as well as increased violence within Indigenous communities. (National Inquiry into MMIWG 2019, 584)

Exploitation of lands and bodies is part of colonialism in Canada, and it is a gendered project. Indigenous women, singled out for discriminatory treatment under *Indian Act* policy, had their identities as "Indian" people made increasingly dependent on the identities of their husbands. They were subject to rules that applied only to them as women; this has been summarized and written about in numerous accounts. For example, Indigenous women "could not vote in band elections; if they married an Indian man from another band, they lost membership in their home communities; if they married out by wedding a non-Indian man, they lost Indian status, membership in their home communities, and the right to transmit Indian status to the children of that marriage; if they married an Indian man who became enfranchised, they lost status, membership, treaty payments and related rights and the right to inherit the enfranchised husband's lands when he died" (Canada 1996, 4:33). This loss of individual identity emphasizes how Indigenous women have been seen as "Other," as "less than," and provides the inherent justification for their objectification. Specifically, it points to how racist ideas about Indigenous women have justified policies, laws, and an underlying belief and political culture that enable violence against Indigenous women.

Numerous scholars have explored the ways in which colonial relationships are inherently gendered and sexualized, demonstrating how the state perpetuates race-based and gender-based violence against Indigenous women (Kuokkanen 2019). Authors have documented numerous accounts of Indigenous women being targeted for acts of violence and sexual exploitation (Kuokkanen 2019; Green 2007, 22; Amnesty International 2004). Yet, as Julie Kay (2013, 67) points out, Indigenous women's "experiences of abuse have been met with indifference by the state and society alike in Canada." Public discourse often claims that violence against Indigenous women is a product of the lifestyles the women live. This negates any sort of structural analysis that examines practices, institutions, and processes that enable an environment in which Indigenous women are victims of violence, victims of rape, victims of homicide, victims of not being protected by police, victims of not getting the resources to investigate crimes perpetrated against them, victims of media bias that puts them in a certain negative light – in short, victims of colonialism. Furthermore, systemic gendered discrimination against Indigenous women undermines their roles in society (Kay 2013). Canada has been condemned for its inaction in relation to high rates of violence against Indigenous women. The Amnesty International report "Stolen Sisters: A Human Rights Response to Discrimination and Violence against Indigenous Women in Canada" (2004), written nearly twenty years ago, substantiated Indigenous women's accounts of specific incidents and systemic issues in the police force, justice system,[4] and Canadian social views. Indigenous people, including Indigenous women, are over-policed and underprotected.

Indigenous women are also negatively affected by the public discourse around their identity and worth. The National Inquiry into Missing and Murdered Indigenous Women and Girls (2019 1a:386) states:

> Negative sexist and racist representations of Indigenous women, girls, and 2SLGBTQQIA people are part of Canada's colonial history. Early representations of Indigenous women in Canada are intimately tied to the process of colonization. Although Indigenous women's connection to the land is used in both Western and Indigenous historical frameworks, the Euro-constructed image of Indigenous women mirrors Western attitudes toward land of "control, conquest, possession, and exploitation." North American images of Indigenous women have been constructed within the context of colonization and have evolved as three different stereotypes: the Queen, the Indian Princess, and the Squaw. All of the early representations of Indigenous women are overtly sexual and charged with colonialist goals and perceptions of land.

Going back to the idea of structural determinism, stereotypes and discriminatory views of Indigenous women can be seen as a thread starting at the beginning of Canadian colonialism and continuing, in various forms, to the present. Sámi scholar Rauna Kuokkanen's 2019 book *Restructuring Relations: Indigenous Self-Determination, Governance and Gender* discusses how Indigenous women have frequently been constructed as "'lascivious, shameless, unmaternal, prostitutes, ugly, and incapable of high sentiment or manners – the dark mirror-image to the idealized nineteenth-century visions of white women.' This characterization of Indigenous women as hypersexual was essential to the justification of colonization" (189). This view has been seen as a way for colonizers to justify treatment of Indigenous women and is based in the fear of the agency of Indigenous women that settlers encountered when they first interacted with Indigenous people on these lands (189).

A policy brief examines how historical representations of Indigenous women related to sexual availability and criminal behaviour have created a society in which Indigenous women are not seen as victims or as facing exploitation but as confronting "a natural consequence of the life that they have chosen to occupy" (Sikka 2009, 3–4). This premise negates and completely ignores the history of racism, cultural genocide, and colonization. Kuokkanen (2019, 190) demonstrates that these racist and dehumanizing discourses continue today in media and police accounts that label missing and murdered Indigenous women, girls, and Two-Spirit + persons as "high-risk, trafficked/prostituted, troubled runaways ... [while] not acknowledging the forced child-welfare policies that put Indigenous people at risk for violence, disappearance, and death"; this is, Kuokkanen points out, "both disingenuous and dangerous." This public discourse also relates to representations of Indigenous women in the media. Media framing is the lens journalists use, beyond the information given in an article, to select other information on which to focus (National Inquiry into MMIWG 2019, 386). The National Inquiry into MMIWG's (2019, 393) final report, *Reclaiming Power and Place,* points to the "early colonial representations of Indigenous women manifest in today's misrepresentation and under-representation of Indigenous women, girls, and 2SLGBTQQIA people; ... [today] media representations can legitimize violence and contribute to the targeting of Indigenous women by silencing their experiences." Furthermore, the Canadian state "commodifies us as victims, builds entire economies around our regulation, patriarchal economies that reinforce old narratives: Indigenous women and girls are promiscuous, available for violence and sex, lascivious tastes, and responsible for our own deaths" (Kuokkanen 2019, 190).

A Canadian statistical analysis finds that Indigenous people are three times more likely than others to be victims of violent crimes, with Indigenous women having the highest rates of victimization (Brzozowski, Taylor-Butts, and Johnson 2006, 5). Indigenous women experience violence at a rate 3.5 times greater than non-Indigenous women (5). In 2016, Amnesty International published a study that found a strong link between resource extraction and exploitation of Indigenous women, stating that "violence toward Indigenous women is a routine part of life" for those in the extractive sector (quoted in Alook, Hill, and Hussey 2017, 10; see also Knott 2018). In "Violence and Extraction: Stories from the Oil Fields," her chapter in the edited collection *Keetsahhnak: Our Missing and Murdered Indigenous Sisters*, Helen Knott from Prophet River First Nation also links the exploitation of Indigenous women to resource extraction. Knott (2018, 153) explains the importance of discussing these issues: "There are many people in my territory who are vocal and knowledgeable on issues related to land protection, but significantly fewer people who are willing to speak about violence experienced by Indigenous women, and ... even fewer who speak to both." Knott brings the words of activist Connie Greyeyes to the forefront of this analysis:

> "I fully believe that the huge amount of resource extraction in this area contributes to the violence committed against women ... There are a high number of transients; men here for work that are new to the area as a result of the resource extraction ... men who have no vested interest [in the community] ... makes this a dangerous place for Indigenous women." (Quoted in Knott 2018, 149–50; National Inquiry into MMIWG 2019, 1a:584–85)

A 2014 study found that oil and gas "man-camps" "breed hyper-masculinity and high rates of substance abuse" and are a "causal factor in violence against women" (Eckford and Wagg 2014). While presenting the report *Violence on the Land, Violence on our Bodies* (Women's Earth Alliance and Native Youth Sexual Health Network 2016) to the National Inquiry into MMIWG, T.J. Lightfoot explained the impact of resource extraction work camps: "So, the influx of workers in these areas, what we have seen is that they have led to increased rates of sexual violence and physical violence, the abduction of Indigenous women and children" (National Inquiry into MMIWG 2019, 1a:585). Against the history of structural determinism, in which racist discourses around Indigenous women justify exploitation of both Indigenous women and Indigenous lands (Knott 2018; Kuokkanen 2019), it is crucial that self-determination include justice for Indigenous women and Indigenous lands. It is also through self-determination that renewed visions of Indigenous women+ have the potential to be realized.

Gendered Self-Determination

The issue of consent is central to self-determination, whether it involves territory or bodies. The Women's Earth Alliance and Native Youth Sexual Health Network (2016, 17) suggest, "In order to increase the recognition of free, prior and informed consent over Indigenous territories, we need to simultaneously build up the ways that consent is supported around people's bodies."

There is potential for a positive correlation between self-determination and Indigenous women's rights.[5] Cree and Métis scholar and poet Emma LaRocque (2007, 62) writes that Indigenous women "have the greatest stake in self-determination, both as part of a people struggling to decolonize and as individuals struggling to enjoy basic human rights." Similarly, Vera Martin, in an interview with Kim Anderson (2000, 245), equates self-determination with respect, "allowing people to make their own decisions, [and] being able to make choices and accepting the consequences." The connection between Indigenous women's rights and safety is highlighted by Amnesty International's (2004, 41–42) recognition that Indigenous peoples' right to self-determination, among other key provisions, would provide greater protection for Indigenous women against violence.

Indigenous women scholars are theorizing alternatives for Indigenous peoples. Setting capitalism aside, Kuokkanen explores the gift paradigm in Indigenous societies, in which gift displays fulfil more than just an economic function; they are applicable to "all my relations" (Kuokkanen 2007, 23). As introduced in Chapter 2, Kuokkanen describes how in many Indigenous world views, "giving entails an active relationship between the human and natural worlds, one characterized by reciprocity, a sense of collective responsibility, and reverence toward the gifts of the land" (23). She also writes about the need to reorient Indigenous governance toward the notion of social economy, which recognizes the intricate ways in which the economy is embedded in social relations (Kuokkanen 2011, 232).

In a study led by Cree scholar Angele Alook (Alook, Hill, and Hussey 2019), the authors explore gendered experiences of work in resource extraction through the lens of miyo-pimâtisiwin ᒥᔪ ᐱᒫᑎᓯᐎᐣ (the good life). Alook and her colleagues link Indigenous people's loss of miyo-pimâtisiwin with severed relationships to the land caused by colonialism (4). In an earlier article, they describe miyo-pimâtisiwin as a good life that balances family, community, and economy (Alook, Hill, and Hussey 2017, 20). The authors explain how there was "a loss of traditional ways of subsistence in which living off the land involved balanced gender relations and was a spiritual, emotional, physical, mental, and economic balance with the Earth" (20). Cree scholar Priscilla Settee (2011, 73) sees social economy models as an alternative to the current economic structure that will reduce poverty and the social exclusion of Indigenous peoples. This developing discourse is quite dynamic and exciting, and there is a need for additional analysis from diverse perspectives, obtained by listening to more voices and Indigenous knowledges connected to place. Further research is needed into Indigenous economic relations that are not exploitative in function or design. Cree scholar Sylvia McAdam (2015, 55) writes that, historically, the Cree women who were part of the okihcitâwiskwêwak were an important part of nehiyawak governance with specific duties, where this Cree women's society would have been consulted over land matters "because authority and jurisdiction to speak about land resides with the women."

Knowledge holder Maria Campbell (2007, 5) speaks to the concept of wahkotowin:

> There is a word in my language that speaks to these issues: "wahkotowin." Today it is translated to mean kinship, relationship, and family as in human family. But at one time, from our place it meant the whole of creation. And our teachings taught us that all of creation is related and inter-connected to all things within it.
>
> Wahkotowin meant honoring and respecting those relationships. They are our stories, songs, ceremonies, and dances that taught us from birth to death our responsibilities and reciprocal obligations to each other. Human to human, human to plants, human to animals, to the water and especially to the earth. And in turn all of creation had responsibilities and reciprocal obligations to us.

On New Year's Eve at the end of 2015, I ran into an inebriated Al. It had been a few months since I ended our relationship. He told me that he would often gain entry to my apartment building and stand in front of my door (I was on the fourteenth floor), trying to decide whether he should bang on it to gain entry. As he said this to me on New Year's Eve, he was holding my arm tightly and would not let me walk away. I felt a mix of emotions, including fear that he had been in my apartment building without me knowing. My friend, Cree scholar Tracy Bear, who was standing by, had had enough and grabbed Al's arm so he would let me go. We left, and I have not seen Al since, although he has tried contacting me. This is just one small story from my own experience.

7

Theorizing Cree Economic and Governing Relationships

AS I WRITE THIS CHAPTER, I am looking out a southeast window at the frozen North Saskatchewan River (2015). This river has historical significance to my family and my Cree roots. On my mother's side, we belong to the sîpîwiyiniwak ᕆᐱᐄᐧᔪᐳᕊᑕ, the River Cree, a subgrouping of the Upstream People, which is the northern regional division of the Plains Cree. Our territory was said to be between the North Saskatchewan and Battle Rivers. Writing and thinking through Cree economic relationships, I am also working toward a deeper understanding of my own roles and responsibilities within this territory. In this process, I acknowledge that there are thousands of years of knowledge within the trees I look at and the millions of footsteps that have walked these forests and all those who have canoed this river. In each story I read in the archives,[1] and in every conversation I had with a Cree knowledge holder, a piece of wisdom was shared. Cree people who shared their knowledge with me included young and old, women and men, those who live in First Nations communities and those who have moved away, those fluent in nehiyawewin ᑕᐦᐊᔭᐁᐧᐃᐧᐣ (the Cree language) and those who are trying to learn. Taken together, these legends, sacred stories, humorous stories, and personal accounts shape and reshape my understanding, like the many pieces of a puzzle. I describe this as a nehiyawak ᑕᐦᐊᔭᑕ peoplehood methodology (see Chapter 1). Knowledge of wâhkohtôwin ᐋᐧᐦᑯᐦᑐᐃᐧᐣ (the laws governing relationships) goes beyond the relationships within Cree political economy. Cree relationships, including economic relationships, include everything the sun touches with its rays.

108

Although I am exploring economic relationships within these narratives, they cannot be understood apart from the social relations in which they are embedded. My research explores Cree economic relationships that include nature's economy, the sustenance economy, and the complex challenges of contemporary economic relationships.[2]

The scope of this research project was ambitious. My goal is to look back in time at historical and continuing Cree economic relations and governance. From that conceptual base, I ask how this knowledge already is and can be enhanced to cultivate contemporary Cree social practices – practices that enable self-determination and economic resurgence for the Cree people. I attempt to explore the resilience within Cree ontological relations that continue in spite of the effects of colonization and economic exploitation. Using a wide selection of Cree narratives, such as written accounts, interviews, and oral histories with Cree knowledge holders, patterns surrounding economic relations emerge from within the stories.[3] In Chapter 1, I presented a pimâcihowin or livelihood economic model (Figure 6), where the pistil and stamen of the beaded okinewâpikonew ▷Pᴜ◁·∧dᴜ° are a visual metaphor representing the interconnections and governance between all beings (human, animal, land, water, spirit). This is understood through the concept of wâhkohtôwin ◁·ⁱⁱd̈ⁱⁱↃ△·².

The first section of this chapter provides a discussion of Cree relationships through the exploration of the Cree concept of wâhkohtôwin ◁·ⁱⁱd̈ⁱⁱↃ△·², specifically practices that respond to establishing, maintaining, opposing, and restoring relationships. I then explore the complexity of Cree economic relationships and look at these through the practices of the giveaway and trade/exchange. As described in Chapter 1, the Cree were a non-state people with, as Val Napoleon (2009, 9–10) writes, a "non-State, decentralized political structure that relies on the maintenance of reciprocal kinship relationships and negotiations rather than on centralized legal and enforcement bureaucracies." At the heart of Cree political economy is wâhkohtôwin ◁·ⁱⁱd̈ⁱⁱↃ△·² – the laws governing relationships. This chapter provides a window into this world view.

Cree Economic and Governing Relationships

Cree economic principles and practices are deeply connected to establishing, maintaining, and restoring relationships, and responding to conflict. These relationship practices occur between Cree people, with other people groups, with nonhuman beings, and with spiritual beings. The often-used phrase

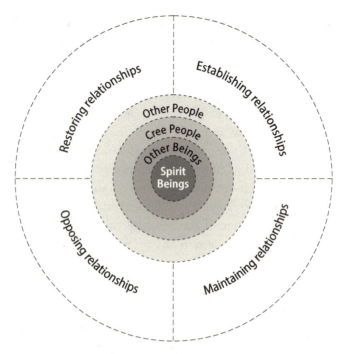

15 Cree economic and governing relationships.

kahkiyaw niwâhkômâkanak ᏆᎵᑫᏲᐤ ᓂᐋᐧᐦᑰᒫᑲᓇᐠ (all my relations) is quite applicable to these findings.

Figure 15 pictorially represents the governing relationships that guide Cree economic practices. The different actors involved in these economic relationships are displayed in the inner circles – these are akin to the pistil and stamen in Figure 6 (Chapter 1). One way to look at this is as if from above and looking down, but you could also look at the spiral from the side, and there are different teachings embedded in this view (see LaBoucane-Benson 2009, 211). In this chapter I will first explore the Cree concept of wâhkohtôwin ᐋᐧᐦᑰᐦᑑᐃᐧᐣ and show how it encompasses the different relationships shown in the diagram. Then I will convey how the giveaway ceremony and trade/exchange are two Cree practices that illuminate these interlocking economic relationships, encompassed by the central Cree principle of wâhkohtôwin ᐋᐧᐦᑰᐦᑑᐃᐧᐣ.

wâhkohtôwin ᐋᐧᐦᑰᐦᑑᐃᐧᐣ

wâhkohtôwin ᐋᐧᐦᑰᐦᑑᐃᐧᐣ involves the laws governing relationships within a Cree world view (H. Cardinal 2007, 74–75). One of the important aspects

110   UPHOLDING INDIGENOUS ECONOMIC RELATIONSHIPS

of this concept is that it does not just include family relationships; rather, it explores how we are all related to each other. wâhkohtôwin ᐋᐧᐦᑰᐦᑐᐃᐧᐣ also extends to the ways we are related to nonhuman beings (i.e., animals, plants, the air, the land). Federal Senator Patti LaBoucane-Benson is Métis from Treaty Six territory and completed her doctoral research with Cree knowledge holders from Treaty Six. In "Are We Seeking Pimatisiwin or Creating Pomewin? Implications for Water Policy," LaBoucane-Benson et al. (2012, 5) explain wâhkohtôwin ᐋᐧᐦᑰᐦᑐᐃᐧᐣ as "Creator's laws that govern relationships between all things" and mîyo wichetowin ᒥᔪ ᐄᐧᒋᐦᐃᑐᐃᐧᐣ as the "laws that direct us to have good relationships between people," to live pimâtisiwin ᐱᒫᑎᓯᐃᐧᐣ "the good life." Then, drawing from H. Cardinal and Hildebrandt (2000) and LeClaire and G. Cardinal (1998), they explain the most common values underpinning these laws, including:

- Kisewâtisiwin: compassion; loving kindness.
- Tapwewin: speaking the truth with precision and accuracy; honesty.
- Witaskewin: living together in harmony.
- Manâtisiwin: respect.
- Miyotehewin: generosity.
- Tapateyimisôwin: humility; humbleness.
- Tipeyimisowin: self-determination; freedom; liberty.
- Wîcihitowin: helping one another; having a partnership or friendship; unity. (LaBoucane-Benson et al. 2012, 5)

Sunney is one of the people I interviewed.[4] He is of the amiskowacîwiyiniwak ᐊᒥᐢᑯᐊᐧᒌᐃᐧᔨᓂᐊᐧᐠ (Beaver Hills People); he is a fifty-five-year-old knowledge keeper, fluent in the language and the Cree world view, and a lodge holder. Sunney took the time to meet with me numerous times; he was very helpful in explaining wâhkohtôwin ᐋᐧᐦᑰᐦᑐᐃᐧᐣ to me. Sunney emphasized how important building relationships and making connections is to Cree society:

> I used to hear men, who didn't know if they were related to one another, sometimes they would call each other mônah-asiskiya: mônaha ᒨᓇᐦᐊ means to dig, asiskiy ᐊᓯᐢᑭᐩ is the dirt; so they are trying so hard, they want to endear themselves to one another so much that they say ah mônah-asiskiya, because they want that relationship, that bonding, that endearment to one another. wâhkohtôwin ᐋᐧᐦᑰᐦᑐᐃᐧᐣ is about that

building relationships, and of course with colonization that system drastically changed, and it became something we were taught about separation: such as great-aunt, great-uncle, rather than grandmother and grandfather. (Sunney 2014a)

Even with colonization, of course, some people are still living out their responsibilities of wâhkohtôwin ᐃᐧᐦᑐᐃᐧᐣ. Sunney started our interview by explaining a trip he took to Kahnawake, bringing his pipe to have a spiritual ceremony with the Haudenosaunee people, specifically to meet with a Mohawk Elder who was part of the Oka crisis in 1990. Sunney explains:

> wâhkohtôwin ᐃᐧᐦᑐᐃᐧᐣ is not just a human dynamic; it is not just a human occurrence ... He [the Mohawk Elder] told us a story about what happened there [during the Oka Crisis in 1990], their side, their reality. I told him, yes, a lot of the pipes went up in Alberta and passed the country ... I wanted this pipe to complete this journey after all this trouble. I brought a pipe down there [to Kahnawake] and I told him I would like to do a ceremony, give thanks to the Creator. He told us all about the military and the Sûreté du Québec, and the actions that the police they took against them. Then he went on to the spiritual side of things.
>
> He said, I have a Grandfather [the sun]; he comes in through a door. There is a great waterway on the East side of Turtle Island and it comes up through that door every day. On the West side of Turtle Island there is another door that our Grandfather goes through when it is done with this day. And my Grandfather says, everything I touch I am related to. That's about symbiosis, of course, in a very practical way, talking about symbiosis and that's our world view. That is how we are related to the trees; we are related to the rocks. We are not just related to each other how we have identified each other as mother, father, child, grandchild, sister, brother, cousin, uncle, aunt, grandfather, grandmother. We are not just related that way; we are all related according to that wâhkohtôwin ᐃᐧᐦᑐᐃᐧᐣ, it is all about that. Now, sihci-wâhkohtôwin ᓯᐦᒋ ᐃᐧᐦᑐᐃᐧᐣ is about your own immediate clan, your own bloodline.
>
> There is also an understanding that we are all related in here, we are also not only related to that; we are also related to the air, the water,

> the sun, the earth, and all that it brings. So we are related to all these things, we are related to what is under the ground, asiskiy ᐊᓯᐢᑭᐩ – all the roots under there. We are related to the stars over there, as farfetched as it may seem, that is what we are related to ... So everything that the sun touches it is related to, but we are also related to the celestial bodies, and they have with our own spirit, they have that name ehokwemeyahk ᐁᐦᐅᑫᐧᒣᔭᕽ,[5] that means that our spirit on this earth, we will call it ahcâhk ᐊᐦᒑᕽ, and what we call the stars, the celestial bodies, the morning star, for instance, what I call it wâpanacâhkos ᐚᐸᓇᒑᐦᑯᐢ. So that's that spirit again. And then there's that spirit again ... So we are related to those Celestial bodies as well, not just here on this earthly thing. There is a belief that we have stardust in our bones. Always, it is all about relationship building. (Sunney 2014a)

In Sunney's words, recounting a trip to the east, we see the expanse of wâhkohtôwin ᐚᐦᑰᐦᑑᐏᐣ – how his trip to Kahnawake Mohawk territory was about establishing a relationship with the Haudenosaunee Elder, while also living out his responsibilities of wâhkohtôwin ᐚᐦᑰᐦᑑᐏᐣ by fulfilling a commitment that was made when he lifted the pipe in 1990 to pray for the Haudenosaunee people. wâhkohtôwin ᐚᐦᑰᐦᑑᐏᐣ is teachings around living well not only with other people, but also with all other beings. This is an example of establishing a relationship between a Cree man and a Haudenosaunee man and maintaining a relationship between a Cree man and a pipe, which within a Cree world view is also a living being. wâhkohtôwin ᐚᐦᑰᐦᑑᐏᐣ includes ways to have good relationships with all beings, and is instructive when thinking about Cree economic relationships.

In terms of miyo-wîcihitowin ᒥᔪ ᐑᒋᐦᑐᐏᐣ, one of the most widely accepted and important practices involves the gifting of tobacco. kinikinik ᑭᓂᑭᓂᐠ is a specific type of tobacco used in ceremonies and that is native to Turtle Island. In a legend called "Ayekis the Frog," the importance of kinikinik ᑭᓂᑭᓂᐠ is explored through the relationship of ayîkis ᐊᔩᑭᐢ and ᐑᓵᐦᑫᒑᕽ (spelled Wesuketchuk in this version, again a story that would be shared in pipon ᐱᐳᐣ, winter):

> Long ago there lived a large frog along the borders of a big lake. He had a very musical voice and was constantly singing merrily every evening. When Wesuketchuk was in the area he liked to listen to Ayekis and sent him many fine gifts of food.

The frog was pleased with this kindness and became puffed up with pride, singing all the more lustily every evening to please his big brother. This continued for some time.

One day Ayekis was puddling along in the water, when it occurred to him that perhaps he was being selfish, always receiving gifts from Wesuketchuk without giving him anything in return. He knew that his big brother smoked so he thought he should send him some kinnekinnic, the inner bark of the red willow. He gathered a quantity of the bark, dried it thoroughly, wrapped it up in a piece of skin, and asked Chekek the Mudhen to carry a bundle to his friend. Wesuketchuk was very pleased with the frog and from then on they continued to exchange gifts while Ayekis kept on his singing every evening. (Brass and Nanooch 1978c)

This legend shows the relationship between an animal and a spiritual being.[6] This relationship was formed through the mutual exchange of music for gifts of food. To maintain this favourable relationship, ayîkis ᐊᔩᑭᐢ presented ᐑᓵᐦᑫᒑᕽ with tobacco, and this facilitated the continued exchanging of gifts.

Tobacco has spiritual significance to Cree people and is gifted to other Cree people, non-Cree people, nonhuman beings, and spirit beings. In Leona Makokis's (2009) book *Leadership Teachings from Cree Elders,* she interviews Skywoman, a Cree knowledge keeper from Saddle Lake First Nation (of the amiskowacîwiyiniwak ᐊᒥᐢᑯᐘᒌᐏᔨᓂᐘᐠ or Beaver Hills People). Skywoman's words show the important relationship Cree people have with the land and how that relationship is maintained through the giving of tobacco. Skywoman explains: "You have all the gifts that will help you each day to provide for life. These gifts are food, medicine, clothing, shelter, water, air, and fire. All of these are life giving ... For every thing you take from the land you must give tobacco" (quoted in Makokis 2009, 68). In terms of establishing and then maintaining relationships with Cree people, giving gifts of tobacco is an important practice. A dialogue between Sunney and me demonstrates this:

SUNNEY: Tobacco is the understanding that there is going to be some kind of negotiation taking place. That is the offering of tobacco, the opening.

SHALENE: After, let's say, you trade something, if I wanted to keep that relationship, what would I do? Like, if I wanted to keep trading with that person?

SUNNEY: You would probably need to re-establish each time.

SHALENE: So, offer the tobacco again?

SUNNEY: Yes. That's what I do, anyway; I still do that if I want something. I have been getting something from someone for a long time, but each time I always offer tobacco. (Sunney 2014a)

Offering tobacco is an accepted protocol that transcends all types of relationships and is important in establishing, maintaining, and even restoring broken relationships. This practice is accepted in many Indigenous societies across the expanse of Turtle Island.

To begin, giving tobacco and other gifts is seen as common practice. Walter, a Cree Elder from the sîpîwiyiniwak ᒉᐱᐃᐧᐁᓂᐊᐧᐠ (River People), is seventy-four years old. Walter lived in his First Nation as a child and as an adult, in rural settings, and in various prairie cities. He has travelled to most of the Indigenous communities in Canada over the last fifty years, is an important public figure, and has been vital to the revitalization of Cree ways of being. We twice had the opportunity to chat about this research project. Walter shared a personal account that really illuminated the importance of gift-giving. He remembered one time when a young man brought a well-known older Crow Elder from the United States to visit him at his house. Walter explains, "As soon as he came in, the old man didn't say anything. He didn't speak. I don't think he looked at us. But because that young man brought him over, he probably shook our hands, and I shook his hand" (Walter 2014a). Walter goes on to explain:

As soon as he sat down, my wife made him tea and brought him some food. A sandwich probably, soup or something like that, and put it in front of him. At the same time, I went and I got a hat, like a polar bear hat, and I put it down beside him. I put tobacco there. I gave him a few other things, I don't remember what. But when he got that he took his cane and he banged it on the floor and he said: "Oh-ta," which meant we will stay here. He stayed for a couple days, visiting.

He didn't [initially know if he] want[ed] to stay because he didn't know if we knew anything. He didn't want to be with anybody that didn't know anything. And he gave me a gift, so that was good, that was protocol, because when you read in our history, that's one thing that we must always do is gift things. (Walter 2014a)

In this account, gift-giving was an important aspect of establishing a relationship. Gifting can also be practised to maintain good relations with non-human beings, such as animals. Walter calls animals like coyotes "our little brothers." He explains to me how in bad winters it can be hard for them if they cannot find food, so sometimes he brings them food; he says: "I knew that it would be so nice for them to find a plate of bones and maybe chunks of meat and fat on the plate somewhere there where they could eat it ... I'd say a little prayer for them." In this way, Walter sees the importance of giving a physical gift of food and a spiritual gift of prayer. I witnessed Walter live out this practice, and I was astonished to see the coyote's response. When the coyote saw us he bowed down, as if acknowledging our presence. It seemed to me that this coyote remembered Walter.

In the narratives of written stories and interviews, I learned about economic principles important to restoring equilibrium. Walter shared a situation that happened to a friend in British Columbia when he was a child:

Yeah, so mankind realized that relationship with everybody, and so today we hear about old people that talk to the animals. Like in British Columbia, this guy was telling me that they were coming home, they were kids having to pick berries all day with their grandmother, and they met a white grizzly bear on the trail, so the grandmother told the grizzly bear: "We have been picking berries all day, we left you some, and we are not here to harm you or do anything, let us pass. We are tired. We want to go home." So, the bear let them pass. (Walter 2014a)

This grandmother had the ability to communicate with the grizzly bear and knew the protocol of gift-giving. The grizzly bear could have inflicted great harm on this family. However, because they intentionally left the bear some of the berries they picked, the bear reciprocated by allowing them to pass on the trail.

Edward Ahenakew, a grandnephew of Cree Chief Poundmaker, was born in 1885. He was a family friend and relative of my grandparents, Lillian and Gilbert Wuttunee. My mother, Loretta, remembers him visiting their house when she was a little girl in the early 1950s. In his book *Voices of the*

Plains Cree, Ahenakew (1995b) shares a personal account told to him by Chief Thunderchild, titled "Indian Laws." This recounting of a complex fight started with a Cree man, Ê-pay-as,[7] stealing horses from a Blackfoot camp, which broke the peace between the Cree and Blackfoot. The Blackfoot retaliated and killed a Cree mother and child. The child's father demanded payment of horses from Ê-pay-as, and after Ê-pay-as would give him no more, the father of the deceased child went to the camp's lawmakers, the Dancers' and Providers' Societies. The decision was made that Ê-pay-as should give his poorest horse to the grieving father. When Ê-pay-as continued to refuse, the camp law was enforced, and there was another injury, which eventually resulted in more death. Finally, Mis-ta-wa-sis, a Chief of the wâskahikaniwiyiniwak ᐊᐧᐢᑲᐦᐃᑲᓂᐃᐧᔨᓂᐊᐧᐠ (House Cree), called the people together, and although he had not done anything wrong himself, he offered two of his own horses to make restitution. They asked Chief Thunderchild's father to bring the horses as a peace offering to Ê-pay-as and then asked him to give two horses to make restitution to Otter-child, whose father had been killed when Ê-pay-as and his two brothers wouldn't follow the camp law. In Chief Thunderchild's words:

> My father said, "Neestaw, I have brought two horses. They are a peace offering, two of the best that Mis-ta-wa-sis has, the best in this country. I implore you that there should be no more trouble. Take these horses and give me two of your common ones for the Old Man's son, Otter-child [the father of the deceased child]. Do this for the sake of your people, our band." As my father finished speaking, the wounded man died. Ê-pay-as said, "Do not cover his face." And he kissed his dead brother. Then he turned to my father, "I will do as you have asked me to do," he said, and he clasped our hands. (E. Ahenakew 1995b, 17–19)

This conflict that arose initially through a Cree person stealing horses in Blackfoot territory resulted in internal conflict among the Plains Cree. This account also displays an example of the legal traditions and legal governing bodies that had the mandate to make decisions on justice, and also authoritative decision makers, in this case Chief Mistawasis who stepped in to resolve the dispute.

Led by the Indigenous Law Research Unit (ILRU), the Accessing Justice and Reconciliation Project (AJR) was a collaboration involving seven different Indigenous communities across six different legal traditions.[8] AJR developed a legal synthesis that draws out the following Cree principles and procedural steps related to Chief Thunderchild's historical account:

- A Wrong-doer, or their family, can remedy harms by paying compensation or restitution directly to the person harmed, or to their family (22)
- When faced with risks of harm or conflict, people seek out and rely on guidance from those with the relevant understanding and expertise to advise and help respond to or resolve the issue (11)
- Avoidance can be employed to avoid the escalation of conflicts, where the conflict might cause more harm than the original concern (20)
- People are responsible to find ways to stop ongoing harms and prevent or mitigate future harms when necessary (33)
- When a person is suspected of causing harm or conflict, Authoritative Decision-Makers confront him or her publically when possible (13)
- Someone who has acknowledged [their][9] wrongdoing and is sincerely seeking resolution, is given the opportunity to be heard (38)
- The appropriate decision-makers are identified and implement a response. This may be a pre-emptive response in some cases. This step includes identifying who is the decision-maker most capable, or best positioned, to respond to the harm or risk of harm, or resolve the conflict in the particular circumstances (14) (Accessing Justice and Reconciliation Project 2013a).

Gifting horses was an accepted restitution practice, and when Ê-pay-as did not follow through on that, there were further consequences. Finally, after the escalation of the conflict and resulting deaths and injuries, restitution was made through the gifting of the best horses from Chief Mis-ta-wa-sis to Ê-pay-as, and to reciprocate, Ê-pay-as agreed to give two of his common horses to the grieving son.

One of the most important relationships to many Cree people is that between them and the spiritual realm or spiritual beings. When I was talking to Walter, he began to sing a Cree song that he had been gifted with, explaining that in this song there is an invitation to the spiritual. Alternating between singing in a strong melodic voice and talking, he explained:

The first part of our song: oh, ho, ho, ho, ha, ha [Walter is singing vocables]. That first part it goes up to hereafter and then any spirits that want to come, then there is a trail made all the way down to earth, and on the last part of that songs is: hey, hey, ha, ha, ha, oh [Walter is singing again], and what that part does? It blesses all of nature. The first part calls anybody that wants to come because they love us so much, they always want to be with us, and then the last part it – it blesses all of nature. So it's built right in the song. When the pipe is smoking, when the Creator was asking everybody what they wanted, the pipe said that the stones said they would like to interpret for mankind. So when we pray with that, then our prayers are interpreted to the Creator. (Walter 2014a)

This song and Walter's explanation demonstrate a way to establish a relationship with the spiritual; within the act of singing there is also the blessing of nature, which is a practice to maintain that relationship with the environment. Many times these songs are sung in a collective, so it also maintains community within Cree society.

Dora is a Plains Cree knowledge keeper, fluent in the language, and a gifted mother, daughter, sister, friend, and teacher – one who teaches and leads by example to both Cree and non-Cree people. She is in her forties (at the time of our interview in 2013), from the sîpîwiyiniwak ᓯᐱᐃᐧᔨᓂᐊᐧᐠ (River People). Dora is a ceremonial person who sees her identity as intimately linked to her responsibilities to maintain good relationships by attending the different Cree ceremonies throughout Treaty Six territory that run through the different seasons as acts of renewal. She sees it as a reciprocal relationship wherein she and her family receive guidance and support from the spiritual practices while also maintaining relationships with the community. Connie is a woman in her mid-thirties, a prominent local public figure and long-time activist from the amiskowacîwiyiniwak ᐊᒥᐢᑯᐊᐧᒌᐃᐧᔨᓂᐊᐧᐠ (Beaver Hills People). Connie is gifted at helping to bring about change by pushing the boundaries in Western institutions and also by sharing grassroots Indigenous initiatives in accessible ways. I had the opportunity to sit down with both of them to hear them share the importance of the ceremonial cycle:

> DORA: We need people aware that these [ceremonies] are still alive, a
> lot of people, some ... say "they don't have those anymore," while

I just had one [of those ceremonies], you know. It is not like the ceremonies are going to come to you; you have to go out to the ceremonies. They are not going to come banging on your door. They are very much alive. Like the giveaway, the Ghost Dance, the Horse Dance, Round Dance, Powwow; there are so many out there. People are not going to them, only the ones who make sure they want to keep the teachings and pass them on, right? People are like, "What, you still have those?" You bet we do.

CONNIE: I didn't realize how many different ceremonies there are, I used to go to sweats, and you always knew about the Sun Dance, it was always there, but the Ghost Dance, the Tea Dance, the Horse Dance – the connectedness to each of those: [for example] the night lodges, each one has a role in the whole.

DORA: There is so much out there that you have to know, you just have to take yourself there. I always take my kids there, so they know the differences in them, the meaning – what they are meant for, so if they need the help they know where to go get it. (Dora and Connie 2013)

Dora sees living out the ceremonial cycle of the Plains Cree as a way for her to maintain miyo-wîcihitowin ᒥᔪ ᐄᒋᐦᐃᑐᐃᐧᐣ (good relationships) with all her relations. Over the last few years, Connie has been more fully immersed in the expanse of Cree ceremonies, and she is recognizing their individual purposes as well as how they all fit into a larger governing system.

pawâmiwin ᐸᐋᐧᒥᐃᐧᐣ (dream power) is another way that Cree people talk about connecting to the spiritual, as well as a way to get guidance. Walter explains how meanings in Cree teachings can come to you in your dreams if you are struggling with understanding them directly:

Nowadays everybody wants to have the teachings ... And so whenever you get a teaching, no matter how small it is, how big it is, take time to think about it. Take time to think about more than the obvious, to actually think about what it really means, and it'll come to you. As a matter of fact, what will happen is when you go to sleep, you don't really remember what it is, then they'll come and they'll tell you in your dream. They will have pity on you. They'll tell you in your dream what the obvious is. Some people don't have to dream because they can understand when they're told intuitively. Some people have to dream because that's the only way they can understand – when they're told in black and white. (Walter 2014a)

Within his words there is the understanding that the one receiving the teaching has a responsibility to try to understand the meaning as well as the acknowledgement that within dreams teachings can appear. To provide an example of the type of guidance dreams can provide, I draw on an account from Chief Thunderchild, who was born in 1849 and shared stories of his life with Edward Ahenakew in 1923 (McCullough 2013). Here, Chief Thunderchild recounts a hard winter, one that included a lot of starvation:

One night I dreamed that someone came to me and said, "You can save yourself. Look to the south!" And looking south, I saw that the country was green, but to the north there was only darkness. I tried to flee to the south. The dream was vivid, and when I awoke it was almost morning. I lay thinking about the dream, and then I told it to my father. "Maybe it is only hunger that made me dream," I said. But my father told me, "Dreams count, my son. Try to go south, all of you; and if I cannot follow, leave me. I will do my best." ...

We camped at the old Sun Dance place, where there was plenty of wood. The women found a buffalo head and neck in the snow, and they made a fire to boil it. I climbed the bank of the river, and as I sat there I saw something that moved and disappeared again in the wind. I went to find out what it was, and I came to a big snowdrift with the pole at the top, from which a bit of cloth blew in the wind. It marked a cache.

I took off my coat and began to dig through the hard crust of snow. Down inside the drift I found hides that covered the meat of two buffalo, cut in pieces. I had to sit down then, for I remembered my dream and was overcome with feeling and with thankfulness to the spirits who had guided us. (E. Ahenakew 1995b, 14–16)

With this recollection, Chief Thunderchild acknowledged the spiritual assistance he received through his dream. Thunderchild's father reminded him of the importance of dreams. In Cree thought, spirit beings are connected to waking and sleeping hours; the veil between the two realities is often quite thin.[10]

This section on wâhkohtôwin and Cree relationships has offered examples of the myriad of relationships among Cree people, non-Cree people, spirit beings, and nonhuman beings. The practices recounted to me during interviews show examples of both diversity and commonalities of protocol, whether it relates to establishing or maintaining a relationship, or attempting to restore a broken relationship. Similar to Chief Thunderchild's story of a winter of hardship, the giveaway ceremony began with a harsh winter in which spiritual help was given. The next section will explore the giveaway, the relationships it includes, and how this can facilitate an understanding of Cree economic relations.

The Giveaway Ceremony

There are many different types of giveaways in Cree society. Giveaways are a ceremony, and in some ways they can also be seen as an institution with spiritual, social, and economic functions.[11] I see this Cree institution as providing key insights into the collective world view undergirding Cree economic principles and practices. As explored above, Cree economy is inherently about relationships, whether they are new, continued, or opposing – and those relationships are with all of creation. In Chapter 10 I explore the mâhtâhitowin ᒫᐦᒋᐦᐃᑐᐃᐧᐣ as a specific type of giveaway, but in this chapter I include an example of the giveaway of centuries past.

Norbert Welsh provided a historical example of the giveaway (Welsh as told to Weekes 1994, first published in 1939). Welsh was born in 1845. During this period on the Plains, it is written that traders and bison hunters were expected to take part in these Cree practices. In Welsh's story, the giveaway explicates how economic principles are involved in restoring oppositional relationships between Cree and Métis hunters. In this personal account, Welsh, a Métis, was confronted by the Cree messenger Pish-e-quat (Blackguard) who was sent by the Cree Chief Shash-apew (Spread Sitter) "to warn the half-breeds not to hunt buffalo in his territory unless they were willing to pay a duty on every buffalo they killed," for the Cree headmen of this band believed they were more entitled to the bison than were the Métis (51). Welsh did not agree. Welsh gave Pish-e-quat some of the finest tobacco, tea, and sugar and told Pish-e-quat to take it to Chief Shash-apew in the dancing tent with the message that if the Indians bothered the Métis while they hunted, there would be trouble. When Welsh's brigade arrived in the territory, they camped by Chief Shash-apew's dancing tent, and the three principal men – Welsh, along with two men named Dumont and

Trottier – were invited into the tent. The bond in Welsh's story was changed to such an extent that Shash-apew and Welsh became family, an uncle to a nephew. Welsh states: "My uncle, Shash-apew, thanked me for the tea, sugar, and tobacco that I had sent. He thanked me also for my message. He said we could go and shoot as many buffalo as we liked, that there would be no trouble" (52). This process shows the importance of the giveaway and how people followed these protocols and procedures to deal with oppositional relationships and to restore relationships, including between different Indigenous peoples.

For a different perspective, the memorial giveaway, or, as some call it, the feast for the dead, is a different type of giveaway meant to honour a loved one who has died. Walter explained to me that the feast for the dead should happen a year after the loved one's death. He said that one year is only a day to those that have passed on, and it is good to let them know one is thinking about them. Reciprocally, in Walter's own words, it also "makes you feel good as a human being on Earth, that you can take enough time to make a feast for them, have a pipe for them, have songs for them, prayers, and then give gifts away on their behalf" (Walter 2014a). Many of the memorial feasts I have attended include a commitment to host them once a year for four years. In the practice of gifting, as seen in the examples above, relationships can be restored through the redistribution of wealth. Walter organized the first memorial feast in his immediate family in his generation. Walter became upset with his sisters, who were not helping him by contributing giveaway items or food, or helping to cook, because they did not know the protocol. He went to get advice from the pipe carrier leading the ceremony, who then went to ask the Old Man for counsel. The Old Man advised Walter to bring all his giveaway items and put them on a blanket, and, when the time came, to ask his sisters to give away all the items to everyone attending the ceremony. Walter was very pleased:

> Well, I told my sisters that, and you should have seen how happy they were. They were all so happy and then they all said to me: "Walter, that was a very nice ceremony that you made." They were happy about everything. Before that I felt they were just hoping I would do everything wrong. But once they had a chance to participate they were so happy. So what I understood was sometimes people don't know how to participate. Right? When I told them to take all my stuff, give everything away, because I had some beautiful stuff in there, expensive

stuff, they took it and they gave it all away ... I found that so interesting that the Old Man gave me that lesson. So I was happy, and I was happy that my sisters were happy. My sisters were happy that I gave them a chance to participate. Isn't that interesting? (Walter 2014a)

By "gifting" his sisters with the items and the opportunity to participate in the gifting, Walter mended his relationship with them, which had been injured by his anger at them for not helping with the ceremony because they lacked the knowledge to do so. Gifting and exchange are tangible examples of socioeconomic practices. Within this practice, they were all able to honour their mutual love for one who had died, as well as restore their own relationships.

The giveaway ceremony, a historical practice that still occurs, illustrates how the Cree engage in different types of economic relationships (establishing relationships, maintaining relationships, oppositional relationships, and restoring relationships). This one ceremony also exemplifies the diversity of actors involved in these economic relations, from Cree people to other peoples, to nonhuman beings, to spirit beings. These are nonlinear relationships, not one-on-one, but interconnected in complex ways. Before moving on to the next section, discussing the practice of trade or exchange in Cree economic relations, I will end with the words of Sunney on the faith component of the giveaway:

There is so much behind it [the giveaway]. It is not to make slaves out of someone or beggars. That is definitely not it. It is much more intricate than that. What do they say: by gifts we make slaves, by whips we make dogs ... It is not like that, though. In a giveaway ... if I give a gift I want my child to be prayed for because I believe so much in that energy – energy of prayer. What I am doing, in my own pitiful way, I am asking for my loved ones to have prayers because I know that it works; it has been my experience that miracles happen. God, you take care of it. I will give away whatever you have given me because I know you will provide. It is that pure faith that you will be taken care of and that your needs will be taken care of. Well then, having said that, you don't go giving away things that will leave yourself or your loved ones in need. You also consider your needs. (Sunney 2014a)

There is an interesting dynamic at play in gifting material items and asking friends and family to pray for a loved one. In this example, there is the relationship between the Cree person gifting another human being to pray (a relationship to a spiritual being) for the Cree person's child. In this one gifting practice, many relationships are being enacted.

Trade or Exchange

The practice of trading is another element discussed in Cree written narratives and oral accounts. When exploring trade or exchange, it is important to note that this includes the exchange of items (such as food or ornamental goods), exchange of knowledge, exchange of ceremonies, and exchange of numerous other things. These exchange relationships took place in the past and continue to take place among many different actors – Cree to each other and to non-Cree people, nonhuman beings, and spirit beings. These exchange relationships can also involve numerous different actors at one time.

There was an accepted normative protocol to be followed among the Plains peoples before any trade activity commenced. The type of protocol or ceremony around trade depended on the material being traded as well as the nature of the relationship involved – for example, whether you were establishing a new economic relationship, restoring one, or perhaps maintaining one. When the Buffalo Dance was bought from the Dakota, the pipe stem carrier led the Cree to the Dakota Warriors' lodge. The Cree gathered in front of the lodge and tied the horses they were giving the Dakota to the tipi stakes. The Dakota came out, gifting the Cree with clothes to "buy back" the Dakotas' ability to continue performing the Buffalo Dance themselves. After the transfer was completed, the Dakota invited the Cree into their lodge to teach them the songs and dance (Mandelbaum 2001, 111–12). Similarly, as introduced in Chapter 3, muskwa (Bear) describes a Plains Cree who travelled to the east to receive medicines. He presented two horses loaded with well-made clothes. In exchange, the Plains Ojibway/Saulteaux/ Anishinaabe took him into their mitewin lodge;[12] they taught him about the many plants useful for medicinal purposes (165). It is said that a Chief had to give freely of his possessions, and "usually set the pace for ceremonial giving" (106–7). These trading accounts demonstrate the importance of certain economic practices and protocols to establishing, maintaining, or restoring relationships.

There was also an accepted protocol followed when the Cree exchanged items with traders – for example, in the fur trade. Welsh recounts how the Plains people would give a trader a tent to himself when he arrived in a camp, and that the first thing the trader would do is present a small amount of sugar, tea, and tobacco. At that point the Cree would make tea, visit, smoke, and tell each other to trade with the trader, and then trade would begin (Welsh as told to Weekes 1994, 10). There is actually a special Cree word to describe the type of tobacco used in these instances; it is called môniyâwi-cistêmâw ᒍᓇᑉ◁· ᒉᓄ∪ᒪ°, which the *Online Cree Dictionary* translates as "White-Man's tobacco, trade tobacco."

The winter of 1878 was a difficult one for Chief Starblanket and his people, with the bison being chased past the Missouri River (Welsh as told to Weekes 1994, 99). By the time Welsh came to trade in the spring, the Cree had only a few items and no ammunition, tea, or tobacco. When Chief Starblanket saw Norbert Welsh, he said: "It is the will of the Manitou that Wa-ka-kootchick turned up at our camp today.[13] Now we can get something to live on" (99). The Chief always had a good relationship with Welsh and referred to him as his brother. As an individual trader, Welsh accepted the chief's request to get credit for needed items (to a value of $789 at the time) until August, when the treaty money would be paid to the nation by the Canadian government. Welsh agreed, as long as Starblanket would be responsible for all the debts of his community. On August 7, 1878, at five o'clock, Chief Starblanket invited Welsh into a tent full of approximately thirty men and thirty women. After drinking tea, Chief Starblanket paid his bill; then every other person paid his or her bill. The next day, Welsh exchanged his buffalo runner horse, which the chief had always wanted, for a common horse worth only twenty dollars, Welsh said that Chief Starblanket "fell on his knees he was so proud" (99–104). This trade example displays how good trade relationships were maintained. It also speaks to the importance of building relationships, trust, and integrity; Welsh said of Chief Starblanket that when he said a thing, he meant it and "always kept his word" (104).

Welsh was recollecting a time of transition on the prairies when the buffalo were being pushed farther and farther south until they became almost extinct. In an interview, Sunney explained to me how his grandmother lived through this change. He describes this transition and then goes on to make clear the freedom and expanse of travel that the Plains people were used to enjoying:

I remember hearing the story about my grandmother, her name was nehiyaw ᗥᐦᐊᕐᐤ and an natopayiw ᖃᑐᐸᕀᐤ, a scout, came back to Saddle Lake and told the community they saw buffalo south of here, so everyone said okay. The decision was made to go to these buffalo. So they went down, they went to the middle of Montana; that was my grandmother who was on the last buffalo hunt. But that is to illustrate my point that there were no borders back then – picikwâs ᐱᖨᐤᐠᐧ [apple] we had; where did those come from? The interior of BC somewhere, and yet we have a name for them, the nehiyawak. Incredible, eh? wâpayôminak ᐧᐋᐸᔪᒥᖁᕀ [rice] didn't grow here, more in Manitoba, the rice, so we had that trade network up and down – to the range and domain of Turtle Island that trade network, and names for those things.

SHALENE: What was the shell you said [earlier]?

SUNNEY: êsa ᐁᓴᐦ – that is abalone shell. (Sunney 2014a)

Sunney's words provide a stark reminder of the extreme change that occurred within three generations of his family. His words also substantiate the extent of trade on Turtle Island before European settlement. Apples, rice, and abalone shell were traded items and became part of Plains Cree society. In a similar vein, Walter explained the eulachon (oolichan) trade to me:

Now with the eulachon oil trade, everybody knew west of the mountains that the Indians over there had something called eulachon oil. That eulachon oil was very good for health. The eyes, the hair, the whole body, skin, everything. It was a good balance. Basically, it was like castor oil because it was made from eulachon fish. So consequently, there was a eulachon trail that Indians from the prairies, they went over to British Columbia and over the mountains and they took gifts along and they traded for oil because that was a very healthy oil. In the meantime, when the eastern Indians came over they were able to trade with whatever they had to trade with. They'd take over [the trail] stuff that they could trade with. (Walter 2014a)

Indigenous nations traded on this continent and developed intricate trade relationships, trade protocol, trade networks, and trading locations that European newcomers relied on, used fully, and then exploited.

Peter Vandall (1987), from wâskahikaniwiyiniwak ᐊᐧᐣᐸᐦᐃᑲᓂᐃᐧᔨᓂᐊᐧᐠ (House People of the Plains Cree), passed on a story titled "A Fast Learner," which came from where his uncle lived. His uncle was one of those who fled to the United States after the Riel Rebellion. Vandall related the following about a conversation he had with his uncle:

"Well, my nephew!" he said to me, "one thing. I cannot give you anything, but one thing I am going to give you," he said to me, "I am going to leave you a little story":

There was this one man who was a real drunkard, he said, he was really drinking all the time, he said. So he had once again been on a binge, and when he went home, he had nothing to eat, he said, well, he was hungry, he was very hungry, he said; well, and he had nothing. "Oh yes, I will go down to the river to fish!" he thought, he said. So he took a fishing rod, he said. He went to where the river was flowing by, oh, but he had nothing to use as his bait, he said, that he could put on the hook, and he was going around looking for frogs [but] there were none, he said.

All at once he saw a snake slithering away, he said, and this snake had a frog in his mouth, he said. Well, he chased him, and when he caught up to him he stepped right on top of his head, and when the other [the snake] opened his mouth, he took the frog out of his mouth, he said. "Oh my! I am truly mean to him," it suddenly crossed his mind, he said, "he must be very hungry too, and here I went and took this out of his mouth when he was going to eat it," he said; "[he must be] just as hungry as I am," he said.

"Anyway, I will give him a drink instead!" he thought, for he had whiskey in a bottle that was in his pocket. He took it out, he said, and when he stepped on him and the other [the snake] opened his mouth, he poured it into him, he said, and so he let him go, he said.

So now he was sitting by the river, fishing, he said. Suddenly he felt something on his knee, he said, something was touching him – and when he looked there, here it was that same snake, he said, with another frog in his mouth, he said, looking at him, he said, to trade it for a drink, he said. (Vandall 1987, 65–69)

This type of story is referred to as a wawiyatâcimowina ᐊᐧᐃᐧᔭᑖᒋᒧᐃᐧᓇ, the Cree genre of funny stories – these can be long and are known to have a relatively short moral or punch line (Vandall 1987, xii). Peter Vandall's uncle gifted Peter with this story. For the Cree, sharing knowledge, like passing on a story, is considered giving a gift, as though a physical object were presented. This humorous account also depicts a trading relationship between a human and a snake. Layers of meaning can be read into a story like this. For example, numerous other archival stories refer to non-Indigenous traders bringing and trading alcohol with the Indigenous peoples of this land (Welsh as told to Weekes 1994). Vandall's account can be a metaphor to link the manipulation, control, and force exerted on the snake (stepping on his head) to the ways that non-Natives unethically used alcohol in trade with Indigenous peoples.

Value in trade can be described as the relationship between the worth an owner puts on something and the reciprocal worth the receiver deems the item has. In Cree thought, there can also be the agency in value for the item itself. When living beings (for example, ceremonial bundles) are traded, there are intertwined relationships involved: owner, receiver, and the elements being traded. Sunney shared an experience in which people from Edmonton started coming to his lodge expecting to trade a ceremonial item, a braid of sweetgrass for a cigarette. To explain through experiential teaching, Sunney took them out onto the land a few years in a row. He said to them while in the country:

> That cigarette you are going to give me for that braid of sweetgrass, take that sweetgrass and now you are going to ask the Creator [Sunney gestures, making two circles in the air], "Creator, I come and get your medicine," and make two more circles, and then you talk to that plant: "Sweetgrass, I come to you and here is a gift for you, I want to take you and I want your medicine, your power ... in the upcoming future." Whatever it is, what kind of blessing for that power to communicate with the ethereal. (Sunney 2014a)

Sunney explains to me that these people would then be taught to pick and clean the sweetgrass, each individual strand, and then start braiding it. One sweetgrass braid could take them a half hour or longer; he told them that they now better understood the cost of picking it – their time. He then shared with them:

> Not only that, you also have to be praying while you are picking the sweetgrass, because you don't know who is going to be crying on the

braid of sweetgrass come wintertime, come fall time, come spring time. Someone is going to be crying maybe, having a hard time, lost somebody, or somebody is sick. Their tears ... while you are picking it, the other thing you are doing is that you are praying to Mother Earth, you are praying to God. You are praying to that plant. You are focusing your entire energy on that – in that way. So what does that cost? Does it cost a cigarette? What is a fair price? (Sunney 2014a)

Value was explained as something that incorporated sentimental worth and the time needed to create, as well as an understanding of the spiritual significance and the connection to the ethereal. Sunney told me that value is more complex than a simple pound-for-pound exchange. Fine Day (kamiokisihkwew ᑲᒥᔪᑭᓯᐦᑵᐤ) was the Plains Cree war leader of the River People mentioned earlier in this book. In his book *My Cree People*, he explained that he once traded a headdress bundle for two fine buffalo-chasing horses, a good-quality rifle, a heavy blanket, a blanket coat, leggings, and [prayer] cloth for the owner to hang. Fine Day explains that the three previous owners were never wounded while wearing the headdress bundle, even in a big fight. Fine Day states that he used the bundle in fighting twice, even when he was out in the open and not in a trench (Fine Day 1973a, 63). This bundle represented a few different relationships – the relationship between traders as well as the relationship to the bundle itself (a nonhuman being), which is shown through the offering to the bundle – the cloth given for the past owner to hang.

In the summer of 2013, I had an opportunity to witness trading relationships at a large Indigenous gathering that happens every summer. I had attended this event in past years, and had often seen people going around seeking to trade different items. There are always thousands of people in attendance; on this day a Cree Elder, Paul, his wife, Gail, and their daughter Sharlene brought me to where they were camping and offered me a beverage. Gail shared with me that while they were at this event, someone asked her if she was selling her dry meat. She said no, but added that she would trade it for tobacco. While we were sitting outside their trailer, a teenager came up to us and said that people camping at the gathering, who were from another community, had just finished making a big feast (wîhkohtowin ᐑᐦᑯᐦᑐᐏᐣ) and had extra, so they were giving meals away. He gave us a few large containers full of meat, potatoes, and other food. Sharlene gave the teenager a pair of earrings she made to give to the cooks, and the Elder gave the teenager ten dollars to give to the cooks. The similarity of the Cree word for feast – wîhkohtowin Ȧ·ᵈⁱᵈᵘᐳᐱ·ᐟ – to the concept of wâhkohtôwin ᐸ·ᵈⁱᵈᵘᐳᐱ·ᐟ is striking, as is the way in which having a feast and sharing food is connected to the living out of wâhkohtôwin ᐸ·ᵈⁱᵈᵘᐳᐱ·ᐟ (the normative principles guiding relationships). Sunney shared experiences in which people have made different things for him and told him to pay what he thinks they are worth, and he says to them: "I think it is worth four, six, ten times as much as, but I can't afford that." He explains to me that there is a balance in the trading relationship in which value is negotiated according to the receiver's means: "I give what I can without putting myself at the risk of needing, being in need of food, or being in need of gas for my vehicle, or being in need of money for my daughter. As long as I don't put myself in need of any of those things, I give as much as I can. There are a lot of things that have been given to me, beautiful things that I have put way more value on" (Sunney 2014a).

Value in this way can be understood as the balance between the worth the owner and receiver of an item perceive that item to have, and the agency of the item (for example, a ceremonial bundle), negotiated in relationship to the means the receiver has to reciprocate the worth. Stated in a different way, the value of an item is mitigated through the means of the receiver (buyer).

Trade with nonhumans can also be explored through relationships with the mêmêkwêsiwak ᑎᑫ·ᕑᐸˋ (the little people). One account states how only Indigenous people of "good character" would see them, and only certain people would be allowed to trade with them (Brass and Nanooch 1978a). The mêmêkwêsiwak ᑎᑫ·ᕑᐸˋ women were known for their exquisite porcupine quill embroidery. There were certain protocols around exchange, and a special trade language was used when exchange occurred between the mêmêkwêsiwak ᑎᑫ·ᕑᐸˋ and the Cree.

> May-may-quay-she-wuk were the stone workers, making arrowheads, flint knives and stone heads for hammers. These they traded with the Indians for buffalo meat, hides, porcupine quills and other things they needed and couldn't obtain for themselves ... Their communication was done by drawing pictures of what they needed in the sand or earth. Only certain privileged individuals were allowed to go and identify the needs of the little people, and he [such an individual] in turn would draw pictures of what his people needed – flint heads, knives, etc. The

trade was made either during the night or the early morning hours. (Brass and Nanooch 1978a)

To maintain miyo-wîcihitowin ᒥᔦ ᐃᐧᒋᐦᐃᑐᐃᐧᐣ (good relationships), the Cree would need to follow the trade protocol outlined by the mêmêkwêsiwak ᒣᒣᑫᐧᓯᐊᐧᐠ. This was especially important since the mêmêkwêsiwak ᒣᒣᑫᐧᓯᐊᐧᐠ were said to have mysterious powers and were known for playing tricks on people.[14] Dora, whom I interviewed, explained that the mêmêkwêsiwak ᒣᒣᑫᐧᓯᐊᐧᐠ are little messengers, and she further elaborated that it was specifically the little people and the giveaway that helped her get through a period of difficulty in her life:

> They were in my hallway, in my house, when John [her husband] was in the hospital and I didn't know what to do. I have these two white beam pillars and a place to sit, I was in my room, this is when John was still in a coma. It was after midnight and close to the morning and they came, I was in my room and I could hear some noises, it was the little mêmêkwêsiwak ᒣᒣᑫᐧᓯᐊᐧᐠ, they were in my hallway, about ten to twelve of them. I was going like this [arms up], "Oh no, I'm going to step on you!" or else they are going to knock me over, right? They jumped on top of the pillar thing and I was scared – what are they going to do to me? They were just chattering and running around, whispering to each other, and they were having fun, and then I woke up but I couldn't see them, I could just hear them, they were laughing. I wasn't scared, I opened my door, those little people were here.
>
> Then I told [the Elder I go to], I told him, "I saw the little people in my house; what am I supposed to do? I think they were trying to tell me something." He said, "They are telling you that everything is going to be good with John and you and the family, so you just have to keep that in your mind and in your heart, not to worry about anything, get that rest and everything will fall into place." I was like, "Okay." (Dora and Connie 2013)

I told Dora that I had read that only good-hearted people see them, not everyone. Connie, Dora, and I started laughing when Dora said that the Elder had said that she should have given them a little ball to play with you, and she responded, "I was like, they would probably have thrown it at me" (Dora and Connie 2013).[15] In this example, we can see that the historical legends of the little people are lived realities for Cree people in the present day. These relationships are maintained through different practices, including gifting. I have been told that people leave jellybeans as special gifts that the mêmêkwêsiwak ᑎᑭᐧᕆᐧᐊᐢ especially enjoy. The legend of "Medicine Boy" is the story of a young Cree girl named pimosais (Little Flyer), who would secretly meet a young man in the forest. The legend says that they were both small in stature for their age, and one day she was curious about where he was from, so she secretly followed him and discovered he was one of the mêmêkwêsiwak ᑎᑭᐧᕆᐧᐊᐢ. Little Flyer says:

> I watched closely until finally I saw some tiny men and women come out to meet him. He resembled them, only he was a little bigger in stature. They were dressed in buckskin clothes and the women had the most beautiful designs on their dresses. I had never seen such work before. They used porcupine quills for embroidering and the colours glowed. I looked hard at the designs, thinking perhaps I could remember and use them on my own dresses. (Brass and Nanooch 1978a)

In this story Medicine Boy knows Little Flyer has followed him, and they agree that they can never be together. He gently rebukes her, saying that she cannot copy their designs, but then gifts her with these words: "You'll always be a fine design worker and your dresses and tepees will always have fascinating figures" (Brass and Nanooch 1978a). There are many teachings in this story, including those around intellectual property. He explains that because he is an extra big mêmêkwêsiwak ᑎᑭᐧᕆᐧᐊᐢ, he was appointed to go out and gather herbs for his people. There are many other instances of stories of exchange or trade occurring between Cree people and non-Cree or nonhuman beings. As seen in the story "Ayekis the Frog," earlier in this chapter, there are also oral accounts of trade occurring between animals and spirit beings (Brass and Nanooch 1978c). The Cree thought it was important to pass down oral histories of trade that did not involve human beings. This reinforces Cree ontology and the ways to relate to all things in creation.

Cree women held power and important societal roles historically; however, most of the archival sources on Cree life are from the perspective of men and ignore the important role Cree women played in the economy. In August 2013, I interviewed Rob, a Plains Cree man who works at a larger Plains Indigenous organization. In our meeting, he elaborated on this gap in historical data: "The other thing, too, is that a lot of the historians were probably male at the time so they wanted to emphasize the male and the trading relationship ... they wouldn't have understood too much [about women's role]" (Rob 2013). A few historical sources make explicit mention of women; for example, War Chief Fine Day, in interviews completed in the 1930s, states that women owned the house (tipi) and were in charge of putting it up: "It is not everyone who knows how to cut a tipi – usually some old woman. I only saw one old man who could do it. When a person wants a tipi made he takes all the hides he has and gives them to the old woman. She measures them out into the desired shape, using the hindquarters for the top. She cuts the hides and then the women sew them together. A lot of food is prepared for the women to eat" (Fine Day 1973b).

In a similar way, Fine Day (1973c, 6) explains that, historically, Cree women had ownership of dogs, which were a means of transportation for the society, and that a man needed his wife's permission to sell a dog. Cree knowledge holder Sylvia McAdam shares how the "*nêhiyawak* believe the women have jurisdiction over land and water" (McAdam 2015, 75). Chief Thunderchild recounted a winter of starvation when the women seemed to be stronger than the men; he says that "though they [the women] were not eating, they kept moving, if it was only to make fires to keep us warm" (E. Ahenakew 1995b). At one point, a lone buffalo is shot but does not go down. Of all the people in the community, Thunderchild's aunt took the gun to follow the trail after the buffalo, and all the other women except one went with her (E. Ahenakew 1995b). There is a significant gap in historical data related to Indigenous women, but this should not negate the notion of Indigenous women's specific jurisdiction and the important and diverse functions and responsibilities they held and hold, including those related to economic relationships.

The interviews excerpted in this chapter attest to the continuities of Cree peoplehood and economic practices. wâhkohtôwin ᐄ·ᐦᑯᐦᑐᐃ·ᐣ is a concept key to understanding relationships, including economic relationships: they transcend human-to-human practices and include a myriad of relations among spiritual beings, Cree people, other people, and other living beings. In turn, different economic practices serve different objectives. These practices help to establish, maintain, or restore relationships, or engage with an oppositional relationship. These practices, which have continuity from pre-contact Cree society, are enacted in the present – for example, through the institution of the giveaway and trade or exchange. These are acts of resilience.

In Chapter 8, my exploration deepens as I delve into the specific principles that guide these economic relationships. We begin to see the tensions through the lens of present-day economic, political, and social struggles. To make sense of how Cree cope with unrelenting challenges, I introduce the concept of colonial dissonance.

8
Colonial Dissonance

THE CONCEPT OF WÂHKOHTÔWIN ⊲ᐧ∥ᑦᐩᑐᐃᐧᑊ is portrayed in Chapter 7 as the laws governing relationships (H. Cardinal 2007, 74–75) that provide a way for Cree people to live in accord with one another, with nature, and with other relations, human and nonhuman. Over time, the persistent strain of colonialism on miskinâhk ministik ᒥᑎᑭᐧᕁ ᒥᓂᑎᑊ (Turtle Island) from first contact caused ruptures in these relationships, creating tensions, internal conflict, instability, discord, and mistrust between the colonizers and Indigenous peoples. A consequence of these ruptures is a settler colonial–induced dissonance, which I will refer to as colonial dissonance. My interviews with Cree knowledge holders and my historical research reveal colonial dissonance as a continuing reality that takes its toll on individuals and on the collective. This colonial dissonance not only affects Cree people (and other Indigenous peoples on Turtle Island); I argue that colonial dissonance affects all the relationships discussed in Chapter 7 – those involving Cree people, non-Cree people, other living beings, and spirit beings on this territory. Following my discussion of colonial dissonance, I discuss the consequences that were revealed by the oral stories and personal accounts I encountered.

There is little debate that the pass system, a policy put in place in the 1880s and continuing till the 1940s (Carter 1999, 163–64), deeply alienated the Plains Cree and damaged their governance system, challenging and dissolving relationships beyond the band level. Implementations of the *Indian Act* disrupted the fabric of Cree relationships with the land, water, air, plants,

136

and animals, among others, and their connections to the expanse of Cree territory that lies beyond reserve boundaries. The pass system also served to alienate relationships between Cree people and non-Cree people. Laws prohibiting ceremonies impinged on Cree people's connection with the spiritual realm as well as the institutions (for example, the giveaway) at the centre of living out miyo-wîcihitowin ᒥᔪ ᐃᐧᒋᐦᐃᑐᐃᐧᐣ (good relationships). The Indian residential school system attempted to destroy personal identity and Cree identities, and therefore the relationship between people and their spirits. The schools also actively attempted to crush the importance of Cree family relationships, legally removing children from families, separating brothers and sisters and destroying the connections between boys and girls. Children in First Nations became wards of the state, and the settler-colonial government considered all members of First Nations to be wards of the state. Mandatory attendance at residential schools, and the oppressive tactics within the schools, forced children to become Christian and to dishonour their own relationships and ways of connecting with kisê-manitow ᑭᓭᒪᓂᑐᐤ (Creator/Great Spirit). To argue more broadly, the colonizers attempted to undermine and destroy wâhkohtôwin ᐋᐧᐦᑰᑐᐃᐧᐣ, the laws governing relationships, totally. The outcome is settler colonial-induced dissonance (or colonial dissonance for short).

Colonial Dissonance

Colonial dissonance is the term I use to describe the breaking of wâhkohtôwin ᐋᐧᐦᑰᑐᐃᐧᐣ, which affects the spiritual, physical, emotional, and mental aspects of Cree personhood and peoplehood. It is also the breaking of relationships among Cree people, non-Cree people, nonhuman beings, and spirit beings. I will begin by exploring the mental aspect of personhood, and then connect this dissonance to the other areas of Cree being.

Sunney, one of the Elders I interviewed, introduced me to the concept of cognitive dissonance, a psychological concept describing the intense mental conflict that occurs when a person holds contradictory sets of beliefs or values (Festinger 1962, 1957; Encyclopedia Britannica n.d.-a). Cognitive dissonance also describes a condition wherein a person or a group holds certain beliefs, but their actions are contrary to those beliefs (Festinger 1962). In Festinger's (1957) theory, individuals will try to reduce their dissonance and may avoid situations that would increase it. By examining the continued presence of settler colonialism, alongside practices and policies inherent in economic exploitation, my research addresses this dissonance. I also explore the implications for and tensions in Cree world view resulting from colonialism.

Related to cognitive dissonance is the concept of cognitive imperialism. Mi'kmaq scholar Marie Battiste (2000, 192–93) coined the term: "Cognitive imperialism, also known as cultural racism, is the imposition of one worldview on a people who have an alternative worldview, with the implication that the imposed worldview is superior to the alternative worldview." She goes on to describe how cognitive imperialism is a type of "cognitive manipulation used to disclaim other knowledge bases and values" (198). Chickasaw and Cheyenne scholar James (Sákéj) Youngblood Henderson (2000, 63–64) states that the imposition of universality creates cognitive imperialism by normalizing the colonizer's belief system and constructing the other's (i.e., Indigenous peoples') as inferior.

The concept of cognitive imperialism is useful for diagnosing the impact of settler-colonial policy and practice on Indigenous consciousness. As noted, settler-induced colonial dissonance affects all aspects of Cree personhood and peoplehood, although I would argue that while cognitive imperialism can be read through its victimization impact, colonial dissonance can be a place of agency. Within the cognitive, spiritual, emotional, and physical tensions lie productive spaces that Indigenous peoples may harness to provide alternatives or antidotes. This chapter explores colonial dissonance and how the resulting tensions can be a productive space in which, I argue, we can draw from our own intellectual resources to respond. This is a place of agency.

Cognitive imperialism and settler-induced colonial dissonance both occur when Indigenous territory is exploited. Youngblood Henderson explains the connection between cognitive imperialism and Indigenous lands:

> Thus arises the consciousness of the immigrant-colonizer and the Aboriginal-colonized, which the colonized have to accept if they are to survive. This binary consciousness justifies the separation of Indigenous peoples from their ancient rights to the land and its resources and the transfer of wealth and productivity to the colonialists and the mother country. (Youngblood Henderson 2000, 63–64)

In this explanation, settler colonialism affects cognition, but it also negatively affects geographic or physical space – land. I see settler-induced colonial dissonance as negatively influencing both physical bodies and physical space.

The exploitation of lands damages Cree (and non-Cree) bodies. Beyond the physical and cognitive, economic exploitation through settler colonialism also harms môsihowin ᒧᓯᐦᐅᐃᐧ (emotions) and manitowan ᒪᓂᑐᐊᐧ (the spiritual). Relationships to the land are an example of connections between the spiritual, physical, emotional, and mental aspects of personhood and peoplehood.

Cree Elders' descriptions of their relationships to land demonstrate perspectives on the land found within specific nehiyawewin ᓀᐦᐃᔭᐍᐃᐧ (Cree language) phrases. The example quoted here demonstrates the connection between Cree economic relationships and the spiritual and material:

> This connection to the land, as described by the Elders, consists of at least the following elements: spiritual, physical, and economic. This connection is rooted in the Cree concept and doctrines related to pimâtisiwin (life). It is a concept that contains many theoretical subsets including among other things, a concept called "pimâcihowin" (the ability to make a living). Land (askiy) is an important source of life for it provides those things required for the physical, material, and economic survival of the people. When treaty Elders use the word "pimâcihowin" they are describing a holistic concept that includes a spiritual as well as a physical dimension. It is an integral component of traditional First Nations doctrines, laws, principles, values, and teachings regarding the sources of life, the responsibilities associated with them, including those elements seen as necessary for enhancing the spiritual components of life and those associated with making a living ...
>
> The teachings related to self-sufficiency (tipiyawêwisowin) provided to the individual direction and guidance and set out the requirements for achieving a sense of self-worth, dignity, and independence – values that were and are essential to a community's or a nation's internal peace, harmony, and security. The teachings (kakêskihkemowina) included unwritten but well-known codes of behaviour for the Cree people in relation to pimâcihisowin (making one's own living). (H. Cardinal and Hildebrandt 2000, 43–44)

In this quotation from the 1990s, Treaty Elders from Saskatchewan provide an introduction to the Cree concepts of pimâtisiwin ᐱᒫᑎᓯᐃᐧ, pimâcihowin

ᐱᒥᕢᐦᐅᐃᐧᐤ, tipiyawêwisowin ᖏᐱᕁᐁᐧᐊᐧᓯᐊᐧᐤ, and kakêskihkemowina ᖃᐣᑫᐦᑫᒧᐃᐧᓇ, which form a conceptual introduction to the ideas discussed in this chapter.

Building on the concepts described above, in my interviews with Sunney, the lodge holder, he contributes to the discussion of Cree concepts with a clear example that illustrates settler-induced colonial dissonance arising from the breaking of wâhkohtôwin ᐚᐦᑯᐦᑐᐃᐧᐤ with respect to family relationships:

> Anyways, back to wâhkohtôwin ᐚᐦᑯᐦᑐᐃᐧᐤ. There was the colonialist period in our history. Unfortunately, it is still that way. I did not know a lot of my relatives; I grew up in this [dissonance] too, people used to pick on me. I didn't even know I was their Uncle. I used to hear old people talk about how relatives look after each other, [and] as I grew up as a man I realized, holy cow, those are my relatives. It sounded good in all its theoretical constructs, and that's all it was at the time, theoretical constructs and new "-isms." And I thought: that's not how my relatives treated me. They treated me bad; some of them were cruel. They are awful to me, some of my relatives. I think, holy cow, those sanctimonious things I used to hear about Native people, that's not true. Then I realized that it is a result of colonization and the divide-and-conquer tactics. We are meant to be that way so we don't know about our own sovereignty. (Sunney 2014a)

Colonial dissonance is created when people learn how they are supposed to treat each other, but that way is not lived out. In Harold Cardinal and Walter Hildebrandt's interviews with Elders about the spirit and intent of Treaty Six, the Cree Elders explained part of the familial aspects of wâhkohtôwin ᐚᐦᑯᐦᑐᐃᐧᐤ. They explained that there should be mutual respect between a mother and child with reciprocal duties of "nurturing, caring, loyalty, and fidelity." With brothers and sisters, there are specific kinship norms, including a practice of non-interference. Cousins and other relatives have different, less-stringent social conduct codes that encourage respectful behaviour and "noncoercive relations" (H. Cardinal and Hildebrandt 2000, 34). With the breakdown of family relationships, directly related to the colonial policies and practices outlined above, many Cree people are not living out these norms.

A Cree concept related to this rupture of knowledge and associated norms is cimâks ᒋᒫᐦᐣ. Sunney explains that kicimâkânês ᑭᒋᒫᐦᑲᓀᐢ is a Cree word for poverty or being poor, but it does not simply have to do with the ability or inability to earn one's livelihood: "poverty for us ... does not [only] mean we go without money; poverty, for us, is – we have a word for poverty: kicimâkânês ᑭᒋᒫᐦᑲᓀᐢ. Did you ever hear that before? Or cimâks ᒋᒫᐦᐣ, ever hear that? That's the word. We have different ways of cimâks ᒋᒫᐦᐣ. If you don't know your history – your blood line – cimâks ᒋᒫᐦᐣ. You are living in poverty" (Sunney 2014a). In Cree society today, there are these dual issues: first, not knowing the kinship norms or wâhkohtôwin ᐙᐦᑰᐦᑑᐃᐧᐣ practices, and second, knowing those teachings but suffering from settler-induced colonial dissonance by not seeing those principles lived out or not living them out in one's own life. In terms of the former, Métis scholar Patti LaBoucane-Benson (2009) interviewed Elders in Alberta, and one of the Elders shared the concern of Indigenous peoples' current lack of knowledge about wâhkohtôwin ᐙᐦᑰᐦᑑᐃᐧᐣ. The Elder said, "That role and responsibility of each individual person in the family, the community and society – that role and responsibility is not easily understood. The children don't under- stand our relationship with mother earth. There has to be a mechanism in place to bring back those teachings to young children. If you don't under- stand your role, how is it your fault?" (115). With this perspective, there is a dual responsibility: knowledge and resurgent action.

Although colonial dissonance is a useful concept for understanding the implications of colonialism for Indigenous peoples, it is important to clarify that not all Indigenous people may be affected by colonial dissonance. For example, some Indigenous people might participate in the extractive resource industry and not experience the cognitive dissonance phenom- enon. I draw from Leroy Little Bear's (2000, 80) words about cognitive diversity here: "Under the custom of noninterference, no being ought to impose on another's understanding of the flux. Each being ought to have the strength to be tolerant of the beauty of cognitive diversity. Honesty allows Aboriginal people to accept that no one can ever know for certain what someone else knows."

Walter, the seventy-four-year-old Cree Elder I interviewed, moves from the current concerns around the breaking of wâhkohtôwin ᐙᐦᑰᐦᑑᐃᐧᐣ related to our relationships with nonhuman beings to teachings found within what Cree scholar Margaret Kovach (2009, 45) describes as nehiyaw kiskeyihtamowin ᓀᐦᐃᔭᐤ ᑭᐢᑫᔨᐦᑕᒧᐃᐧᐣ (Cree epistemology). Walter's words speak to the Cree people's environmental concerns; he also identifies two of the resources we can use (Walter 2014a). One is the acknowledgement that nonhuman beings, without human involvement, provide restoration to "cleanse the earth." (I am turning back to this chapter in the summer of 2020. Although the origins of the COVID-19 global pandemic are still not fully understood,[1] I am struck by how the last four months of restricted human activity have shown improvements in air and water quality and certain animal habitats in various regions of the earth.) The other resource Walter explained is how there are teachings within nehiyaw kiskeyihtamowin ᓀᐦᐃᔭᐤ ᑭᐢᑫᔨᐦᑕᒧᐃᐧᐣ from which we can draw to provide answers to the current obstacles and conflicts facing us.

Colonial dissonance occurs not only with a ruptured relationship between people (and therefore a disconnect between norms of behaviour and lived practices); it can also occur if one cannot live out wâhkohtôwin ᐋᐧᐦᑰᐦᑐᐃᐧᐣ – norms related to relationships between Cree people and the natural environment, such as good relationships with askîy ᐊᐢᑮᐩ (the land). A Cree Elder explains the connection between colonialism and the disruption in Cree relations with the land and how that affects wâhkohtôwin ᐋᐧᐦᑰᐦᑐᐃᐧᐣ:

> Ever since the Europeans have come to live with us – things have changed. No longer can we go to the creek to drink water – everything has been poisoned. The animals have been infected and they pass it on to us. The future doesn't look very good. It's a reality of where we are with pollution and everything else. When we talk about wahkohtowin and witaskewin – it is a lot. In the beginning it was supposed to be that harmony – but how can you have harmony when one party is more dominant – and this dominance is creating conflict for us. (LaBoucane-Benson 2009, 109)

The impacts of settler society have fundamentally altered the land, the animals, and the world, and this directly affects Indigenous people's ability to interact with these nonhuman beings. Colonial dissonance does not end here. Even more insidious (and causing more internal struggle) is how Cree people are now directly involved in altering their relationships with the land. Sunney explains this conundrum, which centrally disconnects

Cree economic relations from the land, and how this affects the cognitive realm of colonial dissonance:

> We have to make a living somehow but then there are traditional people that go out and work on the land, in oil extraction – mostly that is what it is – resource extraction here in Alberta. Traditional people are doing that and it is hard on them, they have to feed themselves, they have to make a living. That causes them to do things to the earth that create cognitive dissonance for some of them. There are a lot of Natives out there running businesses now that service the oil and gas industry and of course we have the bleeding heart liberals back home, maybe some of them don't have nothing, who are criticizing their efforts and yet we have to all make a living.
>
> Then there are the traditional people who are doing these things, and that creates cognitive dissonance. You know, I'm hurting the environment, and here I am a traditional Indian and environmentalist – an environmental Indian, and here I am creating all this pollution. And that is what I was talking about. And there are a lot of things that go on with that idea. There are effects everywhere, like you and I, for instance, we are sitting here eating from porcelain cups, eating from steel utensils. We are driving cars that are polluting things, wearing clothes that come from garment factories that create pollution and taint the waters. We have no place to say: "Oh, those conservatives, they are destroying the land," because we are complicit in the destruction and the polluting of our Mother. What are we doing to be less complicit, to ease our conscience? (Sunney 2014a)

Sunney offers a nuanced explanation of the challenge facing Cree people. On one hand are these norms around good relations; on the other is the reality of living in a society dependent on extractive industry. His warning regarding our complicity with the system is important; we cannot point fingers solely outward. Within Cree teachings there is a concept called ohcinewin ᐅᐦᒋᓀᐏᐣ that helps one think through potential impacts: ohcinewin ᐅᐦᒋᓀᐏᐣ is described as transgressions against nonhuman beings. It can also mean suffering that is in retribution for an action or omission (Borrows 2010, 93). Anishinaabe scholar John Borrows writes about the different kinds of law in the Indigenous legal order, including sacred law, natural law, deliberative law, positivistic law, and customary law. Borrows (2010, 34, 38) explains sacred law as stemming from the Creator, creation stories, and revered ancient teachings, whereas natural law developed through observation of the natural world or environment.

Cree knowledge holder, educator, and activist Sylvia McAdam is of the sakâwiyiniwak ᓴᑳᐃᐧᔨᓂᐊᐧᒃ (Northern Plains Cree), specifically the Big River First Nation. She writes of laws including "pastahowin ... the 'stepping over' or breaking of the Creator's law against human beings; for example, adultery, murder and incest." As well, "ohcinewin is the breaking of the Creator's law against anything other than a human being, such as the abuse of animals, traditional hunting laws, over harvesting of trees and polluting the environment" (McAdam 2009, 8).

In LaBoucane-Benson's (2009, 114) interviews with Elders, they express the belief that Cree society is "living the consequences (ohcinewin) of this contravention of Natural Law (pastahowin)." As one of the Cree Elders she interviewed succinctly explained:

> We are all responsible to live within the rules of Natural Law. Within Natural Law, there is a constellation of laws that govern all relationships, known as wahkohtowin. To transgress Natural Law is known in Cree as pastahowin. The consequences of these transgressions (ohcinewin) are severe and are passed down intergenerationally, until amends are made for those transgressions. (LaBoucane-Benson 2009, 245)

Significantly, the Elders interviewed see these consequences as affecting not only Cree people, but all of society, Indigenous and non-Indigenous (108). In one of my interviews with Sunney, he describes some of the consequences we are living with: "One of the ravages bestowed upon us, is that dysfunction and what we try to do to empower ourselves: to gamble, the multiple sexual liaisons, to drink to excess, to drug to excess. So we are still fulfilling the genocidal policy of the colonialist" (Sunney 2014a). Within this explanation, Sunney touches on some of the afflictions affecting us. Cree Elder Fred Campiou explains further:

> We use the word pastahowin, really what it means is overstepping the bounds, going outside the boundaries that you are entitled to ... In terms of pastahowin, in today's society – there is a lot of that going on ... Society is overextending itself into boundaries, and it is creating

conflict, division, hardship, animosity and resentment. All of those negative feelings that come up when boundaries have been crossed over. (LaBoucane-Benson et al. 2012, 14)

In this description, we can see the connections between pâstâhowin ᐸᐢᒐᐦᐅᐃᐧᐣ and ohcinewin ᐅᐦᒋᓀᐃᐧᐣ; Borrows (2010, 93) explains how these two concepts can be applied to circumstances where Cree law is not followed. Cree legal scholar Darcy Lindberg (2019) further explains how pâstâhowin ᐸᐢᒐᐦᐅᐃᐧᐣ "relates to transgressions toward other humans," while ohcinewin ᐅᐦᒋᓀᐃᐧᐣ "relates to acts against non-human beings and things."

During my interview, Dora and Connie described natural laws and ohcinewin ᐅᐦᒋᓀᐃᐧᐣ:

CONNIE: Because we are not necessarily engaging in fulfilling our obligations this way – that it is eroding, there are consequences, that is: eroding the land, there are detrimental consequences, the ecological management piece: the fish, the water, the reciprocity is so off-balance, because we are not fulfilling our economic relationships.

DORA: Some are going to maintain that [relationship], and some are going to go off-track and go off-balance ... That's where natural law comes from, natural ordering; now, look at the lands today. And this was told by Elders, and it's in books where there were prophecies about what was going to happen, there are stories there saying that they [Indigenous people] want to get wealthy fast, they are losing their ways, and this is going to happen in their future. (Dora and Connie 2013)

The repercussions of not following natural laws include negative impacts on the land, water, and animals. One of the most important Cree–animal relationships has historically been that between the Plains Cree and the paskwâw mostoswak ᐸᐢᑲᐧᐤ ᒧᐢᑐᓴᐠ (bison/buffalo). For Plains Indigenous peoples, life revolved around the buffalo: the hunt, the spiritual ceremony around a kill, and social, economic, and political structures. In the book *All Our Relations*, Winona LaDuke (1999, 143) conceptualizes the ways in which "buffalo determine landscapes. By their sheer numbers, weight, and behaviour, they cultivated the prairie, which is the single largest ecosystem in North America." For the Plains people, the buffalo were a significant part of their livelihood, but this could not be separated from the environment or from their social/kinship structure. They lived in careful balance – praying for the buffalo at a kill and giving respect to the Creator by ingeniously using all elements of the animal.

Cree–animal relationships also include other nonhuman beings. For example, the Manitou Stone has considerable spiritual and material significance to the Cree, with its removal having been foretold to have serious consequences for the buffalo population. The stone is currently held at the Royal Alberta Museum. Sunney explains the fallout of not living by the natural laws around right relationships and the effect on the paskwâw mostoswak ᐸᐢᐠᐚ ᒧᐢᑐᐊᐠ (buffalo):

> I remember a story, speaking of borders, after the Riel Rebellion; see, they had an incident where this sacred item was taken away by Reverend McDougall, and that sacred item had three [parts] – if people moved it, there were three prophecies that came with it: one was that there would be famine; the other was that there would be war; the other was that there would be disease. In rapid succession these happened – famine – our source of food was gone. I remember hearing the story about my grandmother, her name was ᐅᐧᐊᔪ nehiyaw, and an ᖬᑐᐸᔪ natopayiw, a scout, came back to Saddle Lake and told the community they seen buffalo south of here, so everyone said okay. The decision was made to go to these buffalo. So they went down, they went to the middle of Montana; that was my grandmother who was on the last buffalo hunt. (Sunney 2014a)

Prophecy was made to explain what would happen if the Manitou Stone was disturbed and natural law transgressed. The impacts affected the Cree people in fundamental ways.

There were specific rules around ensuring proper wâhkohtôwin ᐋᐦᑰᑐᐃᐧᐣ with the paskwâw mostoswak ᐸᐢᐠᐚ ᒧᐢᑐᐊᐠ. Norbert Welsh, Métis buffalo hunter and trader in the latter half of the nineteenth century, recounts the following:

> The Yankees shot more buffalo for their hides than all the Indian and half-breed hunters put together. The Indians knew better. They did

not want to see the buffalo gone forever. Parties of Yankees used to come up to the North West to shoot for sport. They would sit on a hill and shoot. Once Buffalo Bill came on a shooting trip, and shot five hundred buffalo – just for fun. (Welsh as told to Weekes 1994, 43)

Welsh further explains that Colonel Samuel Cody, known as "Buffalo Bill," killed four thousand, two hundred and eighty buffalo in eighteen months because he had a contract with the Kansas Pacific Railway to supply its labourers with buffalo meat. Cree writer Edward Ahenakew writes that Cree people were also pressured and implicated in the breaking of wâhkohtôwin ᐧᐋᐦᑯᐦᑐᐃᐧᐣ by demands from the newcomers:

Chiefs who were chosen by the Hudson's Bay Company were given more ... and their men brought them their furs to trade. Traders came to our encampments too, and it was always buffalo hides and pemmican they wanted. Hides. Hides. Shoot. Shoot. See who can shoot most. A curse upon man's greed and on the Crees for that inordinate slaughter. (E. Ahenakew 1995b)

The consequence was severe: the near complete extinction of the paskwâw mostoswak ᐸᐢᑲᐧᐤ ᒧᐢᑐᐢᐧᐊᐠ (buffalo). This brought starvation and further pushed the Plains people to negotiate treaties – from a place of need and diminished strength.

There are many Cree legends that teach the consequences of unacceptable practices, including those about Cree–animal interactions related to proper livelihood involving Cree economic relationships. For example, a story called "Musqua and the Greedy Ones" talks about implications when individual interests are prioritized over the collective:

There were always some greedy and grasping individuals who only thought of themselves. Early one morning a couple left the village before sunrise, planning to quietly come back with their berries while everyone was still sleeping. They thought that no one would ever know. They took along their birchbark baskets and were picking at the berry patch when suddenly they heard a loud crash of breaking brush, indicating that something was approaching them. "Musqua! Musqua! A bear! A bear!" cried the man. They became so frightened that they dropped their containers, berries and all. The bear was close on their heels by this time, growling and snorting fiercely. They were so terrified that they ran as fast as they could, finally reaching the camp. The noise had aroused everyone and the people just stood outside their tepees and looked at them. The couple were so humiliated and ashamed that they disappeared into their tepee and didn't show themselves for several days. After this, every time anyone tried to get ahead of the others in picking berries they were sure they could hear the growls and grunts of the bears, reminding them that they must think of others. (Brass and Nanooch 1978b)

In this account there were consequences, not based on human legal systems but on natural law in the physical world. In the report on Cree legal traditions that is part of the Accessing Justice and Reconciliation Project (2013b, 21), it says that one of the general restatements of Cree law is the principle of natural or spiritual consequences, in which, "in some cases, the legitimate response to someone causing harm is to step back and allow the person who caused the harm to experience the natural or spiritual consequence of his or her action." In the above tale, through natural law, musqua (a bear) visited repercussions upon the couple, and facilitated the revelation of the couple's transgression to the community, providing a warning about the importance of considering others within the collective.

The Accessing Justice and Reconciliation Project (2013b, 5) report provides resources within Cree legal traditions to address conflicts and harms among people.[2] Their research revealed that in Cree society, the authoritative decision-makers include medicine people, Elders, family members, and the group. They also explain the procedural steps that often guide legitimate resolutions in Cree society:

1 Recognizing warning signals that harm may be developing or has occurred.
2 Warning others of the potential harm and taking appropriate safety precautions to keep people within the group as safe as possible.
3 Seeking guidance from those with relevant understanding and expertise.
4 Observation, and corroborating evidence.
5 Public confrontation and deliberation by appropriate decision-makers.

6 The appropriate decision-makers are identified and implement a response. This may be a pre-emptive response in some cases. (10)

In this report, they also uncover principles that govern appropriate responses to legal/human issues (legal responses and resolutions). These include the principles of healing, avoidance or separation, acknowledging responsibility as remedy (this can include the family or individual paying compensation or restitution to the harmed person or family), reintegration, natural or spiritual consequences, and incapacitation (rare and only in extreme cases) (20–21). There are also legal-obligation principles to govern individual and collective responsibility, including the responsibility to help, the responsibility to give back, the responsibility to prevent future harms, and the responsibility to warn (31). The first two responsibilities have economic implications embedded in them. There are also substantive and procedural legal rights that Cree people should be able to expect from others. Substantive rights include the right to protection/safety and the right to be helped when incapable/vulnerable (39); procedural rights include the right to have warning signals corroborated by observation or evidence before action is taken, the right to be heard, and the right for decisions to be made through open, collective deliberation guided by appropriate consultation (40). This research also uncovered general underlying principles, including how responses are situationally contextualized and fluid, the inherent importance of acknowledging and valuing relationships, and the principles of reciprocity and interdependence (44–46). The guide Friedland and Napoleon (2015) produced also speaks to Cree legal principles and practices that are enacted when accepted economic relationships are not followed. Significantly, the responsibilities in response to conflict or harm often involve economic sanctions (e.g., restitution) as well as general governing principles, such as ways to be in appropriate economic relationships with others (e.g., helping others).

Fine Day, a Cree warrior writing about life in the late nineteenth century, recounts the legal obligations and procedures within the Warrior Society:

The Warrior Societies had a dance in their tipis that was called "Sitting Up Until Morning" ... The women do not dance [in this specific dance]; they only sing the Society's songs. They keep it up all night. When the morning comes, the criers take the women and sit one down in front of each dancer. If one of the Worthy Men should happen to have a relative among the women, he asks his partner to tell the crier not to give that woman to him. They comb the women's hair, wash and paint their faces. Then they give each woman a present for having kept her up all night. If a Worthy Man doesn't have a nice enough suit of clothes, he may give the woman a good Horse. When this is done, the women go home.

There is no sexual play with the women at all. If one of the Worthy Men should make advances to the woman whose hair he is combing, she might get up and make a speech saying that the Worthy Man had asked her questions. After the women would leave, the other Worthy Men would tear up his [the offender's] clothes and tipi. This did occur twice, but I never saw it myself. (Fine Day 1973a)

In this example, the decision-makers are the members of the okihcihtâw ᐅᐱᐦᒋᐦᑖᐧ (Warrior) Society. The harmed woman would publicly confront the offender by giving a speech. The man's punishment would not occur until the women left; then, as the women had the substantive right to protection/safety as well as the right to receive help, the warriors would administer justice to the man who had transgressed. In this situation, the punishment was the destruction of the wrongdoer's property.

Returning to the discussion of cognitive dissonance at the beginning of this chapter, cognitive dissonance theory holds that the human desire is to create a state of consonance either by avoiding certain knowledge or avoiding the practice causing the dissonance (Festinger 1957). Applying this to Cree people in a perpetual state of hegemonic settler colonialism, one that appears all-encompassing, the choices can at first appear fatalistic. For example, one option is to assimilate into the majority population's (mainly western European Canadian) view on relationships with the natural world – to believe that to alter fundamentally a relationship with the land will not alter who we as Indigenous people are and the specific rights and obligations to which we lay claim. This option is in direct opposition to decolonial resistance thought, writing, and actions. In line with creating decolonial spaces, I am encouraged by the words I heard during a 2013 television interview with musical artist Paul (Bono) David Hewson. He explained that at the centre of tension, lying within conflicted spaces, is an inherently creative place. As colonial dissonance is an undying lived reality for Indigenous peoples, perhaps we should not ignore or run from the mental (or physical, emotional, or spiritual) struggle, but embrace it for the imaginative and ingenious potential that lies at its centre. This creativity manifests itself in knowledge, in spirit, in emotion, and in action. Colonial dissonance is not simply a place of victimization, but a site of struggle. From the struggle can come agency, in which reflection fosters creative thought to enable resistive action that may provide an antidote to colonial dissonance.

9

Principles Guiding Cree Economic Relationships

RUPTURES IN WÂHKOHTÔWIN ᐋᐧᐦᑰᐦᑐᐃᐧᐣ create a settler colonial–induced dissonance that affects all of creation – Cree people, other people, other living beings, and spirit beings on this territory. As we are all implicated, it would be easy to feel paralyzed; however, that is not productive. In this chapter I introduce guiding principles that, considered together, reveal social, economic, legal, cultural, and political practices related to good economic relationships that emerge from the oral stories and personal accounts I gathered. Together these practices are used to mitigate dissonance and to try to maintain wâhkohtôwin ᐋᐧᐦᑰᐦᑐᐃᐧᐣ under the perpetually strained conditions that result from living within a settler-colonial state. Going back to the pimâcihowin ᐱᒫᒋᐦᐅᐃᐧᐣ (livelihood economy) model in Chapter 1 (Figure 6), I see each bead in the beaded okinewâpikonew ᐅᑭᓀᐋᐧᐱᑯᓀᐤ (rose) flower as a visual metaphor representing principles to live out miyo-pimâtisiwin ᒥᔪ ᐱᒫᑎᓯᐃᐧᐣ (the good life).

When I asked Sunney about how we can combat cognitive dissonance, he saw the restoration of the human–spirit connection as being at the core of such practice, and pointed to the importance of opening up a creative intellectual space: "What I do is I pray for scientists. I pray for science to come up with a way to find energy efficiently, efficient ways to power the earth. I pray for those people who are in power to be a little less focused on the upkeep of their own bank accounts. That's all I do – that's all I know how to do" (Sunney 2014a). I go back to Walter's words providing his understandings of the rupture in wâhkohtôwin ᐅᐦᑰᑐᐃᐧ, as well as of the productive spaces that remain:

> What can we do about the air? Because it is polluted. How can we fix that? We don't really know how.
>
> But the fire is the life that is on the earth, because the fire is energy. And that energy, it's a good energy to cleanse the earth and also to make the earth grow again. After wherever a fire goes by, it's a feast for all the animals that eat the hay and grass, because all of a sudden there's all this tender new grass that comes up. Trees that come up. Flowers and all the medicine that come up is all new and tender.
>
> So everything like that is done. So they don't fight fires that are caused by electricity. They let them burn. That's like putting a whole brand new life on the earth. There's an old life that goes away, which is same as us. There's an old life that goes away, but a new life comes, and that new life is young and fresh, and everybody that's on earth enjoys that new life. They have good memories of the old life, but the life is right now for the living, so they enjoy that new life.
>
> So the air, the water, the earth, and the fire. We are aware of that, that they are all good. Even though sometimes everything can be bad if there's too much of it, so we learn. Then the great thinkers; if you think about it, the deep thinkers, and anybody that's in a situation where they would have to think, all those people become deep thinkers. (Walter 2014a)

Walter's words explain the issues and show that the natural agency of non-human beings and processes continues, without human involvement, to restore balance on the earth (through, for example, naturally occurring fires). His words also indicate the value of intellectual work done to restore wâhkohtôwin ᐅᐦᑰᑐᐃᐧ in our current lived reality. This intellectual work can be prolific, but it is fruitless unless it is lived out, and it must be lived out, even though it will be fraught with the dissonance created in knowing that this resistance lies within a hegemonically oppressive system. It is interesting to consider that these resistive actions may provide temporary relief from colonial dissonance, an antidote. Perhaps with enough of these actions, a paradigm shift might occur. In the spirit of Walter's guidance, the next section presents principles embedded in Cree economic relationships.

Before I begin, I would like to provide a caveat. In Chapter 7, I conceptualize Cree economic relationships as deeply connected to establishing, maintaining, and restoring relationships. In this analysis, I include accounts of oppositional relationships and how economic principles and practices are engaged in response to them. In all societies there is conflict, and this is increased by colonialism; I want to acknowledge that there are situations in which it is unsafe (physically, emotionally, mentally, or spiritually) to be in a continued relationship with a person or group of people. I do not want to simplify the complexity of wâhkohtôwin to imply that the goal is always to restore relationships, even where doing so would put a person or people at risk of continued harm. Stated differently, sometimes oppressive actions and behaviours can heighten negative impacts for people in small, confined communities, given sociopolitical history and current circumstances. There are also normative practices related to these situations.

Normative Principles Guiding Cree Economic Resistance

The norms I discuss here emerged from Cree thought, through historical and contemporary accounts, stories, and legends, and through the interviews I conducted with Cree knowledge holders. Blackfoot scholar Leroy Little Bear (2000, 79) writes that "Aboriginal values flow from an Aboriginal worldview or 'philosophy'" and that "Aboriginal traditions, laws, and customs are the practical application of the philosophy and values of the group." The normative principles described in this chapter add to the resistance-and-resurgence literature and speak to how to support individual and collective actions.

With decolonizing and revitalizing work, many stages are required; one step in the process is to recover Indigenous ways of knowing and being in the world. Another step is to collectively deliberate, implement, reflect, and revise these principles (and others) continually.[1] One way deliberative processes can be used for this project is by seeing them as the governance of economic relationships.[2] Deliberation is a cyclical process during which economic relationships are extrapolated (in decolonial work), and then these norms are reasoned through, debated, and lived out in Indigenous societies and in negotiation with other societies.

I draw connections between my intervention in this work and the description of the processes occurring to revitalize Indigenous legal orders. Scholars Hadley Friedland and Val Napoleon (2015, 32) describe how with law "there is never a completely finished product. In all living legal traditions, statements of law are always provisional, not unchanging truths. Indigenous legal principles are no exception to this. They can and should develop, adapt, and transform through time." The normative principles here provide the beginnings of a framework to assist in the revitalization of Cree economic relationships. However, this framework will only come to life through reasoning processes that can only occur in the collective deliberative processes held in Cree societies. The principles in this chapter emerged from within Cree thought (through the oral histories, stories, and interviews I gathered), received ongoing feedback from Cree knowledge holders, and then were supplemented with work from Cree scholars and other scholars who interviewed Cree knowledge holders. This process of feedback is ongoing and cyclical.

pimâcihowin ᐱᒫᒋᕻᐅᐧᐃ: The Ability to Make a Good Living

pimâcihowin ᐱᒫᒋᕻᐅᐧᐃ, introduced in Chapter 1, is described as the ability to make a good living, which is derived from the Cree concept of pimâtisiwin ᐱᒪᐢᑎᐧᐃ, which means life (H. Cardinal and Hildebrandt 2000, 43). Arok Wolvengrey and Freda Ahenakew (2013) explain pimâcihisowin ᐱᒫᒋᐦᐃᓯᐧᐃ as the word for vocation, "that from which one makes a living," To have a good life and to be able to provide for oneself, one's family, and one's community requires the ability to be adaptable, nahiskamowin ᓇᐦᐃᐢᐠᒍᐧᐃ. There are many examples of collective nahiskamowina ᓇᐦᐃᐢᐠᒍᐧᐃᓇ (acts of adaptability) on the part of Cree people. When Harold Cardinal and Walter Hildebrandt interviewed Elders in Saskatchewan, they found that the "teachings (kakêskihkemowina) included unwritten but well-known codes of behaviour for the Cree people in relation to pimâcihisowin (making one's own living). They contained codes of personal conduct designed to enable one to 'make his or her own living.' For example, the code, among other things, describes those characteristics that each person was encouraged to acquire" (45):

- iyinîsiwin: the ability to develop a keen mind
- nahihtamowin: the ability to develop keen sense of hearing
- nahâsiwin: the ability to develop alert and discerning faculties
- nisitohtamowin: the ability to develop understanding
- kakayowâtisiwin: the ability to develop an inner sense of industriousness or inner ability or desire to be hardworking

- atoskêwimahcihowin: the inner desire or need to work
- waskawîwin: inner energy to move or develop a sense of personal initiative
- manâtisiwin: the inner capacity of respect
- kisêwâtisiwin: the capacity to be kind. (H. Cardinal and Hildebrandt 2000, 45)

Cardinal and Hildebrandt go on to explain that the connection to askîy ⊲ᕁᐸ·, the land, is indispensable, and that within the ability to make a living, people must meet the responsibilities in their nation's codes. The first four characteristics (iyinîsiwin, nahihtamowin, nahâsiwin, and nisitohtamowin) are related to kiskinowâpamiwewin.

Pᕁ₽ᒍ⊲·<⅂∇·∆·ᐣ (kiskinowâpamiwewin): Learning through Observation

Throughout the stories I heard the principle of Cree society adapting – learning new things, trading for new items or technologies, exchanging medicines and ceremonies with others. Under this principle, certain protocols guide how new information is gathered and from where. kiskinowâpamiwewin Pᕁ₽ᒍ⊲·<⅂∇·∆·ᐣ describes learning by observing someone or imitating someone's tactics or example. Similarly, kiskinowâpahtam Pᕁ₽ᒍ⊲·<"Cᨆ is to learn by watching something (Wolvengrey 2011). Sunney, Walter, and Paul all shared with me how Cree people learn things by watching animals (Sunney 2014b; Walter 2014b). In Walter's words,

> That's what the old Indian people were able to do because of the time they had on their hands and the things they saw in nature ... They were able to learn so much. And for the medicines that came, just like some of us are good at music, some of us are good in scholastics, some of us are good in intuition. So they would learn.
>
> They would have dreams about a certain medicine, or they would watch a moose eating maskamina Lᕁbᒋᐅ, which are the red rosehip berries. Why do they eat that when there's not much food in the middle of winter? Because there is good vitamin C in there. Why did they eat the bark of trees? Because there is good vitamins in there. So instinctively, the animals who are outside all the time, they know that much more than we do.

So the Indians would watch the animals and they would learn that stuff. They would see the moose sticking his head down and getting the roots of the cattails. And when they would try that, here they would find that big bulb, that pulpy bulb that was in the roots of the cattails. They found out that was a good thing to put in the soup. It would thicken the soup and it was also good to eat. So by watching each other, especially the animals, we learned an awful lot.

Whereas now, we learn mostly from books. But if any person that would go out in nature and live in nature all the time, every day, they would soon begin to learn a lot from nature. So it is good to watch everything. (Walter 2014b)

Plains Cree author Edward Ahenakew explains the legend of the nipâhkwesimowin ᓂᐹᐦᑵᓯᒧᐏᐣ, the Sun Dance. This account speaks to ᐑᓵᐦᑫᒑᕽ (a story told in pipon ᐱᐳᐣ, winter), learning from spiritual beings, and also to kiskinowâpamiwewin ᑭᐢᑭᓄᐚᐸᒣᐍᐏᐣ, observing and then emulating the actions of animals:[3]

Under the spell of the dancing and the drums it had all seemed sublime to him; when he wakened, it was only absurd. He found that it was not a dance-lodge into which he had thrust his head, but an old buffalo skull, and that those who had appeared as human dancers were in reality ants that had made their home in and around the old skull ...

"What I believed I witnessed was a dance in honour of Ma-ni-to, and for the purpose of asking blessing to meet the needs of man and beast. I saw the leaves, and they were young and green; I saw the dancers in their booths, the painted skull, the singers, and the leaders of the dance; and as I saw it, let the ceremony be.

"The Thunderbird with his flash of lightning released me from my predicament. It is by his agency as the ruler of the air, that Ma-ni-to waters the earth, in response to man's appeal. Only rain then can slacken the thirst of those who dance, as a sign of faith that the Ma-ni-to will send rain in response to prayer.

"I suffered distress, though it was not from a dangerous source. So must man sustain trials to open himself to the store of mercy that is in Ma-ni-to. In days to come, when the earth is well-peopled, at the time of year when the leaves are first out, let mankind as a whole perform this great act of prayer, the dance that shall be known as Nē-pa-kwā-se-mo-win (All-night-thirst-dance)." (E. Ahenakew 1995a)

In this full teaching, Edward Ahenakew explains the origin of one of the most important renewal ceremonies for the Plains Cree, one that still goes on, a ceremonial practice in which very important governing principles and practices are displayed. As Sunney explained to me, "the ones where we get our lessons are the lodges and pipes, and then we learn things from animals" (Sunney 2014b).

Similarly, Walter told me that Cree people often get lessons from dreams – for example, about certain medicines (Walter 2014b). One important Cree concept that Sunney shared with me is that of kiskinowâcihcikan ᑭᓂᑯᐋᐧᐦᐃᒃᐞ:

SUNNEY: Anyways, that is where we get our lessons from; from nature, anything that is circular, what we call those things, like the ones you find the rocks there, they are in a circle like this [shows the shape with his hand], there are spokes. Those spokes, they tell a story to something further over here, there is something over here that is a certain distance. You're going to find something depending on what is in that circle of rocks and those spokes. We call those kiskinowâcihcikan ᑭᓂᑯᐋᐧᐦᐃᒃᐞ.

SHALENE: Each one or the whole thing?

SUNNEY: Those rocks that are like that, the pipes, the lodges, those are now making it plural, talking about all of them: kiskinowâcih-cikana ᑭᓂᑯᐋᐧᐦᐃᒃᐊ.

SHALENE: Can I ask you what the word is based on? Is there a root in that?

SUNNEY: Yes, the visual, when someone shows you something – believe them. kiskinowâpamêw ᑭᓂᑯᐋᐧᐸᔪᐤ, look at them, observe them, it's an observance. kiskinowâcihcikan ᑭᓂᑯᐋᐧᐦᐃᒃᐞ, is not only is it something that you observe, it's also a teaching wheel, from that observing – from what you guys, you intellects, call it – from time immemorial.

kiskinowâcihcikana ᑭᓂᑯᐋᐧᐦᐃᒃᐊ, that is what they are there for, for us to observe. Like I said, if somebody shows you who

158 UPHOLDING INDIGENOUS ECONOMIC RELATIONSHIPS

they are, believe them, kiskinowâpamêw ᑭᐣᑮᓄᐘᒥᐤ. kanawâpa-
mew ᑲᓇᐘᒥᐤ look at them, observe them. (Sunney 2014b)

Sunney explains the different types of teaching wheels and how Cree people have used them to observe and learn. The next norm speaks to obligations to others.

mâmawi-h-itêyihtamowin ᒫᒪᐄᐧ·ᴵᴵ ᐃᐅᕯᴵᴵᒪᐅᐧᐤ·ᑐ: Thinking about All
The collective needs to be considered, and this can come in the form of obligations.

The stories and interviews I gathered provide numerous examples of the importance of considering the collective in economic relationships. The Cree Legal Traditions project explains the responsibility to help as a legal obligation that governs individual and collective responsibilities (Accessing Justice and Reconciliation Project 2013b, 28). Similarly, the project's researchers found that a substantive legal right is to receive help when a person is vulnerable or incapable: They write: "This Right can be inferred from the inverse obligation to help those when capable and to ask for help" (43). Interestingly, the researchers found that this responsibility to help includes helping non-Cree people as well (36). In *Voices of the Plains Cree,* Plains Cree author Edward Ahenakew (1995b) shared a personal account from Chief Thunderchild, titled "Indian Laws." This account provides a clear example of this obligation to the collective.

> The men who had horses chased the buffalo for the others and every-one got some of the meat, which would be hauled into the camp by the dogs. There was no selfishness. It is an Indian custom to share with others. That has always been so; the strong take care of the poor; there is usually enough for all.

We see the collective perspective in Thunderchild's words, as well as the principle of the vulnerable being taken care of. Fine Day (1973a) also wrote about the requirements of looking after the collective in terms of being inducted into the Warrior Society:

> Then an old man said to those of us who had just been taken as Warriors, "From now on your homes and your possessions are not

your own. From today, these two old men, the servers, are the owners of your goods. If a poor Person comes for help and you are not at home, these men may give away your things.[4] You must look after all the People. If their moccasins are torn you must supply new ones. Any clothing you may have must be given to those who come for help and who need it. If you see an old Person stranded while camp is moved, you must get off your Horse and put him on. Then the Horse is his." And I did give away a lot of clothing as a Warrior should.

This principle of being collective-minded includes both the practices and commitments of sharing, generosity,[5] and helping those in need.

There are also accounts that include helping non-Cree people. These examples describe Cree people sharing with or helping non-Cree people as well as, reciprocally, non-Cree people helping the Cree. Thunderchild recounts a winter of hardship when there was starvation, and at one point that winter he came upon a Nakoda man named Chō-ka-se; after Thunderchild told Chō-ka-se of his people's state of ill health, Chō-ka-se (a non-Cree Indigenous person) said, "Come with me and I will lend you horses and carts." Thunderchild explains that "this is the Indian way" (E. Ahenakew 1995b). In this way, the obligation to help others in need was shared among different Plains Indigenous peoples. Cree Chief kah-payuk-wah-skoonum (One Arrow) – who had fifty-sixty lodges in his camp at the time – invited Métis hunter Norbert Welsh and his men to participate in their buffalo pound. Once the buffalo were run into the pound, the buffalo were shared among the people, including the men of Welsh's team. He states, "The buffalo were shared. My men got twelve" (Welsh as told to Weekes 1994, 20).[6]

In terms of the norm of helping, there are accounts that substantiate how this extends beyond humans and includes Cree–animal relationships as well. For example, kâ-kîsikâw-pîhtokêw (Coming Day), a Plains Cree from the sîpîwiyiniwak ᓯᐱᐅᐃᓂᐊᐧᐠ (River Cree), recounts the Bear-Woman story. He characterizes this as a sacred story. In this account, a lonely man went out hunting, and whenever he saw a buffalo he would kill it and bring home the tongue and thigh bone (presumably leaving the rest, and not following the principle of civility toward all relations). One day he found a handsome woman in his dwelling, and she asked him why he only brought home a little bit of the meat; he replied that he did not know anyone was there, and as he lived alone, he only brought home a little. She said she came from a long way off, and her father and his people were in need of food and asking for his help. He agreed and she became his wife. He would bring home more buffalo that she would then prepare. In time, they brought the food to her father's people, and the hunter was amazed at his wife's strength and the ingenious way in which she was able to transport the food. In the springtime, he realized that his wife and her family were actually bears, and he was sad that he would not always be able to be with them (kâ-kîsikâw-pîhtokêw [Coming Day] 1930). This story illustrates many things, including how the obligation to help those in need extends to animals.

There are also specific norms around sharing that inform the collective perspective. For example, in a legend it is said, "When the fruit was plentiful, Indians picked them without any set rules. On the other hand, when lean years caused a scarcity, scouts were sent out to search for berry patches. When they located some, the camp was informed, whereupon rules were enforced, including the provision that no one was to go out until the whole camp was prepared to go on a berry picking expedition" (Brass and Nanooch 1978c). The rules around harvesting were contextualized to the specific availability of the resource, year to year.[7] In another Cree legend, a similar norm around harvesting practices is shared: "The Summer was very dry and growth was slow, so there were only a few berry patches and the berries themselves were small. In seasons such as these, it was customary for a camp to go together to pick all the berries they could, so that everyone would have an equal chance to get some food for the family" (Brass and Nanooch 1978b). In both of these accounts by Brass and Nanooch there is a consequence enforced by different animals – a bear in the first legend and a serpent in the other – when the norm around collective harvesting (in times of scarcity) was not followed.

The qualities of sharing, generosity, and helping, which inform collective obligations, are still valued in teachings and norms today. In my interview with Rob, the younger Plains Cree man who works for a large Indigenous representative organization, he states that "there is more of a collective push than an individual, it is almost like they would rather see a band business succeed than an individual person become wealthy themselves" (Rob 2013). He goes on to explain:

> In terms of the role of the Chief, when you are looking at giveaways and that sort of thing, it is kind of a different system now with the

> Chief being a higher position. The band members don't give everything to the Chief and have them redistribute, I think that is a little different nowadays but yet a lot of the band members ask the Chief for these things. It is a little different in terms of that, the Chief doesn't take all the meat and distribute it to those in need. It is kind of a different system; the current government system doesn't really work with the old ways of doing things. A lot of it is to do with the attitudes of the membership is not lining up totally with the new system or the old system too. In a lot of cases, because of the poverty of the First Nation people, the bands have to take a collective approach because they are the ones that have the resources ... I think that the collective approach still does work and is needed. (Rob 2013)

Rob's words point to the tensions in Cree economic relations and governance, as well as to the continued importance of Cree economic norms. The principle of mâmawi-h-itêyihtamowin ᒫᒪᐃᐧᐦ ᐃᑌᔨᐦᑕᒧᐃᐧᐣ (thinking about all) means more than thinking about all Cree people; it includes non-Cree people, and nonhuman beings like animals. Thinking is not a passive activity; it is also acting on these obligations to help, share, and consider the collective.

manâtisiwin ᒪᓈᑎᓯᐃᐧᐣ: Civility and Showing Respect to All of Creation

One apparent lesson from the stories I heard is the importance of showing respect to all creation and protecting nonhuman beings,[8] which involves principles of not overusing resources, taking only as much as one needs, and using resources properly. This element was found in each type of story – sacred, legend, and personal. Sunney explains to me how "ecological management is to be civil to the earth. To be compassionate, because it provides us with so much, so that reciprocity, we need to be civil to it" (Sunney 2014b). He said that this is manâtisiwin ᒪᓈᑎᓯᐃᐧᐣ.

This principle extends from Cree people to all nonhuman relations. Plains Cree scholar Leona Makokis (2009) explains that reciprocity and respect guide how the Cree relate to the land. As Bernie, a Cree Elder she interviewed, said, "it is a nurturing land. How we treat it will always come back to us and our future generations" (Makokis 2009, 126). Walter, a Plains Cree Elder, explains how his mother-in-law practised civility in the sustenance economy:

I know about economy in science, spirituality, mentality, and physical. First of all, the economy of science, I remember my old mother-in-law, when she would gather wood she would only gather as much as she needed. She wouldn't stockpile for a month. She'd only gather what she needed right now. When she was picking berries, she wouldn't take every berry out of the tree. She would leave some for the bears.

I remember watching that. I used to be so impressed because she was always thinking of nature too. We are part of nature, but everybody else needs to participate in the bounty of everything that is there. (Walter 2014b, 2)

Walter's mother-in-law only took as much as she needed in terms of harvesting. Walter attributes this respect to an acknowledgement that humans are not separate from nature but part of it.

One of the principles already mentioned in this chapter is related to enforced and natural consequences, and one of the examples provided explains the effects on the Cree of the loss of paskwâw mostoswak <ᐣᑎᐧᐤ ᒎᐣᑐᐣᐊᐧ (the buffalo). It is thought that fifty to sixty million buffalo roamed the Plains in the pre-contact era (Bryan 2005, 40). Historically, Cree people were respectful toward the paskwâw mostoswak <ᐣᑎᐧᐤ ᒎᐣᑐᐣᐊᐧ. In 1935, Plains Cree War Chief Fine Day explained one way to show respect for the animal was to try to use all its different parts, therefore avoiding waste (Fine Day 1935a, 5).

In her book *The People of the Plains*, originally published in 1909, Amelia McLean Paget records the words of her grandmother, Anne Campbell Murray:

What the Indians did not owe to the buffalo one can hardly imagine. This noble beast provided them with almost everything they required in the olden times. Every part of its flesh was converted into food, dried and preserved so that it could be kept for years ... the hides of the animals were worn instead of blankets ... The buffalo skins were ... used in making their wigwams or tepees, and for their bedding ... Clothing and footwear ... saddles and bridles ... lassoes and thongs. The horns were shaped into spoons and drinking cups. The brains were used in the tanning of the skins. The bones were used for the different implements required in the tanning and dressing of the skins, for saddle horns, and for war clubs ... The sinews were dried and used

> for making thread for sewing their garments, as well as for strings for their bows. The feet and hoofs were boiled for the glue they contained, which the Indians used for fastening their arrow points ... The long hair from the head and shoulders was twisted and plaited into halters, and the hair was used for a brush with which to kill flies and mosquitoes. (Paget 2009, 68–69)

This description explains the specific ways in which the Plains peoples, including the Plains Cree, showed manâtisiwin ᒪᓈᑎᓯᐏᐣ (civility) toward the life of the paskwâw mostoswak ᐸᐢᒁᐤ ᒧᐢᑐᐢᐘᐠ by using many different parts of the animal for food, shelter, clothing, and tools (Saskatchewan Indian Cultural Centre 2011, 75).

Another example of manâtisiwin ᒪᓈᑎᓯᐏᐣ is shown in how the Cree and other Plains peoples showed respect to manitô sâkahikan ᒪᓂᑑ ᓵᑲᐦᐃᑲᐣ (Creator's Lake or Lake of the Spirit), a place of healing. Although they wanted to gather there, they showed their respect by camping at another lake eighteen kilometres east instead, along the historic trails. The geographical region in and around the Edmonton area was historically known as amiskwacîwâskahikan ᐊᒥᐢᑿᒌᐚᐢᑲᐦᐃᑲᐣ, meaning Beaver Hills (or Mountain) House in the Cree language. Historical evidence shows many Indigenous peoples have inhabited the wider Edmonton area for over twelve thousand years (Goyette 2004, 11) whether at intervals, in a village, at a seasonal camp, or for ceremonies. amiskwacîwâskahikan ᐊᒥᐢᑿᒌᐚᐢᑲᐦᐃᑲᐣ has been known to Indigenous peoples for thousands of years as a meeting place for hunting, trading, medicine lodges, feasts, Sun Dance ceremonies, and other events.

An extensive Indigenous trail system predates European contact throughout North America. As discussed in Chapter 3, these trails were migration routes, trade networks, access to hunting grounds, and locations of warfare. This large network was throughout Turtle Island and provided the infrastructure on which the fur trade and then the settler road systems were built. The Old North Trail (also known as Wolf Tracks or Blackfoot Tracks) is one of the most extensive and best-known historic networks from Edmonton to Mexico.

Research has documented that a branch of the Old North Trail passed by Wabamun Lake, and that Lac Ste. Anne was a significant gathering place for those travelling on these historic trail systems (Coutu 2004, 71). Before the arrival of Europeans, Lac Ste. Anne (manitô sâkahikan ᒪᓂᑑ ᓵᑲᐦᐃᑲᐣ,

Lake of the Spirit) was a historical gathering place where "ceremonies that celebrated life, including the sun dance and marriages, took place. People traded roots and herbs used for medicine and special stones needed for tools and arrowheads" (Simon 1995, 2). Lac Ste. Anne still boasts the largest gathering of Indigenous peoples in Canada, with up to forty thousand Indigenous people gathering in this space for two weeks every summer. These gatherings encompass a diversity of spiritual, economic, and kinship relations. Métis author Philip Coutu (2004, 71) provides a useful connection between Lac Ste. Anne and Edmonton: "Edmonton, a major river crossing situated along the North Saskatchewan River, was easily accessible by river or road from Lac Ste. Anne and so appears to be a significant junction that connected the Wolf's Track to the North."

Sunney took the time to explain to me the civility Indigenous peoples showed toward manitô sâkahikan ᒪᓂᑑ ᓵᑲᐦᐃᑲᐣ:

SUNNEY: So [this is] the history that I heard about manitô sâkahikan ᒪᓂᑑ ᓵᑲᐦᐃᑲᐣ. Say this is manitô sâkahikan ᒪᓂᑑ ᓵᑲᐦᐃᑲᐣ here [points to an item on the table], that's the lake. And over here, east of manitô sâkahikan ᒪᓂᑑ ᓵᑲᐦᐃᑲᐣ, there is another couple of lakes, there's a nice valley in there, they call it Devil's Lake. That is where people used to camp.

They will camp out there or on the reaches. Okay, now say this is manitô sâkahikan ᒪᓂᑑ ᓵᑲᐦᐃᑲᐣ [points to one item] and this is what we call Devil's Lake now [points to another item on table to show the distance, eighteen kilometres]. They started a propaganda why they named it that [Devil's Lake]. Now look at the distance here. See the distance from there. That's how far the people would camp away from Manitou Lake.

SHALENE: Why?

SUNNEY: manâtisiwin ᒪᓈᑎᓯᐃᐧᐣ. They were civil towards that lake and that's about ecological management. Here is another thing about manâtisiwin ᒪᓈᑎᓯᐃᐧᐣ, when you go and pick rat root, what are you supposed to do: of course you do your ceremony, you've got your tobacco and pray, after you finish your prayer to the Creator, and to the mother earth, and then you address the plant and give that plant instructions while you're snipping it, and then you tell that plant that this tobacco is for you and then you give that plant that tobacco, right?

Now when you go and harvest the roots, because the roots are what you want, and it's all mucky in there, it is like this [shows with hand], all these roots. So you break off, and say this is the plant here and say this is the root here [shows with hand], and it is long here ... what we're instructed to do is snip off that plant, take the root out, now finish harvesting that. After you've done that then – our law is to go and put that root back into the water so it can replenish. That is our manâtisiwin ᒪᓂᑎᓯᐘ.

Then each one like the horse sweetgrass, that one ... you call it sage, right? You snip it off here but leave the roots on that one, there's a different way. Buffalo sweetgrass, you just rip out the roots and everything. Beaver sweetgrass is what you call mint, same thing, just rip out the roots and everything in there. So there are different ways about manâtisiwin ᒪᓂᑎᓯᐘ, hay sweetgrass, the one you braid, try to take the roots out of that one. It's kind of tough. Anyways that's about manâtisiwin ᒪᓂᑎᓯᐘ.

So these people used to camp that far away; the healers, whoever they were, whatever system they came from, would take their patients to there along with their oskâpêwis ᐅᐢᑳᐯᐏᐣ (helpers), whoever they needed, [they would] go to the ceremony for that amount of time and then leave that lake, Manitou Lake.

Catholics came along and saw this, how it was revered there, and they said, "Oh, Saint Anne was seen here." Saint Anne was, I don't know, Mary's mother. People began to go there and the Catholics didn't respect that manâtisiwin ᒪᓂᑎᓯᐘ. They just go there and they set up their churches because they saw the power, yes, and the tradition that went along with it. So that eventually as we got colonized and conquered, and of course the main thing we do when you are colonizing is you take our God away, take the peoples' God away. So they recommended their own God, and this God had a white big beard and a staff and had a gated community up there, a place called heaven, and only a few lucky ones got to go up to that gated community, and those are the ones that gave away all their possessions to the corporations.

So, that is about manâtisiwin ᒪᓂᑎᓯᐘ. What I told you about. I went a couple of years ago, a few years back, I used to go harvest wîhkask ᐃᐧᑭᐢᒃ (sweetgrass) at that lake, and I went there and I just cried. What happened? Somebody had harvested it [wîhkask

166 UPHOLDING INDIGENOUS ECONOMIC RELATIONSHIPS

ᐑᐦᑲᐢᐠ] and had just thrown the plant on to the side. They just picked it and that was the end of that plant's life right there. So that's a little bit about what ecological management is about, that ecological management is to be civil to the earth. To be compassionate because it provides us with so much, in that philosophy you need to be civil. (Sunney 2014b)

Sunney's teachings provide a concrete example of the principle of manâtisiwin ᒪᓈᑎᓯᐏᐣ related to manitô sâkahikan ᒪᓂᑑ ᓵᑲᐦᐃᑲᐣ (now known as Lac Ste. Anne), as well as how to show civility when harvesting medicines.

The last three principles outlined in this chapter are (1) following protocols, (2) gift-giving, and (3) reciprocity. These principles emerged from the Cree stories I analyzed and the knowledge holders I interviewed, and were substantiated by secondary sources written by Cree people or grounded in their knowledge, like the dissertation by Plains Cree scholar and Elder Leona Makokis (2001), "Teachings from Cree Elders: A Grounded Study of Indigenous Elders," which I quote from next. In that text, Leona Makokis shared her wisdom as well as the words of various Elders from her community of Saddle Lake related to these principles.

> In the words of Charles [names mentioned are Elders Makokis interviewed], "In destroying Mother Earth, you destroy all humanity." This statement reflects the interdependency between human beings and the land. Vincent suggested, "We really do not profit from the earth itself because we live in harmony with it."
>
> The relationship with the land is represented by gift-giving, or offerings made to the spiritual forces of Nature. The earth gave all types of gifts to the people in bountiful, unconditional ways. Skywoman affirms this in the statement, "You have all the gifts that will help you each day to provide for life. These gifts are food, medicine, clothing, shelter, water, air, and fire. All of these are life giving." In thanking the earth for these life-giving gifts, Florence said, "We give back to the earth what we take, we make offerings." "For every thing you take from the land you must give tobacco," stated Skywoman. Mike makes the physical connection of man to Earth as follows: "The earth is a living entity. The trees are the lungs of Mother Earth, their job is to provide us with oxygen."

... He [Mike] noted, "Our relatives the animals and plants are the spiritual beings. They are here because every day they remind us. They are our teachers." Skywoman emphasizes the importance of our obligation to the land. "Furthermore, we assume the responsibility and authority entrusted to mothers, grandmothers, and daughters as provided in our Natural Laws, for we are keepers of the land." (67–68)

This excerpt explores humans' relationship to the earth and everything that is connected to it. The importance of sustaining the earth to nourish all other life forms is at the core of most collective Cree identity, as shown in the language, and is also aptly illustrated by Skywoman relating the Cree to their territory when she says iyiniwaskamkohk ᐃᐱᓂᐊᑲᒼᑯᐦᐠ "means it is a healing land, the land itself, they call Turtle Island and the turtle is part of healing" (Makokis 2009, 54). When discussing Cree protocols, the wisdom keepers' words show the primary relationship with the Creator and how certain protocols flow from that relationship in the way people interact with the earth, with each other, and with all other beings. One way to honour the relationship with the land is to gift okâwîmâwaskiy ᐅᑳᐃᒫᐊᐢᑭᕀ (Mother Earth) with offerings of tobacco and (prayer) prints; this will be explored by Sunney in the section on gift-giving. The connection with and between all life-beings on okâwîmâwaskiy ᐅᑳᐃᒫᐊᐢᑭᕀ is explored in the section on symbiotic relationships. Mike explains symbiosis when he conveys the important cyclical relationship of okâwîmâwaskiy's ᐅᑳᐃᒫᐊᐢᑭᕀ lungs providing oxygen, and how humans (and other mammals) exchange carbon dioxide in perpetuity (Makokis 2001, 67–68). This was also described in Laura Calmwind's teaching on the first treaty in Chapter 3.

nâcinehikewin ᐋᒋᓀᐦᐃᑫᐃᐧᐣ: Protocol and Proper Procedures

What is protocol, in a Cree context? Sylvia McAdam (2009, 12–13) explains, "Protocols and methodologies are the foundations to accessing sacred teachings, knowledge and understanding of the culture, ceremonies and traditions." Sunney described it to me this way:

Say I want a song, you have a song and I want it. I would bring you tobacco. I will bring you offerings as a gift and I'd start with the tobacco and I tell you, "You sang a song and I would really like to sing that song, if you agree to give it to me and show it to me." If you said yes,

168 UPHOLDING INDIGENOUS ECONOMIC RELATIONSHIPS

then I would give you the gifts. Then you would show me. That's about nâcinehikewin ᐅᠤᠮᐊᑫᐃᐧ.[9] (Sunney 2014b)

Elders speak to the time-honoured "ways, procedures, and processes that First Nations persons are required to follow when seeking particular kinds of knowledge that are rooted in spiritual traditions and laws" (H. Cardinal and Hildebrandt 2000, 2). To do these teachings correctly and precisely is important. In terms of asking questions about sacred knowledge and teachings, generally the protocol is to present tobacco and cloth to the Elder or knowledge holder and a gift (McAdam 2009, 10). In one of my interviews, Sunney shared how he taught some young Indigenous people about protocol:

> There were students, back in the twentieth century, these students were complaining, they said the Elders wanted an honorarium. They asked me, what do you think? Some of them were outright angry for being asked to give an honorarium. They thought, "How dare they, they are supposed to be Elders, they are not Elders if they are asking for money." They asked me my opinion. I said, "Okay, you guys sound like really traditional people, this is what you do: get a little cardboard box and you find out who is all living with them at their place. Find a little what goes on at their place, then you put enough food in there – meat, potatoes, a little bit of flour, sugar – in this box. Put a little bit of tobacco in there too, so they can have a smoke, not too much tobacco, so they can roll one smoke. Then go get a buffalo robe from Helford hides, because you guys sound traditional." They stopped, they said, "How much does a buffalo robe cost?" I said, "Well, you can get a real ugly one for about $450 or $500 ... ; you guys are really traditional, so you want to get a nicer one; they are about $1,600 to $5,000." So they decided to go with the honorarium. (Sunney 2014b)

Sunney indicates here the importance of following protocol, as well as the colonial dissonance that Indigenous and non-Indigenous people grapple with when trying to incorporate Indigenous teachings into a contemporary context. Sunney's teaching method is also instructive: instead of simply telling the students to provide an honorarium, he provides an analogy of comparable costs under more traditional forms of payment, enabling the students to deconstruct their assumptions.

Tobacco is considered one of the sacred gifts that the Creator gave Indigenous peoples on Turtle Island, as it is believed to establish a direct link between the user and the spiritual realm (McAdam 2009, 16). Before tobacco was introduced, there was also kinikinik ᐳᓯᐳᓯᐤ or mihkwâpe-makwa ka pihtwâtamihk ᒥᑲᐧᐸᐱᒪᑲ ᐸ ᐱᑌᐧᒉᒐᒉᑫ, the bearberry plant. It was often used in pipes and for offerings (17). On August 5, 1935, Dr. David Mandelbaum interviewed Cree leader Fine Day, who explained, "The leaves used in kinnikinnik are called akagicipagwa 'anigaci' leaves. They are tied in bunches and put on a rack to dry over a fire. When they want to do them in a hurry they are roasted in a pan. They are used to make the tobacco milder" (Fine Day 1935b). Historically, Fine Day explained, in the spring tobacco was sent to the different bands as part of a governance function, to explain when and where to gather: "When the People come together, the 'ogihtcitau' (or warrior society) tipi is put up. If there was a very big crowd there might be three ogihtcitau tipis belonging to different Bands – River, Prairie, and West People" (Fine Day 1973a).

Tobacco is offered to establish, maintain, and restore human-to-human relationships, but it is also offered to establish, maintain, and restore human-to-nonhuman relationships. This is explained beautifully in *Cultural Teachings: First Nations Protocols and Methodologies*:

> Tobacco is also offered when a First Nations' person takes medicines, plants, stones or other such items from the earth. Every time you pull a plant from Mother Earth, she feels that pull, and you must always make the proper offerings of tobacco and prayers. By offering tobacco in gratitude and thankfulness, you are ensuring that this pulling of Mother Earth's hair will not hurt her too much. She must understand that you comprehend your relationship to her and that you know what she is giving you is one of the parts of her body. Through honouring and understanding that relationship to Mother Earth, you also honour and understand your reciprocal relationship to all of life and creation. (McAdam 2009, 17)

This teaching explains proper procedures for maintaining good relationships with all of our relations, including relations with the land. Giving tobacco acknowledges this relationship by giving a gift in exchange for items taken from the earth.

emekinawet ᐃᐧᑭᓇᐁᐧᐧ: Gift-Giving

Gift-giving is a continuous process in relationships, a process that occurs in Cree society not only between people (Cree and non-Cree) but among all living beings. In Chapter 7, I write of the different giveaway ceremonies as examples of Cree institutions that have spiritual, social, and economic functions. Here, I discuss gift-giving that occurs outside these institutionalized processes.

When I asked Sunney to talk about gift-giving, he immediately linked this to the gift of tobacco from the Creator:

> **SUNNEY:** Probably one of the oldest of our traditions is to honour that gift-giving and here is how for us ... tobacco was given to us, that was the first gift Creator gave to us. I told you quite a few times already, if you're going to get berries, you go talk to the Creator, talk to the earth and then talk to that tree, that plant, the one who you're going to pick from first.
>
> The first thing you do is that gift[ing]; you honour that gift – that gift, that life that plant is going to give you, that tobacco. Creator saw us, that we didn't have anything. We hadn't understood those laws yet. One of the things that was so important was honouring all of creation, if I go and get a rock for the sweat, the first thing you do, the first four rocks is tobacco – enough tobacco to fill a pipe, you put that tobacco down.
>
> So that was our first gift, and the law of tobacco is this, we're commanded by our Elders to smoke and we are forbidden by that law of tobacco to inhale it in to our own lungs.
>
> **SHALENE:** I don't understand.
>
> **SUNNEY:** We just ate ... the metabolized things are going through your liver and kidneys, there's change of energy there. And it's going through your stomach and it will go to your big intestine and small intestine, all the while creating energy. Everything that we ate, that we drink. Your energy, what happens there, again, is practical, right? We're living – to live another day as a result of that exchange, now tobacco when you blow it out, that goes to the ethereal – the energy around it, that's their food. That's their sustenance. So when we go like this [demonstrates inhaling while smoking], we are withholding that.

SHALENE: Oh, okay, thanks.

SUNNEY: So we're commanded by the elders to smoke, and why? To keep that relationship going. Not all the time, but – and then we're forbidden by the law of tobacco to inhale into our own lungs, it would be like withholding food from a child. So that was the first gift we were given. Now, we give that tobacco to everything; when we make a kill the first thing we did, tobacco. Even before they go out on a hunt, smoke a pipe, or smoke a cigarette for that animal spirit to pity us. Once you get that, and then you are free to hunt. (Sunney 2014b)

Tobacco is seen as a mekinawewin ᖸᑭᐤᐁᐧᐃᐧᐣ; in English this word is defined as a "gift from a higher power" (Wolvengrey 2011).

In my interviews, I found that one of the standards around gift-giving is the importance of giving the best of something, something that the giver values. Walter, the seventy-four-year-old Elder to whom I spoke, explains the different types of gifts:

So now, if I was to give a gift away, I don't give away anything that's cheap or anything. I always give away something that's nice. That way, you just feel better for yourself. You feel happier knowing that you've given somebody something that they can use and maybe that they want and can appreciate, whereas a cheap gift, then you don't really feel that good. All you know is you gave away a cheap gift, or it wasn't your very best gift or something like that.

Maybe it's a matter of feeling, how it makes you feel. And when you look at yourself in the mirror you can look at a guy that's real cheap that gives away cheap stuff, or you can look at somebody that gives away good stuff. If you give away good stuff you will have that feeling when you look at yourself. If you give away good stuff you will know that it's not you so much as a good spirit that's come with you, and you give away good stuff. Then you recognize and value that good spirit more than ever before. Does that make sense? (Walter 2014b, 2)

In this teaching, Walter shares how gift-givers need to give the best thing they can, something that they consider valuable. When you gift "the best," he believes you will feel better. He also acknowledges that a generous spirit enables the gifting to occur. Walter also shares a story in which an important teaching around gifting came to him in a dream:

> So whenever you have something, give away the best. Now, one time, dad came to me after he had passed away and he asked me for a shirt. Now, somebody had just given me a beautiful ribbon shirt. It was not very fancy, but it had a beautiful turquoise ribbon through it. Two. One had turquoise green and the other one a beautiful reddish colour. It was so nice. The background was so artistically beautiful. I loved it.
>
> So I put it into my clothes closet and I didn't wear it in front of anybody. I didn't want anybody to see how nice that was, right? So I put it away. And then one night Dad came to me and said, "Son, do you have a shirt I could borrow?" And I offered every shirt I had in the closet and he kept saying, "No, not that one. Is that all you have?"
>
> And I thought of that shirt I had, which I knew all the time, but I wasn't giving it to him because I didn't want to give it to him. So I went and I got it and he said, "That's perfect. That's the one I want." I said, "Where you going, Dad?" He said, "I'm going to a wedding." So then I knew that weddings were on the other side, or what we call a wedding down here on earth.
>
> So then about three weeks later, ... [my sister and her husband] came to the house ... They came to the house and he asked me for a shirt. So I didn't hesitate. I just went and got the very best I had, because Dad had already taught me about two or three weeks previous to that, give the best you have. Don't fool around. Just give the best you have. So [my brother-in-law] got the best I had right away, and I didn't worry about it because Dad had already showed me that. (Walter 2014b)

This account from Walter speaks to generosity in giving. It seems to be a sacrificial giving, in which Walter was taught through a dream that he needed to let go of the material possession he was holding. In Cree ways of knowing, knowledge through dreams is given much significance (Kovach 2009, 58). Dreams can provide direction, information, and understanding.

In Cree custom, when a person compliments an item one has, it is common to give that item to the person who complimented it. In Walter's account above, I wonder if that was the reason why he did not want to wear his prized ribbon shirt in front of people. The act of him "squirreling away" the ribbon shirt was tested first in the dream world, and then three weeks later in the nondream world. Walter tried to explain to me the philosophy behind this practice. He said, "If somebody really likes something you have, you might as well just give it to them right now, because if you don't somebody will steal it and it'll go away from you. As soon as somebody likes it, it is no longer yours, it is that person's" (Walter 2014b).

There are limits to the practice of giving an item(s) away to a person who admires it. Both Walter and Florence provided different ways to deal with this. In Walter's words:

> Some people say it [a compliment], not trying to get anything off you, they just can't help themselves, but there are other people that know that you are the kind of a person that will give it to them, so they will say that to you with hopes of getting that in the intention that you take it out and give it them. But what you can do is you can give them twenty-five cents. Sometimes they are insulted by that, but that's all that their comment was worth. (Walter 2014a)

Within this Cree custom, Walter shows a way to respond to someone who is trying to take advantage of a person's generosity. Florence is a Plains Cree woman, from the the sîpîwiyiniwak ᕈᐱᐃᐧᐃᓂᐊᐧᐟ (River Cree), who is now in her mid-seventies. In a similar vein to Walter, Florence recalled a time when she was being taken advantage of and how she responded:

> I can remember what I didn't do. Everybody knew I used to give my things away. Anyway, my son one time was on a trip with his Aunt Sylvia, and I had just given her all these clothes. All the way there, Sylvia said that my son bothered her. He would say, "That's my mom's blouse you have on." "You have my mom's purse ... " "You have this and that." She added, "By the time we got there, I was so sick of listening to him reprimand me because that is all he kept saying." Anyway, Sylvia had people at her house and she said to them, "Florence will give me anything I want. See those shoes she has on her feet, she got them in Europe and she really likes them. But if I ask for them, she will give them to me." But I was hearing this, eh, and I think, "Oh, no I won't." So when Sylvia said, "Honey, do I ever like your shoes!"

174 UPHOLDING INDIGENOUS ECONOMIC RELATIONSHIPS

I responded, "Really?" Sylvia said, "Yeah, could I have them?" and I said, "No" [laughing]. She was so shocked that I had refused her which made the people at her house laugh. (Florence 2014)

There are thus limits to these acts of generosity. One does not have to give items away, especially if one feels that the intent behind a compliment is objectionable.

miyohtwâwin ᒥᔓᐦᑕᐁᐧ (kindness) is a key value behind gift-giving. Walter told me that kindness supersedes everything, even oneself. He equated kindness to living. He went on to say, in relation to gift-giving, that "when you do kindness there is the energy of kindness, and that's a beautiful energy to have. Kindness in spirit, kindness in thought, kindness in action and deeds, and kindness in words" (Walter 2014b). When interviewing Florence, I asked about obligations around gift-giving, and she related those back to kindness:

SHALENE: Did you feel obligated to [give things away] or it was just what you knew?
FLORENCE: Personally, for me, I felt good to give things away. I was happy to do it.
SHALENE: And was there ever the expectation, did you ever feel because maybe you [had more] –?
FLORENCE: Yes, that's true.
SHALENE: Was there the expectation that you should give?
FLORENCE: No, there was never the expectation; it was my expectation that I knew I was better off, so if they needed something it didn't hurt me to give it to them.
SHALENE: And how did you decide what to give?
FLORENCE: I would know if they were short of blankets or something, or I would know if they didn't have enough clothes, and I had lots, I would just give it; "Do you like this?" "You can have it." But I got carried away and sometimes gave other people's things away [laughter]. One time, my mom had just bought herself two new purses, and my sister's purse was falling apart. I said to my sister, "Hey, which purse do you like?" She said, "This one" and I said, "Take it." It was my mom's purse [laughter].
SHALENE: When was that?

FLORENCE: When I was about twenty-three. So then my mom goes, "What happened to my purse?" and I said, "I gave it to Sylvia." She was not impressed.

SHALENE: Did you ever see that happening with other people, giving stuff away?

FLORENCE: My dad was sort of like that, and Sylvia always helped me, anyway. It is like when people are kind to you, you want to help, not because you feel obligated to. They don't have to help you; it's kindness that does it. That's the thing. (Florence 2014)

From both Walter's and Florence's perspectives, it is miyohtwâwin ᒥᐧᐦᐨᒐᐃᐧ or kindness that motivates Cree gift-giving practices. Walter shared with me that this principle can be enacted anywhere, including in the downtown core of large urban cities on the prairies. He gave an example of how he carries some fur-lined leather gloves in his car in the winter, and if he sees someone walking without gloves, he says, "Hey, come here. I have another pair of gloves here. You can have them if you want. They're extra, here." He told me, "They always take them" (Walter 2014b).

I also asked about the idea of reciprocity in gift-giving. Both Florence and Walter clearly explained that if one gives a gift, one should not expect something in return, but there is still a principle of reciprocity. Here is an excerpt from my second interview with Walter:

SHALENE: Do you think sometimes, when you give a gift, or when someone gives you a gift, is there ever a kind of expectation that you'll get a gift back or they'll give you something in return at a later date?

WALTER: Yeah, that's right, because that's almost like a visit. When somebody comes to visit you, they know that one day you're going to come and visit them. Or if somebody comes to visit you and you feed them, you know that one of these days they're going to feed you. Same thing with that, if somebody gives you something then you're going to give them something back. It's not that it's expected; it's just that that's the way it is. (Walter 2014b)

In response to my question about reciprocating a gift, Walter mentioned visiting someone. Florence was very clear with me that in her understanding, there is no obligation to return a gift. However, she said that a gift-giver could reciprocally expect to stay at people's houses as a guest. Here is part of our conversation:

> SHALENE: Is the idea that you give something away, but you know you will get something back at some point?
>
> FLORENCE: No, it is because, historically, our people sometimes had nothing to eat, and so they would share everything that they had. First of all, the kids would get it, and then the old people, and then them.
>
> SHALENE: So it's not like, okay, I will give this something away, but then when I need something, then I can ask for something?
>
> FLORENCE: Well, I was not around then, but I don't think it was like that, I think it was just natural; you just shared what you had. And that [sharing] was actually one of the qualities of a Chief, if they looked after the people good. That's why with orphans, someone would always look after them ...
>
> SHALENE: What about reciprocity – how, if I give you something, I know you will give me something? Or if I help you out, then I know in the future you will help me out?
>
> FLORENCE: But it's not like a law. It is just if you feel like it.
>
> SHALENE: So you wouldn't feel like – let's say one of your relatives, if they lent you twenty dollars, that sometime in the future they could ask you for money?
>
> FLORENCE: Well, my thinking is, "What, you want to borrow twenty bucks off me because you happened to lend me twenty bucks?" You know, like, that's why [incredulously]? Now, if it is just because you want to help them – a lot of old people were like that, they would just give and share their stuff. And their homes were always open. That is why we had everybody's kids in our house.
>
> SHALENE: The open house thing, if you had people at your house, and they could come over anytime, then was the idea that you could go to their house?
>
> FLORENCE: Well, we didn't expect it ... well, maybe. Our feelings sure would have been hurt if we showed up and they turned us away. (Florence 2014)

It seems that the concept of Cree gift-gifting is different from some of the wider literature on gifting; in Cree gifting, there is not always a notion that a gift will create a type of future obligation.[10] Reading and analyzing my notes now, I wonder if having an open house for family and friends is a Cree custom, and that is why it is expected, as opposed to being a reciprocal response to letting someone stay at one's house. When exploring differences, it is important to distinguish the giveaway ceremony (e.g., the mâhtâhito ᒪᐦᒉᐦᐊᑐ ceremony) from gift-giving: in the former, there is a form of reciprocity or obligation to give back, whereas there is not a formalized expectation in the latter. I will explore this more in the last principle discussed in this chapter.

kahkiyaw kâwâhkôhtowak ᗷᐦᕆᕀ· ᗷᐊ·ᐦᗡᐦᑐᐊ·ᕀ: We Are All Relatives

There is a Cree proverb:

> ka-kí-kiskéyihtétan óma, namoya kinwés maka aciyowés pohko óma óta ka-hayayak wasétam askihk, ékwa ka-kakwéy miskétan kiskéyihtamowin, iyinísiwin, kistéyitowin, mina nánisitotatowin kakiya ayisiniwak, ékosi óma kakiya ka-wahkotowak.
>
> Realize that we as human beings have been put on this earth for only a short time and that we must use this time to gain wisdom, knowledge, respect and the understanding for all human beings since we are all relatives. ("Plains Cree Elders Quotes" n.d.)

The English language has innate limitations when exploring Cree ways of thinking and being in the world. When I was analyzing the oral histories and archival as well as contemporary writing on Cree people, the term "reciprocity" came to the forefront as a guiding principle. However, when I talked to Cree knowledge holders, they did not seem to have the same connection to this concept as they had to the other principles. One of the issues relates to what reciprocity actually means. The *Oxford English Dictionary* defines reciprocity as "the practice of exchanging things with others for mutual benefit, especially privileges granted by one country or organization to another." Merriam-Webster's definition of reciprocity is "a situation or relationship in which two people or groups agree to do something similar for each other, to allow each other to have the same rights, etc.: a reciprocal arrangement or relationship." When examining the idea of reciprocity for Cree people, the term does not always relate well, as an equal exchange does not always occur – there is not necessarily "sameness" in value or "rights."

Although making offerings is a Cree custom, there is no notion that the offering is equal in perceived value to what has been given. This can also be seen in offerings made before hunting an animal; this is not necessarily seen as an equal exchange. miyo-wîcihitowin ᒥᔭ ᐄᐧᕋᐦᐃᑐᐃᐧᐣ has been translated as reciprocity or "helping each other in a good way" (McLeod 2007, 35). This concept and definition resonate with the stories I heard and what was told to me in interviews. Makokis (2009) translates sharing as wîcihitowin ᐄᐧᕋᐦᐃᑐᐃᐧᐣ. In her section explaining natural laws, she states that "the third teaching is about sharing; the Cree word is 'wîcihitowin.' This stems from the verb, wîcih, to help; and 'towin' makes the root word into a noun and refers to having everybody involved" (59). This is similar to the Cree term mâmawi-wîcihitowin ᒫᒪᐃᐧ ᐄᐧᕋᐦᐃᑐᐃᐧᐣ, which is defined as "all helping together, general cooperation" (Wolvengrey 2011).

When sharing the Cree stories related to this norm, Sunney told me that he saw this as symbiosis. Symbiosis is a way to think through how we are all related (humans, more than humans, etc.). Sunney talked to me about symbiosis in both interviews I conducted, in January 2014 and March 2014. In the first interview, he began with a teaching from an Elder from the east that is also instructive here:

> Then he went on to the spiritual side of things. He said, I have a grandfather; he comes in through a door. There is a great waterway on the east side of Turtle Island and it comes up through that door every day. On the west side of Turtle Island there is another door that our grandfather goes through when it is done with this day. And my grandfather says, everything I touch I am related to. That's about symbiosis, of course in a very practical way, talking about symbiosis and that's our world view. That is how we are related to the trees; we are related to the rocks. We are not just related to each other, how we have identified each other as mother, father, child, grandchild, sister, brother, cousin, uncle, aunt, grandfather, grandmother. We are not just related that way; we are all related according to that wâhkohtôwin ᐊᐧᐦᑰᑑᐃᐧᐣ is all about that. (Sunney 2014a)

One aspect of the all-encompassing relationship Sunney mentions here is the chemical, biological, physical, and spiritual ways beings are connected to each other:

> SUNNEY: A long time ago, we would look at bees, for instance ... Bees have a very important function, they are part of, well, every one

of them is part of keeping the earth balanced, right. Mosquitoes, we need them, but people hate them and poison them and yet they are so important; symbiosis, eh.

SHALENE: What does symbiosis mean?

SUNNEY: That sun, it affects everything, touches the plants, touches the earth. Photosynthesis is taking place, it goes into the roots and it comes back out. Plants thrive, animals eat from there, and it goes back to the sun. That's symbiosis; we are all part of that. (Sunney 2014b)

In this teaching, Sunney conveys how Cree people learn from animals. The teachings from the bees, Sunney also explained, relate to the respect that men should have for women. Sylvia McAdam (2009, 41) writes, "Historically, First Nations' women had highly respected roles in aspects of society. Women were advisors, mentors, and leaders involved in all levels of governance ... Women were more than nurturers; their roles were endless and varied from community to community." In Sunney's teachings, the ways we are related to everything have profound implications for how we live our responsibilities to all of our relations.

When I asked Sunney to explain to me what symbiosis meant in the Cree language, he explained it as pimâtisiwin ᐱᒫᑎᓯᐃᐧ, which means life:

SHALENE: Life? And how does that relate to symbiosis? Because all of life has symbiosis?

SUNNEY: It's all symbiosis. It's a real simple one for you to understand, okay? What is that stuff that you breathe out, carbon dioxide?

SHALENE: Yes.

SUNNEY: So we breathe in oxygen. If we were just to breathe and if we had to breathe back in carbon dioxide, that will kill us. If trees were to breathe back in oxygen, that would kill them. So what would kill them is what gives us life. What would kill us is what gives them life. (Sunney 2014b)

We are connected to everything else in extremely profound ways. Within these relationships, there is also an inherent interdependence. This can be part of the teachings when Cree people say "all my relations" or kahkiyaw niwâhkômâkanak ᐚᑭᐧᐢᔪ ᓂᐋᐧᐦᑰᒫᑲᓇᐧ. In the words of Cree knowledge keepers in Saddle Lake:

First Nations' relationship to the land is one of reciprocity and respect. As Bernie said, "It is a nurturing land. How we treat it will always come back to us and our future generations." This is echoed by Florence's statement, "When you take something from Mother Earth, you give back something in return." If one is not connected to the land, it is simpler to continue abusing the land for its resources without taking responsibility for the consequences on the future generations. A Cree saying is, "Only when the last fish is caught, only when the last tree has been cut, and only when the last river has been poisoned, only then will people realize you cannot eat money." (Makokis 2009, 126)

This Cree adage is a strong warning about the profound ways in which we are connected to all living beings. What we do to others – not just human relations but also nonhuman beings – will have implications for us through the process of symbiosis.

The discussion in Chapter 8 about colonial dissonance showed how mental, physical, spiritual, and emotional conflicts can be seen as consequences of settler colonialism. There was a specific focus on economic exploitation. Within the tensions of colonialism that can cause a perpetual state of collective colonial dissonance for Indigenous peoples, I argue that principles drawn from a nehiyawak ᐅᐦᐃᔭᐤᐠ world view can be a buffer against the oppressive aspects of settler economies and can provide alternatives that can shape renewed Cree economic relationships.

With decolonization, many people are learning and relearning their Indigenous language(s), renewal cycles, connections to territory, and histories (see the descriptions of peoplehood in Chapters 1 and 3). Without this knowledge, there can be a tendency to see only the negative impacts or social problems resulting from colonial dissonance, and not the strengths within Cree society. This self-reflection and action reclaim individual and collective agency. The principles described in this chapter emerged from Cree perspectives, passed through historical and contemporary knowledge holders, Cree stories, and interviews. In the next chapter, I will discuss stories that illustrate both moments of tension and the ways in which such moments construct a creative space to bring Cree principles and practices into economic relationships.

10

Renewed Relationships through Resurgent Practices

I AM WRITING THIS CHAPTER in the mountains; it is the first day of niskipîsim ᓂᐢᑭᐲᓯᒼ, the goose moon (March 2018). I am in a library at the Banff Centre, looking out floor-to-ceiling windows at a panoramic view of various mountain ranges on a beautiful, sunny day. I am in front of Buffalo Mountain; it is a powerful place. In this book, I have presented a few over-arching arguments. The first is that economic exploitation was the first and most enduring relationship between newcomers and Indigenous peoples. This set the stage for settler colonialism to take hold. Connecting the first and second arguments is the belief that our economic relationships are constitutive; by this I mean that the relationships we have to land, people, and other beings creates and co-creates who we are as individuals and as peoples. Based on this belief, the second argument relates to what Indigenous peoples' knowledge has to share with others. What gifts are embedded in Indigenous world views to speak to miyo-pimâtisiwin, the good life, and specifically to good relations in terms of the economy? In the previous chapter I talked about principles that guide Cree normative economic practices related to miyo-pimâtisiwin ᒥᔪ ᐱᒫᑎᓯᐃᐧᐣ. Going back to pimâcihowin ᐱᒫᒋᑚᐃᐧᐣ and a model for economic livelihood introduced in Chapter 1, with the beaded leaves of the rose as a visual metaphor of the interlocking aspects of a nation's peoplehood (territory, living histories, ceremonial cycles, and language), we need to reimagine our economies today in ways that reconnect and uphold our relationships to all beings, and that also provide a resurgence of these four key aspects of peoplehood. This chapter provides examples of these principles in action today.

The Giveaway Ceremony

There are many different types of giveaways in Cree society. Giveaways are a ceremony, and in some ways they can also be seen as an institution with spiritual, social, and economic functions. The following section provides further insight into the practice of giveaways from the perspectives of the Cree knowledge holders I interviewed.

The mâhtâhitowin ᒪᐦᒋᐦᐃᐅᐧ is one specific type of giveaway. Memorial giveaways, Round-Dance giveaways, and giveaways that happen at powwows are other examples. mâhtâhitowin ᒪᐦᒋᐦᐊᐅᐧ (gifts exchanged are a blessing) is mentioned in historical accounts and still takes place, and is explained to me as the only giveaway based on ᐸᐦᑲᑖᐣ or the "Skinny Man" (Connie 2013). Mike recounted the beginning of this specific giveaway ceremony to Leona Makokis; Mike is an Elder from Saddle Lake Cree Nation, which historically is part of the amiskowacîwiyiniwak ᐊᒥᐢᑯᐚᒋᐯᐃᐧᓂᐊᐧᐠ (Beaver Hills People):

> During a very harsh winter, a camp found themselves unable to find any source of food. All men took turns going out to hunt, but were not successful. The situation in the camp was getting very serious, and without food all the members would starve. Finally, as a last resort, one of the hunters decided he would venture out on his own. When the hunter had been out in the woods for many days, and unable to find any animals, he spent an evening just sitting by the fire and thinking of his dilemma when he noticed a little skinny man sitting just outside of his circle. He tried to befriend this little Skinny Man but was unable to. During the night when the Skinny Man thought the hunter was asleep he crept up to him. Very quickly the man captured the Skinny Man. This Skinny Man is really fearful of anything that a woman touched. The hunter had tied Skinny Man up with a woman's leggings. The Skinny Man was helpless, so he began to beg and plead with the hunter to let him go. He promised the hunter a ceremony that would assist him in his hunt if he was freed. The hunter decided that he would free the Skinny Man. In return the Skinny Man taught him songs, he taught him to use the pipe. The hunter was taught all the procedures

of this ceremony. He was told that if anyone is to practice it, that also is life giving. The hunters use the songs that were given. This ceremony is where the hunter was given the life of the animal in order for his tribe to survive. In order to give thanks for the gifts that Cree people receive during the year, this is a ceremony where they bring gifts to share with other people attending the ceremony. (Makokis 2009, 64)

The Skinny Man is also referred to as ◁ᐦbdᐣ, or the hard luck spirit; this Giveaway Dance is completed to win or regain his favour (E. Ahenakew 1995b). This is an example of an economic practice that can occur in response to an oppositional relationship, as well as a practice to restore relations between a Cree person and a spiritual being. It is said that the Skinny Man can be directly offended by a person (spirit-to-Cree relationship), or that he may be responding to a person's offence against another person in a camp.[1] The giveaway ceremony is partially to restore or establish a favourable relationship with the Skinny Man.

There are many aspects of this ceremony that can be discussed in terms of Cree economic relations. One element is the redistribution of wealth within the community. Another is related to the connection between this redistribution and success on a hunting trip, or to give life to a person. The giveaway ceremony is also a practice that maintains relationships within Cree society. It is said that "the giver would dance towards the person for whom the gift was intended. No gift could be refused. The receiver was then to give a gift of equal value to someone else" (Cuthand, Federation of Saskatchewan Indian Nations, and Deiter-McArthur 1987, 23). Value is more complex than simply a monetary value in a capitalistic system. The principle of reciprocity and equality in gift value is a way to redistribute goods within Cree society; this is about maintaining relationships within Cree societies, including gifting nonhuman beings, such as horses. It is said that this is an example of "giving in order that the poor and the destitute may have" (E. Ahenakew 1995b, 95). It is interesting how items that might not be traded before the ceremony would be gifted during the ceremony. For example, in an account by Norbert Welsh, after the receiver danced, the giver put shaganappi (long strips of rawhide) through the door (of a tipi) attached to a horse that the receiver had tried many times before to buy but was denied, as it was the giver's favourite horse (Welsh as told to Weekes 1994). This seems to illustrate the importance of generosity within the giveaway practice, even to the point of self-sacrificial giving.[2]

184   UPHOLDING INDIGENOUS ECONOMIC RELATIONSHIPS

In my conversation with Dora and Connie, who were introduced in Chapter 7, Dora explained how she made a commitment to host the mâhtâhitowin ᒪᐦᒐᐦᐃᐳᐃᐧᐣ or mâhtâhito ᒪᐦᒐᐦᐃᐳ every year for four years. She made this commitment when her husband was in a coma; the final ceremony was completed the year of our interview (2013). Dora remembers: "When John [Dora's husband] was in the hospital ... and we didn't know if he was going to make it, I asked ᐸᐦᑲᐟᐣ to give John his life back and I will pledge to do the four years in the community, and I'm asking for everyone's help to do this. The thing is I didn't really go around to everyone [to ask for help], it just fell into place" (Dora and Connie 2013). Dora's husband lived; this ceremony is said to be life-giving.

During the first three years of the usual four-year cycle for this ceremony, the ceremony itself is two evenings long, and in the fourth year, it lasts for four nights. Below is a conversation Dora, Connie, and I had in 2013 about the mâhtâhito ᒪᐦᒐᐦᐃᐳ. Our questions to Dora underline the significance of the ceremony.

> DORA: My final one (mâhtâhitowin) is this coming year. If you want to come, see what it's all about – pihtikwe ᐱᐦᑎᑫᐧ. I think just seeing, being a part of it, being able to see it means more than just reading about it. Seeing exactly what happens at the beginning, even putting it together is a whole big process. With the Elders, the singers.
>
> SHALENE: Does it only ever happen one time a year?
>
> DORA: Yes, in the winter. There has to be snow.[3] So that's a good way to restore, gift-giving, to share, you giving life by giving gifts. But it is also not about just giving to somebody else, it's remembering who gave you that gift. They gave you life, so you find something, and give them back life as well. So you have to remember who gave you something, and you're going to go back and give something back to them.
>
> SHALENE: During the same ceremony?
>
> DORA: Yes.
>
> CONNIE: So what happens if you don't?
>
> DORA: It's fine, but just try to.
>
> CONNIE: But what if you don't continuously?
>
> DORA: Well, you have to. Try to remember.
>
> CONNIE: What if you don't, what if you break the protocol? Do you get kicked out?

DORA: No, no, you keep going until you are broke, if you have nothing left then you leave.

SHALENE: Even if you are the one hosting it?

DORA: No, well, you can't be broke, you make sure you are prepared to do the whole thing, right. Even if it is giving your jacket away. Giving your shoes away. Your moccasins, here you go.

SHALENE: So you had to bring lots of stuff?

CONNIE: Thousands of dollars in preparation, food.

DORA: The feast, the Elders, the oskâpêwis ᐅᐢᑳᐯᐃᐧᐢ [Elder's helpers], inviting singers, a lot of preparation in doing that, and not forgetting what you have to do to get it together. You can't miss anything, for four years consecutively.

CONNIE: I did not know that ᐸᐦᑲᑰᐢ meant the hard luck spirit?

DORA: Yes. Shalene, you should come and see ᐸᐦᑲᑰᐢ.

SHALENE: Yes.

CONNIE: Does the tree have significance?

DORA: That's life, right.

CONNIE: For the economy? So, for how reciprocity is distributed, is that governed by the tree, is that central?

DORA: You give that tree life as well, so you will see people giving gifts to the tree as well.

SHALENE: So in that diagram [Figure 15 in Chapter 7], that's the non-human relations, the tree is in a relationship with the humans?

CONNIE: But I would say it is more powerful than the human-to-human.

SHALENE: Oh, okay. So, like a hierarchy of importance of relationships.

CONNIE: What do you call this spot, the tree spot?

DORA: You just call it that Mî-tos.

Dora talks about restoration through gift-giving. The ceremony is also deeply connected to living, as a person who is seriously ill may have his or her health restored; significantly, the giving of gifts is a metaphor for giving and receiving life. I had the opportunity to attend a mâhtâhito ᒫᐦᑖᐦᐃᑐ with Dora's family this year (2014). This ceremony was in a First Nation in the Beaver Hills territory. When I arrived, I noticed the ceremonial fire outside, tended by helpers. The actual event was in the basement of a church in this Cree community. The host had made this commitment when her child was in a coma for many months and the doctors did not think the child would live; in fact, the child was still alive and participated in the ceremony. Dora had given me advice on the protocol and what sort of gifts I should bring to the giveaway. The first gift I gave was to a woman sitting by me. She seemed genuinely happy and excited to receive it, and I was also filled with joy; I could not wait to give another gift. I was told that night that when you present a gift in this way, you are giving life, and when you accept a gift you are receiving life. I found people to be very thoughtful about the gifts given.

These events build community – establishing, maintaining, and restoring relationships among the people attending, with nonhuman beings (e.g., the tree that was represented there), and with the beings in the spiritual realm. It is also an intergenerational event, with a wide distribution of all age groups represented. There were young children, four or five years old, dancing and exchanging gifts with each other and with people of different ages. A few different times during the night, someone would make a proclamation that someone else was so generous that they were now broke, and at that point almost all the people would gather around and dance and give a gift to that person. There were also little jokes played – for example, a tiny pair of newborn baby jeans was gifted to a big man. Laughter was shared at these moments. There were the male Elders, drummers, and helpers at the front. At one point during the night, the mother of the hostess spoke, explaining the history, story, and meaning behind the mâhtâhito ᒫᐦᑖᐃᗒ; she had a teaching role during this part of the ceremony. Dora excitedly shared that "it is great, especially when the whole community is bringing themselves together as they are having fun; they are laughing, dancing, exchanging, then when it is all finished and over, the year's done, they are pretty sad. They say: 'See you at the next mâhtâhitowin ᒫᐦᑖᐃᗒᐅᐃᐧ.' So that's good" (Dora and Connie 2013). This practice is an example of Cree people and others from different communities gathering in a Plains Cree community to renew relationships among themselves, and between themselves and other beings.

kâ-ohpawakâstahk ᗠ ᐅᐦᐸᐧᐊᐦᑕᕽ

The next grounded practice I will discuss comes from a Plains Cree community that is renewing its relationships with the land, each other, and other peoples who enjoy their produce.

kâ-ohpawakâstahk ᗠ ᐅᐦᐸᐧᐊᐦᑕᕽ (Flying Dust First Nation or FDFN) became party to Treaty Six on September 3, 1878, under the leadership of

Cree Chief kopahawakemum (Thompson n.d.). There are many examples of colonial policy specifically and directly affecting FDFN. The Beauval Residential School opened in 1921, taking Flying Dust children, and it did not close until 1995 (Flying Dust First Nation and Dalhousie University 2007, 23–24). Flying Dust's land was expropriated, starting with unmet land entitlements after Treaty Six, and then further, in 1952, with a discriminatory enfranchisement policy affecting veterans returning from fighting for Canada in the Second World War (22). Cree territory and livelihood practices were severed with the creation in 1954 of Primrose Lake Air Weapons range (4,490 square miles of land in Northern Saskatchewan and Alberta expropriated by the federal government for air force bombing and gunnery),[4] uranium development in northern Saskatchewan, and numerous other industrial resource extraction developments.

kâ-ohpawakâstahk ᑲ ᐅᐱᐋᐧᐊᐧᐸᐣᑕᕁ signed a Treaty Land Entitlement (TLE) agreement on September 22, 1992, as compensation for lands that were never provided under Treaty Six. These negotiations were conducted under the leadership of the Federation of Saskatchewan Indigenous Nations (now called the Federation of Sovereign Indigenous Nations, FSIN), who represented over twenty First Nations in the TLE process. The result for Flying Dust was compensation valued at 33,910 equity acres, with Flying Dust having bought and turned 10,965.7 of these acres to reserve status ("Flying Dust First Nation" n.d.).

In 2007, Flying Dust and the community planning department at Dalhousie University completed the Flying Dust First Nation Community Plan, also named "kopahawakenum mamawīcihitōwin." mâmawīcihitōwin ᒫᒪᐃᐧ· ᐃᐧᒋᐊᐧᑐᐃᐧ·ᐣ means "to help all together." Their vision statement is "mamawīcihitōwin ekwa kēhtēyak okiskinohamakēwin kakaskihtānanaw kasokīsihtamasōwak miyomacihowin ēkwa wīcīsowin iyinito ayisīnīwiyak [Through teamwork and the teachings of our Elders, we will build a strong, healthy and self-sufficient Nation]" (Flying Dust First Nation and Dalhousie University 2007, 51). In the community plan, they explain that a root cause of negative community wellness outcomes is a loss of traditional hunting and gathering methods (44).

Renewed Relations with the Land: Cooperative Gardening

Citizens of Flying Dust have said that growing their own food is a historical practice. In 2009, a group of community members decided to bring back some of their community's gardening and harvesting history more formally.

Their ideas originated from a need and desire to have readily available, healthy foods for them and their fellow citizens; this is a move toward Indigenous food sovereignty. At the first Indigenous Peoples' Global Consultation on the Right to Food and Food Sovereignty in Guatemala (2002), food sovereignty was defined as "the right of Peoples to define their own policies and strategies for sustainable production, distribution, and consumption of food, with respect for their own cultures ... and [this] is considered to be a precondition for Food Security" ("Declaration of Atitlan" in Honor the Earth n.d., 19). Susan Merasty, community member and co-manager of Flying Dust Cree8 Worker Co-operative Ltd. (FDC8WC), explains how "community Elders had maintained small gardens in the past, but the practice had dropped off and had even been discouraged by the federal government's Indian Affairs agents" (Levy 2011). In her book *Lost Harvests,* Sarah Carter (1993) meticulously documents how during the time of numbered treaties, Plains Indigenous peoples had a sustained interest in agriculture; it was Canadian government policies that continually attempted to thwart this. Also significant is how, before European contact, 75 percent of Indigenous peoples' food (including that of the Cree) in North America came from agricultural production (37). Engaging Cree agricultural practices to increase food sovereignty is an act of self-determination. Indigenous food sovereignty maintains and restores relationships between Cree people and the land, as well as providing ways to connect to the different aspects of Cree personhood (spiritual, physical, mental, and emotional) and Cree peoplehood (territory, ceremonial cycles, language, and living histories) positively. In a guidebook by the Indigenous organization Honor the Earth (n.d., 22), the authors write: "The recovery of the people is tied to the recovery of food, since food itself is medicine, not only for the body, but for the soul, and for the spiritual connection to history, ancestors and the land."

Leading up to and during the negotiations of Treaty Six, agriculture was a main issue for both the settler representatives and for the Plains Indigenous peoples. Elders from Treaty Six explain how "the Commissioner said that he came not to take land." Another Elder said, "The settlers would share the land and could use it to the depth of a plough – about one foot. The British wanted top soil for agriculture, grass for animal fodder and some trees to build houses and fences" (International Work Group for Indigenous Affairs 1997, 36). As discussed in Chapter 4, on August 18, 1876, the official proceedings for negotiating Treaty Six began. On August 23, the Indigenous peoples' counter-offer was presented. This included an ox and cow for each

16 Flying Dust Co-operative Garden.

family, as well as "four hoes, two spades, two scythes and a whetstone for each family. Two axes, two hay forks, two reaping hooks, one plough and one harrow for every three families. To each Chief one chest of tools as proposed. Seed of every kind in full to every one actually cultivating the soil. To make some provision for the poor, unfortunate, blind and lame ... [and] all agricultural implements to be supplied in proportion" (Morris 1880, chap. 9). These negotiations document how important agriculture was to the Cree people. The final agreement contained new concessions over previous treaties, including provisions for agriculture, a medicine chest, and assistance during famine (Hildebrandt 2008, 16). For the Cree, agriculture was an important part of Treaty Six, despite the fact that the settler government did not honour its commitments.

Flying Dust began its community gardening initiative in 2009, with two acres. In 2013, the community cultivated twenty-eight acres. That summer (2013), I had the opportunity to spend time with and interview one of the garden's founders. These are Susan Merasty's words:

> I grew up here on Flying Dust ... I left my reserve for, I think, 15 years, but regardless of where I have lived or where I've gone, I've always

been gardening. Even in the cities, whether it is on my balcony in boxes or whatever, I've always managed to grow food for my family. The biggest thing for me, I guess, is teaching what my Elders taught to us. I'm a big gatherer; I gather berries, roots, herbs, and medicines; this was all taught to me by three grandmothers in my life. My grandfather took me on his trap line and taught me how to trap, how to skin; these are things that I want to pass on to my immediate family and anybody that will listen. A lot of times we are taught that this is how we pass on our knowledge to teach others. (Merasty, G. Cardinal, and Sawatsky 2013)

Susan then delves into the realization of the impacts of unhealthy food, which can be seen as part of the physical implication of colonial dissonance. She continues:

I came back to my reserve because I was diagnosed with chronic illnesses, I was in the first stages of diabetes, so I came home, and I started gardening with the garden group here. We had always had community gardens here before, they weren't really successful because people didn't really give it their all. So when Gladys [Cardinal] and I and our group came on the scene we decided that our community really needed it, a better way of sustaining ourselves, another choice of food other than what you find in the stores because of all the GMO products. Prepared foods, that weren't available for us before, are not as healthy as we think they should be. It is causing a lot of illnesses in our families. So when I came home I changed my diet, I was a borderline diabetic, now I don't have diabetes. It is just a matter of changing my diet and my lifestyle. I exercise now on a regular basis. I used to be really obese and overweight, over 200 pounds. Now I sustain my weight at an even level, so for me it has been a healing journey. I continue to go further into healing: spiritually, emotionally, health wise and then to pass this on to my community – to share all of that with them. (Merasty, G. Cardinal, and Sawatsky 2013)

Susan then links her response (an act of resistance against colonial dissonance) to a renewed relationship with the land and how this correlates to her physical health and the health of the land. She also discusses ceremonial practices around relationships with the land:

With our garden practices and beliefs, we try to take care of Mother Earth first and foremost. We do a lot of our gardening in a traditional sense, where we are mounding things, planting in mounds or in raised rows or in beds. We're doing a lot of experimental things with our garden area, we've tried different seeds, planting at different times of the season, we are trying to figure out what works best for our area and then stick to those veggies that were successful. From our teachings we try to train our people. We do see consequences when we don't follow the teachings of our people, like offering tobacco when you are harvesting a medicine. A lot of times it comes back to bite you in the butt. I am really strict when I am teaching it and gathering, I make sure I say the right prayers for what was taught to me and given to me by my Elders. I make sure I'm doing it correctly out there when I'm gathering and passing on what I've gathered. I do not sell anything; I trade. I won't sell a braid of Sweet Grass to you but I will trade for something, whether it is tobacco, anything. A lot of times I will ask for beads, hide, because I am a crafts person and that was another gift that was passed on to me by my Elders, I was forced to learn that and it has come back, it helps to have those skills. I've been teaching at the schools, to pass on that gift. It has been quite the journey just to be home. (Merasty, G. Cardinal, and Sawatsky 2013)

Susan's words are full of wisdom and illustrate thoughtful adaptation. Her personal experience demonstrates many of the normative principles related to Cree economic relations, as introduced in Chapter 9. She begins by talking about the teachings she received through her relations; how her three grandmothers taught her about gathering food and medicines, and her grandfather taught her how to trap. It is not just about learning these elements, but also passing these gifts of learning on to others. Susan also describes the natural consequences for Indigenous peoples of our change in diet, from eating natural foods to eating processed foods. One consequence of this is related to health issues like diabetes. Instead of being passive, Susan is taking action, for her own health as well as the health of members of her community.

One of the elements that stands out in Susan's words is the importance of being in good, thoughtful relations with the land. Through their practices, they try to demonstrate manâtisiwin ᒪᓈᒋᓯᐃᐧᐣ (civility) for creation. The importance of following nâcinehikewin ᓈᒋᓀᐦᐃᑫᐃᐧᐣ (protocol) is demonstrated through specific prayers offered when harvesting and the importance of gifting tobacco. In terms of medicinal items, Susan follows the practices of trading and gifting as opposed to having these items become part of the capitalist system. I was also struck by how she and her colleagues are revitalizing Indigenous planting and harvesting techniques while also trying experimental ideas, by first observing the environment, kiskinowâpamiwewin ᑭᐣᑭᓄᐃᐧᐸᒥᐁᐧᐃᐧᐣ (learning through observation), to see how different methods work in their territory.

I also had the opportunity to talk to Gladys Cardinal, a community member who has been involved with the garden since its beginning. She is a single mother with two teenage boys. A striking element from this interview is how connecting with the land helps her reconstitute her identity, world view, and view of Cree economy. These are her words:

> My name is Gladys Cardinal and I am from Flying Dust here. When I first started with the garden, it was nothing more than just a job, but now that I am into my fourth year with the Riverside Market Garden I have grown in a lot of ways, more or less; I have grown to not let money motivate me but to actually work with my hands and work with the ground, the earth, and trying to be reconnected with the land. Because I was brought up by my grandparents, I was adopted when I was just a baby, I was taught traditional ways to a certain extent, but my grandparents believed in Pentecostal ways, going to church, going to camp meetings and such, but I was definitely taught you are to respect Elders and the people you came in contact with. Respect was a big thing for me that was taught to me. Growing up with my grandparents I learned a lot. From my grandpa I learned how to skin a moose, or deer, how to pack it out of the bush – how to work hard – gather berries, my grandmother taught me that. She taught me how to tan hides, how to gather the wood, the right type of sod you were supposed to use to tan a hide with. I was taught that, a lot of different things, from that way. (Merasty, G. Cardinal, and Sawatsky 2013)

Gladys explained how, through community gardening, she has renewed her relationship to the land. Elder Elmer Ghostkeeper refers to this as Spirit Gifting (see Chapter 5) – living *with* the land as opposed to living *off* it (Ghostkeeper 2007). This is a psychological process as much as it is a material one. You do not need to live a completely subsistence lifestyle to, in Ghostkeeper's words, revitalize your Indigenous world view to the land.

Gladys also acknowledged the valuable Cree teachings from her grandparents. Like Susan, she sees great importance in mentorship and involving youth – passing on this knowledge and creating the environment for others to grow:

> Being with the garden has also taught me a lot of things, how to grow certain vegetables, when to harvest it, and having my kids involved as well because my kids used to come to the garden, my sons, I tried to get them involved as well. That is what we tried to stress as well, with our garden, try to get the youth involved. There are presently two youth summer students that are working with us. It is always nice to work with the youth; they are always willing to learn. Their minds and brains are like sponges – they always want to learn ...
>
> I am still learning and it's an ongoing learning experience for me. I have grown in a lot of ways. Our motto for the Riverside Market Garden is *growing people, growing produce*. I can say for myself that I have grown, matured, and I want to set an example for my children as well because they are so bombarded by fast food, pop, and all these foods that are not good for you. I am trying to set an example in that way where I can say, hey, this is not good for you, you should be eating this instead. Even the vegetables and fruit that we buy in the grocery store, they have herbicides and pesticides on them, they make them look so good, so the customer will buy the product. Us, we as a community garden, we want to stipulate that ... our vegetables, fruits, are pesticide-free. (Merasty, G. Cardinal, and Sawatsky 2013)

Young people are also engaging in this initiative. One aspect of the principle of mâmawi-h-itêyihtamowin ᒩᒪᐃ·ᐦ ᐃᐅᔦᐦᑕᒧᐃᐧᐣ, introduced in Chapter 9, is the importance of sharing, thinking of the collective, and critically observing the world with agency. Gladys's words point to the value of sharing knowledge regarding renewed relationships with the land and healthy food with the younger generation.

In Chapters 3 and 7, I explored Cree historical and contemporary trading practices. This can include trade in items, songs, ceremonies, and information. Gladys talked to me about trading knowledge related to Indigenous gardening:

Also, I just recently went on a trip to Manitoba, with several people from the garden, the group; it was a very eye-opening experience for me. The way they live, they are really down to earth, and being able to go there and trade knowledge, I guess in a way, in a sense, it was an Indigenous food-gathering mission. Me and seven other people travelled over there last week for four days. It was a two-day gathering, but it took about twelve hours to travel there, it was quite the drive. We met other people that are going through the same struggles as us, promoting community gardens like this, having to promote healthy lifestyle because our First Nations people are so susceptible to diabetes and other things, like obesity, and other health problems like heart disease. It was a really nice experience to go over there and learn how they live and how similar they are in a lot of ways. It was a very good experience. There was one lady there, we usually started our day with a group discussion, we sat in a circle and the people from the different First Nations' communities talked, and they talked about what they are doing in their communities. There is this particular lady, her name is Audrey, she was very knowledgeable, and she grows her own herbs, vegetables. She is pretty much self-sufficient in her own way, and she did some research on some seeds that were found and they were 6,000 years old. It goes to show that gardening happened years and years and years ago. (Merasty, G. Cardinal, and Sawatsky 2013)

In Flying Dust's community garden, they do not see their gardening activities (including harvesting berries) as something adopted from the non-Native community, but as a productive way of bringing something back that had a historical basis in their community. The five founding directors of the project developed relationships with those in their community and also with others to make this initiative a reality – establishing relationships with both Cree and non-Cree people. For example, they brought Len Sawatzsky in to co-manage and to teach a certificate program in partnership with North West Regional College (Levy 2011). Len explained to me how they are using organic practices and how this is Indigenous. He says, "I've said to some people, organic may be a nice progressive, left-leaning word, but you know, when they ask me how is this Indigenous ... well, for one thing, it is organic. I tie that more to Indigenous ways of living and growing than I do to some trendy movement called organic. It is Indigenous" (Merasty, G. Cardinal, and Sawatsky 2013). Although their produce meets the technical requirements for organic labelling, it does not officially have organic status due to the overly arduous certification process.[5] There are critiques that charge that the organic food movement is embedded in neoliberalism (Ventura 2012, 137–140). Organic farming practices were originally part of a social movement focused on taking control away from agro-food corporations and moving it toward "small-scale food production, community engagement, and ecological responsibility" (J. Johnston, Biro, and MacKendrick 2009, 510). Scholars have criticized the corporatization of organics, with large factory farms supplying distant markets while marketing products based on the movement's original ideals (J. Johnston, Biro, and MacKendrick 2009). Within this new corporate organics model, corporate power continues to marginalize communities, favours elite social classes that can afford the high-priced organic food market (J. Johnston, Biro, and MacKendrick 2009), and potentially still disposes peoples and lands. The corporate organic model is not about Indigenous food sovereignty, which allows Indigenous peoples to have access to nutritious goods that are "ecologically, socially, economically and culturally appropriate" (First Nations Development Institute 2013, 6). Flying Dust's community garden is not based on a neoliberal corporate governance model. Rather, its cooperative gardening is primarily conceived around subsistence food practices, and secondarily around selling the excess. There are also many ways in which the gardeners are using specific Cree teachings in their practice. Below is an excerpt from a conversation between Len, Susan, and me about Cree gardening practice.

> LEN: Well, we heard some stories a few years ago from an elder and he heard it from his grandfather. This guy is in his seventies. They [community members] actually planted in mounds [historically]. He told a funny story about it as well. These white people would come to these villages and, already, a mile away, they would start holding their nose, [like] "What do these Indians think? This is awful." They come close to the village and they have to go there because of making treaties or trade or whatever. It was them [the settlers] trying to get their [the Indigenous people's] land from them in some way ... or another.
>
> Upon further investigation, they [the settlers] found out that their [the Indigenous people's] fish, their leftovers, anything that they didn't use from the fish, they put in their pile, covered it with

earth, and then in the spring, they put seeds in there. They composted. And they put the seeds in there and that stuff of course would rot and heat up and even in the unfriendly winters and everything; they could grow vegetables here. And so they would find out what was compatible with each other through thousands of years, of course.

So what they did is they grew corn, of course the corn is Indigenous to here [Turtle Island]. And then they would take the vine-type beans, the pole beans, and the beans would grow off the corn stalk, and they needed protection around these sites, so they grew squash. And the squash provided shade and kept things moist and reduced the weeds.

SHALENE: I heard that gardening in mounds helps to reduce weeds.

LEN: There were all compatible kinds of stuff, and now people write books about these vegetables as compatible. What is this knowledge again that was here before white people came? So we tried mounds this year and some of it is working. Now that we've tried it we'll do it again next year and perfect it.

SUSAN: The thing is too, as you sit and watch, I couldn't figure out why my kohkom ᑰᑯᒼ (grandma) used to always put ashes in her garden. Because they always heat with wood, right? So they gather all their ashes, even in the wintertime, wherever the garden was, they put ash on top of the snow. And then it would melt and it would go into the garden, and finally I asked her, "Why do you do that?" She said, "Because it gets rid of the bugs and it controls the acidic levels, the alkaline and all those different things in the ground to help your plants grow better."

All those things are coming back to play in what we're doing now. And we're putting all these practices that our Elders used in their gardens because they've learned through years of gardening, and we are now using it in our garden. And it is a way to fight and control worms, control bugs and stuff like that.

But that's when I'm thinking back to what my kohkom ᑰᑯᒼ used to do. She kept all her books [accounts] on paper in Cree. So we'd sit there and we'd look and see these Cree figures and empty sheets [that] would have numbers beside them, and I never could figure out what she was doing. But also her books, she kept her own books. She was a seamstress, a gardener, and she used to raise chicken and sell her eggs. So she had three different forms of income. In the meantime, mosôm [nimosôm ᓂᒧᓯᒼ, my grandfather] was the hunter and he was a farmer ...

So they were well-known in our area here, and I've learned so much from that. And then being able to pass that on, given the opportunity with our group to pass that on has been such a blessing for me. I'm passing on teachings that were taught me years ago, and I never ever thought as a child that I would eventually have to use these in my life later on. But like I said, it's a blessing to be able to pass [on] those gifts. (Merasty, G. Cardinal, and Sawatsky 2013)

This excerpt from our conversation demonstrates how their community garden is drawing from historical practices of agriculture, from their territory, and from their people. Susan's words also relate to the principle of kiskinowâpamiwewin ᑭᖏᓄᐋᐸᒥᐍᐏᐣ, learning from observation and imitating someone's example. Susan learned from watching her kohkom ᑰᖓᒼ and kimosôm ᑭᒧᓯᒼ. Her kohkom also demonstrated a detailed method for keeping track of her own observations.

In Chapter 9, one of the norms discussed is emekinawet ᐁᒣᑭᓇᐍᐟ (gift-giving). This practice is intimately connected to establishing, maintaining, and restoring relationships. Different thoughtful examples of this practice are demonstrated in the community garden project. For example, Susan explained how important it is to follow protocol when harvesting and make sure to gift specific songs and tobacco to different nonhuman beings (for example, the plants). Len also told me how they have giveaways, for example to the Elders in the community (Merasty, G. Cardinal, and Sawatsky 2013). This practice of gifting and providing for the Elders is also found in numerous historical accounts, and can be seen as an important aspect of revitalizing the norms related to mâmawi-h-itêyihtamowin ᒫᒪᐃᐧᐦ ᐃᐟᐁᔨᐦᑕᒧᐃᐧᐣ (thinking about all). Ways in which the collective needs to be considered can come in the form of obligations: "Now, not only does the garden provide free vegetables to people in the Flying Dust First Nation, but there is enough surplus to sell" (Levy 2011). In 2017, the garden in Flying Dust donated two tonnes of potatoes to the Saskatoon Food Bank (Petrow 2017). Susan told me how, during their first year, "we just fed our people, basically ... We did make some money in sales, but our goal was to feed our

198 UPHOLDING INDIGENOUS ECONOMIC RELATIONSHIPS

people back here. And that's exactly what we did. And then we've continued to feed them every year since. So at the end of October or somewhere in October, we'll have a great big harvest fall that we try to make it an annual thing now" (Merasty, G. Cardinal, and Sawatsky 2013).

The gardening project is also part of the market economy, though this is balanced with principles of the giveaway. The harvest giveaways are a practice that used to happen regularly on the Flying Dust First Nation and are now being renewed – the principle of emekinawet ᐃᒣᑭᓇᐍᐟ. Susan says,

> I remember going to gatherings like that with my elder son. They put all their garden stuff together and what they had extra they gave away to other families that didn't have a garden for the season. I don't know if you remember that [to Gladys]. They used to gather a chair and dance after at night. We used to have a lot of fun [laughter]. We need to bring that back to our communities, the sharing and the giving and the caring. We seemed to have lost it here. It's a lot of work to bring it back but we're getting there. (Merasty, G. Cardinal, and Sawatsky 2013)

Susan acknowledges the loss of community values and principles. This is a result of the dual logics of settler colonialism – bureaucratic control and economic exploitation. Control comes in the form of forced systems of governance through the *Indian Act* and residential schools, for example, while economic exploitation comes through numerous impacts on traditional and reserve lands. Insidiously, through neoliberal governmentality, policies such as Treaty Land Entitlements and self-government negotiations can at first appear to be enabling "freedom" from the first settler-colonial logic and to be righting past injustices. However, upon further examination, these new policies uphold and increase settler colonialism by further embedding Indigenous peoples into the second colonial logic, economic exploitation. Through neoliberal governing policy and practices, Indigenous peoples can be implicitly or explicitly coerced into practices that may go against their teachings around responsibilities to more than human beings. These ruptured relationships create conflicts within communities, especially with those who are attempting to live with the land, not off it. These exploitive practices also negatively affect relationships with nonhuman beings that live on the land and in the water. Together, these practices create colonial dissonance for Cree people.

There are also examples, such as the community gardening project, of people renewing relationships with the land and of how this can be constitutive and can challenge the impacts of market citizenship. These acts of resistance are not total, but neither is neoliberal governmentality. Dene scholar Glen Coulthard (2014b, 172) provides an analysis of political-economic alternatives and the three ways in which these practices can disrupt capital accumulation on Indigenous lands:

> First, through mentorship and education these economies reconnect Indigenous people to land-based practices and forms of knowledge that emphasize radical sustainability. This form of grounded normativity is antithetical to capitalist accumulation. Second, these economic practices offer a means of subsistence that over time can help break our dependence on the capitalist market by cultivating self-sufficiency through the localized and sustainable production of core foods and life materials that we distribute and consume within our own communities on a regular basis. Third, through the application of Indigenous governance principles to non-traditional economic activities we open up a way of engaging in contemporary economic ventures in an Indigenous way that is better suited to foster sustainable economic decision-making, an equitable distribution of resources within and between Indigenous communities, Native women's political and economic emancipation, and empowerment for Indigenous citizens and workers who may or must pursue livelihoods in sectors of the economy outside of the bush.

Coulthard's (2014a, 172) analysis of "resurgent Indigenous economies" can be readily applied to Flying Dust's community gardening and harvesting practices. The gardeners and harvesters indicated the importance of education and mentorship during the interviews I conducted. The harvest provides alternative food sources for the community members involved, as well as for other community members who are gifted with the food. The cooperative model under which they work also implies a sustainable and equitable decision-making process. Cree women have been leaders and instigators in this process. The example of Flying Dust's community garden draws on Cree normative principles and practices, but also reinterprets them in original ways. It is too early to tell the long-term impact of these practices of resistance and renewal.

The ᐊᐧᐦᑯᐟᐅᐃᐧᐣ wâhkohtôwin Project Intensive: miyo-wîcêhtowin Principles and Practice

One of the main learnings I absorbed while writing this book is the importance of renewing good relations, especially with the land and with our nonhuman relations. The concept of symbiosis that Sunney shared with me (Sunney 2014b) is a lived reality when we "live *with* the land" (Ghostkeeper 2007). For those of us who do not live a completely subsistence-based life, it is still of extreme value to renew these relationships. This can be done in a myriad of ways, as the last two examples have demonstrated. These renewal practices provide a healing antidote to colonial dissonance.

From 2016 to 2018, I was involved in the ᐊᐧᐦᑯᐟᐅᐃᐧᐣ wâhkohtôwin and ᒥᔪ ᐁᐧᐟᐅᐃᐧᐣ miyo-wîcêhtowin Project: Pedagogy and Practice through Community and Academic Indigenous-Based Learning Collaborations (see Jobin et al. 2021). This project was a partnership between the University of Alberta and a Cree community. In the project's first twelve months, a team composed of community and university participants applied for funding to complete an on-the-land camp in Aseniwiche Winewak Nation Cree territory.[6] This for-credit university course provided community-led and university-led teaching in the Cree concepts of wâhkohtôwin and miyo-wîcêhtowin, and then community knowledge holders and Elders applied these concepts, teaching the students how to tan moose and elk hide at their hide-tanning camp in their community. We started the course in Treaty Six territory and then, through an established relationship, we took the course to the Aseniwiche Winewak Nation Cree community in the Rocky Mountains. This is from our 2021 article:

> The fifteen students enrolled in the course spent two full days in the classroom and four days in the community. Prior to and during the first two days on campus, students were required to read books and academic articles about Indigenous laws and governance as well as land-based learning. They listened to lectures, participated in classroom activities, and summarized a paper for a presentation. Once the students arrived at the camp, the community team took over instruction almost completely. For four days, students participated in hide tanning and other activities led by our community-based team of instructors. The students observed and experienced Cree law and governance principles in practice as the Elders and helpers led them through the process of brain-tanning a hide, from the first step to the final smoking. When

the students returned to campus, there was a half-day integration seminar, and they then wrote a final reflective paper, integrating their learning from both academic and community sources. (Jobin et al. 2021, 55)

This course was transformative for many of the Indigenous studies and law students who participated. It spoke to me of the importance of bringing the classroom to Indigenous territories and of having the land and the Indigenous ontology to create the pedagogy. Below are a few of the comments that a student shared from her student journal, which she has allowed me to share here:[7]

> I am so exhausted, on all levels. There was so much for us all to take in. It was a profoundly beautiful experience, all of it. It is a lot to process though because of how complex all of this learning is ... not necessarily the knowledge but the meaning it has to my life and my perception of my own identity as a Cree woman. I feel humbled by this experience. I loved watching the elders and knowledge keepers work on the hides. They made the process seem effortless, they scraped the hair as if it was butter. The sharing circle at the end was definitely the most profound part of the whole event for me. To see how much the experience touched everyone in so many ways, and to be a part of that was amazing. It was so nice to see a shared experience in so many others as well, to know that I am not alone, and to see so many tears showed me just how profound and transformational the experience was for us all, the laughter; always the laughter. So much has happened over the past few days ... so much knowledge gifted to us. I think it might take weeks before I have fully processed all that I have experienced. It really does feel like in some ways we are all family now – and these memories we have created will be what holds each other in our hearts for the years to come. I sincerely hope that this is just the beginning of a lifelong journey for all of us and we take what we learned to the rest of our lives. So grateful. ninanâskomon mistahi. (Native Studies Student)

This excerpt circles back to my belief that our relationships, including our relationship to the land, create and co-create our identities, individual and collective. This student talks about how participating in these practices renewed her identity as a Cree woman. The importance of establishing good relations was an important component of the experience. For Indigenous students, renewing these relationships was a very significant experience. It has been encouraging to see these relationships continue beyond the classroom. For example, students have continued to visit the community and participate in renewal events, like a Memorial Round Dance that happened in the fall of 2017. Students also started a group that could continue traditional hide-tanning on campus in the city of amiskwacîwâskahikan ᐊᒥᐢᐠᐧᐋᒌᐧᐋᐢᑲᐦᐃᑲᐣ (Beaver Hills House or Edmonton area).

Sharing Cree knowledge with non-Cree and non-Indigenous students was also seen as very valuable. One of the ways reconciliation can happen in truly meaningful ways is to have Canadians receive the gifts of knowledge that Indigenous peoples decide to present to them. Below is an excerpt from the journal of one of our non-Indigenous master's degree students; he is also an accountant:

> In many ways, practicing and learning traditional Cree hide tanning is a form of Indigenous resurgence, but I want to think about it here as explicitly destabilizing to the colonial establishment. Darcy Lindberg refers to the use of the "old tools" of hide tanning as a "form of resistance";[8] building on this, I think the hide scrapers and fleshers and sewing needles and water-wringing sticks we used in our weekend on the land can be viewed not only as tools that rebuild/reclaim Cree law, governance, culture, and so on, but also weapons in a fight against the colonial establishment.
>
> This idea of the tools as weapons could be unpacked in many ways, but I will just provide one example: the challenge traditional Cree hide tanning poses to capitalism. As an accountant, I think I am at least somewhat qualified to assert that it would be very difficult to economically rationalize the hide tanning process we learned. Presumably, however, literally no one has ever tried to prepare such a rationalization, because, of course, capitalist economics are not what the hide tanning process is about. The continued practice of traditional hide tanning at Susa Creek (and the participation of our class in learning the process) asserts that the colonial establishment's methods of cost accounting and profitability analysis are not the only way to assess value. (Master's student)

This experiential course, exploring Cree legal and governing concepts, was also able to destabilize the notion that capitalist economic principles and practices are the only economic system happening on the landscape. Through this pedagogy, Cree economic relationship principles based on miyo-pimâtisiwin ᒥᔪ ᐱᒫᑎᓯᐎᐣ (the good life) were experienced as a lived reality still happening in this community.

One question I get asked relates to scale. How do we translate these small initiatives into a large scale? My reflections through this work have me believe that part of upholding Indigenous economic relationships is to draw from Indigenous historical practices that were intentionally localized. Instead of thinking of macro initiatives, we should be thinking of networks of place-based economic endeavours. Our historic trade and trail networks could be re-engaged to facilitate regional and inter-nation knowledge exchange and trade of goods to sustain the livelihoods of all of our relations.

The tensions generated by colonial dissonance can ignite creative resistance among us as nehiyawak ᓀᐦᐃᔭᐘᐠ, and among other Indigenous peoples, too. Through the telling and retelling of stories, we remember the principles and practices of how to live miyo-pimâtisiwin ᒥᔪ ᐱᒫᑎᓯᐎᐣ. These principles are based in our languages and, by learning these core concepts, we uphold nehiyawak ᓀᐦᐃᔭᐘᐠ world view. Practices found in various ceremonies, like the different types of giveaways, provide important social, cultural, spiritual, and economic functions. There are also the different practices being engaged or reengaged to renew relations with the land, and to teach others how to do so as well. These "daily acts of resurgence"[9] (Corntassel 2012) are constitutive – they create, re-create, and renew who we are as individuals and who we are as peoples. They are social, cultural, political, legal, and economic acts of self-determination. They create different pathways forward.

11

Upholding Relations

IN THIS BOOK I NAME economic exploitation as the first and most enduring relationship between Indigenous peoples and settler society. This exploitation does many things, including limiting the options for miyo-pimâtisiwin ᒥᔪ ᐱᒫᑎᓯᐃᐧᐣ (the good life). Economic exploitation limits the options for providing livelihoods for a person's family and a people's community. When exploitation has ravaged the land and water, the options for food can appear as no option at all. It is in this spirit that I offer these words. We all live in our dissonance, as individuals and as communities. The problem with writing a book like this is that I have no desire to build walls; I believe, where possible, we achieve so much more through bridges. My words might not come across that way, but that is the spirit in which I hope to write.

I want to situate the normative principles in Chapter 9 in the importance of deliberative processes, explaining this as the governance of economic relations. I see deliberation as a cyclical process in which Cree normative principles are reasoned through, debated, and lived out. In the case of Indigenous societies today, there are competing interests at play that are in part a consequence of seemingly insurmountable pressures from economic exploitation. In the tensions resulting from colonial dissonance, it is vital for Cree peoples to find a way through these seemingly dichotomous positions. This requires continual dialogue and collective reflexivity regarding both the internal and external power dynamics at play. I believe in self-determination, with each Indigenous community deciding (ideally through processes like deliberation that are seen as legitimate to the people) what economic endeavours work for them given the different socio-political contexts they are in.

We have agency and responsibilities. The tensions arising from colonial dissonance can ignite creative resistance; in our oral stories, we unearth the Cree principles and practices to live out wâhkohtôwin ᐋ·ᐦᑯᐦᑐᐃ·ᓐ. We also continue to survive as nehiyawak ᓂ·ᐦᐃᔭᐊ·ᐠ, claim responsibility, take agency into our own hands, and innovate. Cree women like Susan and Gladys (see Chapter 10) are finding solutions and ways to live out wâhkohtôwin ᐋ·ᐦᑯᐦᑐᐃ·ᓐ by reinventing and reinvigorating Indigenous practices. Cree women like Dora and Connie (Chapters 7, 8, and 10) live out their responsibilities through annual communal ceremonial practices that follow the seasons to establish, renew, and restore relationships. Intellectual processes are also being engaged and reengaged. These "daily acts of resurgence" (Corntassel 2012) and practices of resistance may be obscured by the dissonance of living in late-capitalist settler society, but they are still important. They renew our relationships with each other, the land, the water, and other living beings. They transform. These acts create momentum; they provide important reminders and knowledge for individual and collective reflexivity, and ways to resist the constitutive effects of continual economic exploitation. Participating in these acts of resurgence is an antidote to colonial dissonance.

17 Beaded okinewâpikonew ᐅᑭᓂᐋ·ᐱᑯᓂ·ᐤ

With pimâcihowin ∧ᒐᑊᐅᐃᐧ, a model for economic livelihood, introduced in Chapter 1 with the metaphor of a beaded okinewâpikonew ᐅᑭᐅᐧᐣᐧᐁᐨᐅᐤ (see Figure 17), we uphold that all elements need to be considered and valued, and we acknowledge the inherent interconnections and interdependence of all beings. The economic sphere of society is not prioritized over the cultural, social, political, and legal spheres, and a livelihood economy may bring new life or resurgence to our living histories, ceremonial cycles, territories, and languages.

One of the benefits of this type of research is that it adds a distinctly different dimension to the conversation about Indigenous economic "development." I see the ethos of development, the idea of continued exponential growth, as part of the problem. However, my work seeks to go beyond critique and draws on Cree intellectual resources to provide a more situated understanding of both the critique and intellectual norms, as well as grounded practices embedded within our epistemologies that shed new light on economic relationships. Non-Indigenous societies are increasingly recognizing the pitfalls and gaps of unfettered capitalist logics. Indigenous societies that continue to draw on place-based knowledges situated within the historical and continuous relationships in their territories provide alternatives. I echo this sentiment: "This study has helped me in my quest to develop a renewed relationship with the timeless values and principles that have been kept alive for Western society by the very people Western society has tried to destroy" (Ghostkeeper 2007, 85).

I completed this study through a decolonization and resurgent methodology I refer to as the nehiyawak ᐅᑊᐃᕀᐋᐧ peoplehood methodology. Specifically, this research process is centred on Cree knowledge that encompasses the interlocking components in peoplehood: language, territory, ceremonial cycle, and living history. Peoplehood is also discussed in the literature as an Indigenous theoretical paradigm (as used in Chapter 1). This methodology can be drawn on by others, reframed, and centred on other Indigenous knowledges. My intervention in the field grounds a critique of economic exploitation in a Plains Cree context, while also providing understandings of Cree-centred resurgence. Although this book is focused on the Plains Cree, other Indigenous peoples may find useful the method of revitalizing Indigenous economic relationships by drawing from intellectual resources in their own society's world view and from their knowledge holders.

Since 2016, I have been able to take some of these resurgent research learnings and apply them to Indigenous community-led research on governance initiatives. By community-led I mean projects where the community has approached me or the teams I have worked in, and then we have collectively and collaboratively developed the process. I am especially interested in supporting the development of grounded resurgent methodologies and methods that draw on the strengths of an Indigenous community's own ontological and epistemological knowledges. I see an Indigenous resurgent methodology including the development of innovative Indigenous research methods, led by an Indigenous community (or communities), that honour and apply their Indigenous language(s), Indigenous lands, ceremonial cycles, and living histories in the research process while also meeting their applied research needs. The process of using an Indigenous resurgent research methodology and method(s) can revitalize place-based Indigenous languages, Indigenous lands, ceremonial cycles, and/or living histories (and other aspects of Indigenous societies) in the process, as well as the outcome. There are many Indigenous peoples leading this kind of work in ethical and meaningful ways.

When it comes to settler colonialism and economic exploitation, most scholars and the general populace tend to see only the tip of the iceberg – Indigenous economic relationships that fall within the capitalist lens. Those Indigenous practices that fall principally outside capitalism, such as ceremonial practices deemed to fit only within the spiritual realm, are seen as noneconomic. But governance and economic relationships are embedded in ceremonies of renewal. Settler colonialism makes silos of these different practices; by removing the blinders to recognize Cree economic relationships in everyday actions and in sublime practices, we witness acts of resurgence as strong antidotes to colonial dissonance. For example, giveaways can be seen as a Cree institution with spiritual, social, and economic functions. This Cree institution provides key insights into the collective world view, and a foundation for understanding Cree economic principles and practices.

I look at Plains Cree governance based on historical systems that predate the intrusion of the *Indian Act*. Exploring governance in this way creates a new old-way for thinking through self-determination, governing processes, and social organization, one that revitalizes kinship practices found in the core Cree concept of wâhkohtôwin ᐊᐦᑯᐦᑐᐃᐧ. Colonialism affects more than the mental, physical, spiritual, and emotional aspects of Cree people and Indigenous peoples; it ruptures all relationships on the territory – among people, nonhuman beings, and spirit beings. All aspects of Indigenous societies are impacted: social, cultural, political, legal, and economic. These ruptured relationships create colonial dissonance that affects all the relationships discussed in Chapter 7.

In that chapter I explained how Cree economic relationships based on the concept of wâhkohtôwin ᐚᐦᑰᐦᑑᐏᐣ surround distinct economic practices, whether a person or people are (1) establishing, (2) maintaining, or (3) restoring relationships, or (4) interacting in a conflicting relationship. These practices regulate relations not just between Cree people, but also among Cree people, non-Cree people, spirit beings, and nonhuman beings. For example, the ceremonial cycle, discussed as an integral part of peoplehood in Chapters 3 and 9, can be seen as both an instance of Cree practice and an act of resistance to market governance. The social, cultural, and political practices I introduce in Chapters 9 and 10, considered together, are examples of historical and contemporary acts of resistance. The redistribution of goods that occurs in the mâhtâhito ᒫᐦᑖᐦᐃᑐ and giveaway ceremonies, and the continuity of different ceremonies through each season, are also ways to maintain relationships in families, in community, with external guests, and with nonhuman beings, including land and territory. Each seasonal practice reasserts nehiyawak ᓀᐦᐃᔭᐘᐠ (Cree people) on their territory through practices of Cree governance that are apparent in the ceremonial cycles. These practices predate capitalism. Although purchased material goods might be involved, the way in which they are (re)distributed and the logics behind them are primarily non-capitalist. These practices are not privileging the capitalist market; they privilege relationships. nehiyawewin ᓀᐦᐃᔭᐍᐏᐣ is spoken during these events (although not exclusively), history and place are reasserted in the present, and responsibilities to territory and to land and nonhuman beings in the landscape and waterscape are lived out. During these events, all aspects of peoplehood are enacted – language, living histories, connection to territory, and ceremonial cycles. As Coulthard (2007, 456) writes, a critically "self-transformative process" takes the gaze off the state and moves it to the on-the-ground practices of resistance and freedom. Ceremonial practices – for example, the mâhtâhito ᒫᐦᑖᐦᐃᑐ (ceremony and seasonal ceremonies) – are continuously renewing relationships between people and with the land. The totality of these ceremonies, described by Sunney in Chapter 9 as ᑭᐢᑭᓄᐚᒋᐦᒋᑲᓇ (kiskinowâcihcikana), persists as modes of resistance and agency, and as enduring practices that continue in the face of economic exploitation.

As I started to write this final chapter, I was at a rustic log cabin in the heat of summer (2014). At the same time the year before, I was interviewing Cree knowledge holders in different locales within Treaty Six territory. It is now four years later (2018), and a winter storm has blanketed my surroundings in fresh snow. We live in renewal. Four years ago, in the fall, I was in a personal season of change, and I felt drawn to the North Saskatchewan River; these were my words:

> As I write and edit the final words of this dissertation, it is now late fall 2014. I am on my last writing retreat for this dissertation, sitting in a room above the North Saskatchewan River and watching the golden leaves in all of their end-of-life glory. The passing of this season also represents the ending of one season in my life and a transition to a new one. A few weeks ago I paddled down the North Saskatchewan River. I feel deeply connected to this river, and I remember that I am of the River People (sîpîwiyiniwak ᓰᐱᐃᐧᔨᓂᐊᐧᐠ). We have roles and responsibilities to this place and to this space. These roles and responsibilities include those with family and community, and they also include relations with non-Cree people, nonhuman beings, and spirit beings. As a people – together – we have resilience.

It is now 2018, and I feel inexplicably drawn to the forest. I do not have the teachings yet to understand this, but I trust that the teachers will come, as nehiyaw knowledge holders Dora, Sunney, Walter, Florence, Rob, Gladys, Susan, Sylvia, Gail, Sharlene, Paul, and Connie did; they also come as sîpiy ᓰᐱ and mistik ᒥᐢᑎᐠ. The canvas on which I have painted these words is damaged; however, there is such beauty within. Elder Maria Campbell has a story that is a powerful metaphor for the situation in which we live (Campbell 2017). When she was a young activist and single mother, an Elder of hers came to her house, and there was a completed jigsaw puzzle on the table. She asked the Elder about colonialism, and he threw the completed puzzle into the air. All the pieces were scattered. Under colonialism, we are living with these fractured pieces and relations. He shared that we all have to play our part to rebuild this puzzle. We create new relations and fix the broken ones. I believe we all have gifts to share, and with each

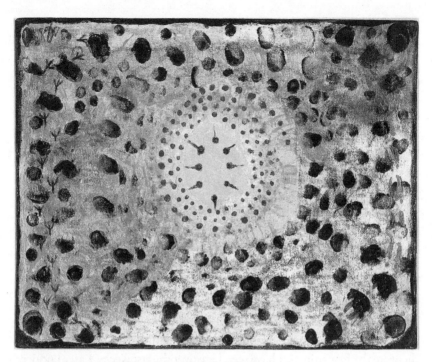

18 nihtâwihcikewin pîcicîwin: Creation's Round Dance

of us offering a puzzle piece, even while knowing we do not see the full picture, collectively we can rebuild.

It is mikisowipîsim ᒥᑭᓯᐘᐱᓯᒼ, the eagle moon (February 22, 2018), and I am writing these words from a cabin that the Cree architect Douglas Cardinal designed. A spiralling shell inspires the cabin on Buffalo Mountain. Cardinal's design statement on the wall explains how the "design takes the form of a spiralling shell that seems to grow out of the ground and wrap itself around the composer, like a sea shell around a sea-urchin, turning its back to the road and pathway." To reflect on this experience, my thinking in this book, and the creativity in this place, I decide to paint this piece called *nihtâwihcikewin pîcicîwin: Creation's Round Dance*.[1] The ahcâhk ᐊᐦᒐᕽ behind this is to show all the "foot" prints of different beings dancing in a Round Dance.

It is now niskipîsim ᓂᐢᑭᐱᓯᒼ, the goose moon (March 6, 2018), and I am finishing my writing retreat at Buffalo Mountain. Moments ago I was sitting on the small couch in the rounded cabin and smudging with sage and the last of a sweetgrass braid. There was what sounded like a rap at the door. At first I ignored the sound, as no one would visit me here, but it was

19 Deer tracks around the perimeter of the Douglas Cardinal studio.

so intrusive that I got up to look. There were two âpiscimôsisak ᐊᐱᒋᒧᓯᐢ (deer) that had come to visit me and were standing on my doorstep. We looked at each other for what felt like a minute. I literally wondered whether they were waiting to be invited in, so I started to open the door (now this makes me chuckle). They slowly walked around the front of the cabin where a large window is, and then they carried on with their day. Besides birds, these are the first animals I have seen here over the last weeks. Later I noticed the deer tracks around the rounded cabin; the tracks in the snow make it look like a Round Dance has occurred. Indigenous peoples have unique knowledges regarding living *with* this land (Ghostkeeper 2007). The animals and other beings have unique knowledges. Theirs are the stories that paint the landscape and waterscape. Canadian society will be coming to hear these stories and, I believe, one day good relations, *with all our relations*, will be lived out again. As each season changes, we experience renewal.

Postscript

I STRUGGLE WITH A FEW aspects of putting this book into the world. One is the permanence of the written word when I, as we all do, continue to learn; this can make putting something in print seem slightly incongruent. As well, orality is alive, and I am not fully reconciled to how oral communication can truly be transferred to the written page. Colonial dissonance around economic relationality is also a struggle. The seemingly insatiable hunger to buy can feel addictive; there is a sort of rush that comes with purchasing something. Capitalism, where we need a perpetual demand to ensure the continued production of goods and services, can create a state of addiction, individually and collectively. I currently exist in the colonial dissonance of living in spaces framed through a capitalistic lens; although there are always more economic relationships at work, capitalism is still hegemonic in practice and design. I feel addicted.

Our ways of relating are constitutive – they make and remake who each of us is as persons, and who we collectively are as peoples. The okinewâpikonew ᐅᐱᓄᐋᐧᐱᑯᓄ° (rose), which grounds the theoretical framework for this book, is more commonly called the wild rose and is the provincial flower of Alberta, one of the prairie provinces that include Plains Cree lands and peoples. One of the anonymous reviewers of this book commented how "in Alberta the wild rose is also used to symbolize white capitalism." I had not previously made this association with the okinewâpikonew ᐅᐱᓄᐋᐧᐱᑯᓄ°, but perhaps this is serendipitous. The work to reclaim the wild rose based on teachings embedded in the okinewâpikonew

ᐅᑭᓀᐚᐱᑯᓀᐤ can be seen as a microcosm of the work to reclaim economic relationality in a way that upholds all of our relationships.

It is opâskahopîsim ᐅᐹᐢᑲᐦᐅᐲᓯᒼ, egg hatching month (June 2022), and I am sitting in a hotel room in amiskwacîwâskahikan ᐊᒥᐢᑿᒋᐚᐢᑲᐦᐃᑲᐣ, looking over the bend in the kisiskâciwani-sîpiy ᑭᓯᐢᑳᒋᐘᓂ ᓰᐱᕀ, North Saskatchewan River. This river has been an important place of grounding for me over the ten years of writing this book. I love her. Sitting here, with this glorious view, it all feels so familiar. I am reflecting on all the changes that have happened in my life over the course of writing this book. I remember a writing retreat in a different hotel room a few blocks west, looking out at the same river in fall of 2014, and I knew there was a breaking of wichetowin ᐏᒉᐦᑐᐏᐣ with my ex. In Chapter 11, I said:

> As I write and edit the final words of this dissertation, it is now late fall 2014. I am on my last writing retreat for this dissertation, sitting in a room above the North Saskatchewan River and watching the golden leaves in all of their end-of-life glory. The passing of this season also represents the ending of one season in my life and a transition to a new one.

A handful of weeks after writing those words, I moved to a 410-square-foot bachelor pad, in the building next door to where I am sitting now. It was a small space where I could look down and see kisiskâciwani-sîpiy ᑭᓯᐢᑳᒋᐘᓂ ᓰᐱᕀ from my window – providing a healing and comforting presence in my new solitary life. Two seasons later, I moved to another small apartment looking at the bend in the river from the south side. Two seasons after that, I first met ninâpem ᓂᓈᐯᒼ Kevin. We later moved to an apartment with a northwest view of kisiskâciwani-sîpiy ᑭᓯᐢᑳᒋᐘᓂ ᓰᐱᕀ; I still wanted her healing. In 2018, we moved a half an hour north to a home with a backyard and a view to the trees; it is also good, but I miss seeing her every morning and every night. Since then, Kevin and I have made kin, through wâhkohtôwin ᐚᐦᑰᐦᑐᐏᐣ to a beautiful little boy with ties to the communities on both sides of my family (and a kohkom holding kinship to Kevin's community). His family and our family are now made-kin. wâhkohtôwin ᐚᐦᑰᐦᑐᐏᐣ.

> kahkiyaw niwâhkômâkanak ᑲᐦᑭᔭᐤ ᓂᐚᐦᑰᒫᑲᓇᐠ
> (all my relations)

Glossary of Cree Terms

THIS PLAINS CREE (Y dialect) glossary is drawn mostly from translations found in the *Online Cree Dictionary* (*nehiyaw masinahikan* ᐅᐦᐃᔪ ᒪᓯᓇᐦᐃᑲᐣ) at creedictionary.com, from my interviews with Cree knowledge holders, and from the quoted material I include in this book. I try to be consistent in spelling, but as Cree is developing in terms of standard roman orthography, this has proven difficult. Dorothy Thunder has edited my spellings for consistency. I rely on the reference materials in the dictionary listed above; however, I have retained spelling as is within quoted material, even if it does not match the dictionary spelling. Correspondingly, the spelling in quoted material may be different from the way I spell the same word throughout the rest of the book.

achakosis	ᐊᒡᐦᐁᑯᐢᐣ	little star
ahcâhk	ᐊᐦᒑᐦᐠ	our spirit on this earth
amiskowacîwiyiniwak	ᐊᒥᐢᑯᐊᐧᒌᐃᐧᔨᓂᐊᐧᐠ	the Beaver Hills Cree People
amiskwacîwâskahikan	ᐊᒥᐢᑲᐧᒌᐋᐧᐢᑲᐦᐃᑲᐣ	Beaver Hills (or Mountain) House (Edmonton)
âpiscimôsisak	ᐋᐱᐢᒋᒨᓯᓴᐠ	deer (plural)
asiskîy	ᐊᓯᐢᑮᕁ	all the roots under there
askîy	ᐊᐢᑮᕁ	land, earth, world, country
ayîkis	ᐊᔩᑭᐢ	frog

cahkipehikanak	ᒐᐦᑭᐯᐦᐃᑲᐣᓇᐠ	the Star Chart Method: encompassing forty-four syllabic symbols and fourteen consonant syllabic symbols
cimâks	ᒋᒫᐠᐢ	(diminutive form) poverty or being poor (see also kicimâkânês)
ehokwemeyahk	ᐁᐦᐅᑫᐧᒣᔭᕽ	related to the word okwêmêsiw ᐅᑫᐧᒣᓯᐤ, to have the same name
emekinawet	ᐃᒣᑭᓇᐍᐟ	gift-giving
êsa	ᐁᓴ	abalone shell
itâtisiwin	ᐃᑖᑎᓯᐏᐣ	their own nature, conduct, behaviour
iteyimikosiwiyecikewina	ᐃᑌᔨᒥᑯᓯᐑᔦᒋᑫᐏᓇ	treaties inspired by our Creator
îyinewiwin	ᐄᔨᓀᐏᐏᐣ	being human
iyiniwaskamkohk	ᐃᔨᓂᐗᐢᑲᒼᑯᕽ	it is a healing land
kâ-ohpawakâstahk	ᑳ ᐅᐦᐸᐘᑳᐢᑕᕽ	Flying Dust First Nation
kahkiyaw kâwâhkôhtowak	ᑲᐦᑭᔭ ᑲᐘᐦᑐᐘᐠ	we are all relatives
kahkiyaw niwâhkômâkanak	ᑲᐦᑭᔭᐤ ᓂᐚᐦᑰᒫᑲᓇᐠ	all my relations
kakêskihkemowina	ᑲᑫᐢᑭᐦᑫᒧᐏᓇ	teachings
kamiyokisihkwew	ᑲᒥᔪᑭᓯᐦᑵᐤ	Fine Day, a Plains Cree war leader of the sîpîwiyiniwak ᓰᐲᐏᔨᓂᐘᐠ
kanawâpamew	ᑲᓇᐚᐸᒣᐤ	look at them, observe them
kasispowicikew	ᑲᓯᐢᐳᐏᒋᑫᐤ	bringing the past to the future, west (direction)
kayâsês	ᑲᔮᓭᐢ	long ago
kicimâkânês	ᑭᒋᒫᑳᓀᐢ	poverty or being poor (see also cimâks ᒋᒫᐠᐢ)
kimosôm	ᑭᒧᓲᒼ	your grandfather
kinikinik	ᑭᓂᑭᓂᐠ	tobacco
kisê-manitow	ᑭᓭᒪᓂᑐᐤ	Creator/Great Spirit
kisêwâtisiwin	ᑭᓭᐚᑎᓯᐏᐣ	the capacity to be kind
kisiskâciwani-sîpiy	ᑭᓯᐢᑳᒋᐘᓂ ᓰᐱᕀ	swift-flowing river

kiskinowâcihcikan	ᑭᓄᐳᐊᐧᐦᐦᐸ	ceremony
kiskinowâcihcikana	ᑭᓄᐳᐊᐧᐦᐦᐸ	ceremonies
kiskinowâpahtam	ᑭᓄᐳᐊᐧᐸᐦᐸᐦ	to learn by watching something
kiskinowâpamêw	ᑭᓄᐳᐊᐧᐸᑌᐤ	describes when you learn from observing someone or imitating someone's tactics or example
kiskinowâpamiwewin	ᑭᓄᐳᐊᐧᐸᑌᐁᐊᐧᐃᐧ	learning through observation
kitatamihin	ᑭᐦᐦᑌᐦᐊᐧᐃ	I thank you
kohkom	ᑯᐦᑯᐦ	your grandmother
kôsisim	ᑯᓯᐦ	your grandson
mâhtâhito	ᒫᐦᐦᐊᐧᐅ	(diminutive form) gifts exchanged are a blessing; specific type of give-away ceremony
mâhtâhitowin	ᒫᐦᐦᐊᐧᐅᐊᐧᐃᐧ	gifts exchanged are a blessing; specific type of giveaway ceremony
mâmawi-h-itêyihtamowin	ᒫᒪᐊᐧᐦ ᐊᐅᐸᐦᐦᐊᐧᐃᐧ	thinking about all
mâmawi-wîcihitowin	ᒫᒪᐊᐧ ᐊᐧᐦᐦᐊᐧᐅᐊᐧᐃᐧ	to all help together, general cooperation
mâmihkiyiniwak	ᒫᐦᐦᑭᔭᓄᐊᐧᐤ	the Downstream People
manâtisiwin	ᒪᐊᓄᔭᐊᐧᐃᐧ	civility, showing respect to all of creation, creation
manitô sâkahikan	ᒪᓄᐅ ᓴᐦᐦᐊᐧᐸ	Creator's Lake or Lake of the Spirit
manitowan	ᒪᐅᐊᐧᐃᐧ	the spiritual
maskamina	ᒪᐦᐦᑲᓄᐊ	red rosehip berries
mekinawewin	ᑌᐸᐊᐧᐁᐊᐧᐃᐧ	gift from a higher power
mekiwin	ᑌᐸᐊᐧᐃᐧ	gift
mêmêkwêsiw	ᑌᑌᐊᐧᔭᐤ	a little person
mêmêkwêsiwak	ᑌᑌᐊᐧᔭᐊᐧᐤ	the little people
mihkwâpemakwa ka pihtwâtamihk (kinnikinnick)	ᒥᐦᐦᑲᐊᐧᐸᑲᐊᐧ ᑲ ᐱᐦᐦᐦᐊᐧᑕᒥᐦᐦᐠ ᑭᓄᑭᓄᐤ	tobacco (see also kinikinik ᑭᓄᑭᓄᐤ)
mikisowipîsim	ᒥᑭᐊᓄᐊᐧᐸᔭᐊᐧᐦᐦ	the eagle moon
miskinâhk ministik	ᒥᓄᐸᐸᐦᐠ ᒥᓄᐦᐦᑎᐤ	Turtle Island

GLOSSARY OF CREE TERMS 217

mistasiniy	ᒥᐢᑕᓯᓂᐩ	Big Rock, a large rock in the Qu'Appelle Valley in the shape of a buffalo
mistik	ᒥᐢᑎᐠ	tree
mistikwak	ᒥᐢᑎᐠᐘᐠ	trees
miyo-pimâtisiwin	ᒥᔪ ᐱᒫᑎᓯᐃᐧᐣ	the good life
miyo-wîcihitowin	ᒥᔪ ᐤᐄᒋᐦᐃᑐᐃᐧᐣ	living in harmony together, good relations, good relationships
miyohtwâwin	ᒥᔪᐦᑖᐃᐧᐣ	kindness
mônah-asiskiya	ᒧᓇᐦᐊ ᐊᓯᐢᑮᕀ	to dig at the dirt
mônaha	ᒧᓇᐦᐊ	to dig
môniyâwi-cistêmâw	ᒧᓂᔭᐃᐧ ᒋᐢᑌᒫᐤ	white-man's tobacco, trade tobacco
môsihowin	ᒧᓯᐦᐅᐃᐧᐣ	emotions
môsomin	ᒧᓱᒥᐣ	Moosomin Cree First Nation
mwâc esakapayikini	ᒖᐨ ᐁᓴᑲᐸᕀᑭᓂ	jurisdiction within each nation's sphere of influence
nâcinêhikêw	ᐋᒋᓀᐦᐃᑫᐤ	"s/he gets spiritual help, assistance or counselling (from s.o.) by offering appropriate gifts or payment" (Wolvengrey 2011)
nâcinehikewin	ᐋᒋᓀᐦᐃᑫᐃᐧᐣ	protocol and proper procedures
nahiskamowin	ᓇᐦᐃᐢᑲᒧᐃᐧᐣ	the ability to be adaptable
nahiskamowina	ᓇᐦᐃᐢᑲᒧᐃᐧᓇ	acts of adaptability
natimîwiyiniwak	ᓇᑎᒦᐃᐧᔨᓂᐊᐧᐠ	the Upstream People
natopayiw	ᓇᑐᐸᕀᐤ	scout
nehiyaw	ᓀᐦᐃᔭᐤ	Cree person
nehiyaw iskwew	ᓀᐦᐃᔭᐤ ᐃᐢᑫᐧᐤ	Cree woman
nehiyaw kiskeyihtamowin	ᓀᐦᐃᔭᐤ ᑭᐢᑫᐧᔨᐦᑕᒧᐃᐧᐣ	Cree epistemology
nehiyaw masinahikan	ᓀᐦᐃᔭᐤ ᒪᓯᓇᐦᐃᑲᐣ	Online Cree Dictionary
nehiyawak	ᓀᐦᐃᔭᐊᐧᐠ	the Cree People/Cree peoplehood
nehiyawaskiy/ nehiyaw-askiy	ᓀᐦᐃᔭᐊᐧᐢᑮᕀ	Cree territory
nehiyawewin	ᓀᐦᐃᔭᐁᐧᐃᐧᐣ	the Cree language

218   GLOSSARY OF CREE TERMS

nehiyâwiwin	ᑐᵘᐧᐰᐁᐧᐁᐧᐃᐧ	"Creeness"
newo	ᑐᐅᐧ	four
nicâpân	ᓯᒳᐸᐧ	my great-grandparent
nihtâwihcikewin	ᓯᵘᒡᐃᐧᵘᕈᕀᐁᐧ	Creation
nikâwiy	ᓯᐱᐁᐧ	my mother
nikosisinân	ᓯᒜᔲᒌᐧ	our son
nimosôm	ᓯᒍᔭᐨ	my grandfather, grand uncle
ninâpêm	ᓯᐅᐧᐯᐨ	my husband
nipâhkwesimowin	ᓯᐸᵘᕠᐧᐧᒍᐃᐧ	the Sun Dance (Nee-pah-quah-see-mun), described as "dancing through a day and night without quenching one's thirst" (Paget 2004, 5)
niskipîsim	ᓯᐣᕒᐱᔲᐨ	the goose moon
nohkom	ᗬᵘᑫᐨ	my grandmother
nôsisim	ᐉᒜᔲᐨ	grandchild, my grandchild
ohci	ᐅᵘ ᕑ	from there, from
ohcinewin	ᐅᵘᕑᑐᐁᐧ	transgressions against nonhuman beings
okâwîmâwaskiy	ᐅᐱᐃᐧᐧᐯᐃᐧᕒ᠊ᐣᕀ	Mother Earth
okihcihtâw	ᐅᕒᵘᕑᵘᒼᐤ	warrior
okihcitâwiskwêwak	ᐅᕒᵘᕑᵘᒼᐤ ᐃᐣᕈᐧᐧᐄ	Cree woman's society
okimâw miyo-wîcihitowiyicikewin	ᐅᕒᐱᗝ ᕑᐁᑦ ᐊᐧᕑᐃᐧᐊᐧᐃᐧᕒᕈᕀᐁᐧ	an agreement to organize good relations between sovereigns
okinewâpikonew	ᐅᕒᑐᐧᐊᐧᐃᐧᐊᐧᐣᑐᐤ	rose
opâskahopîsim	ᐅᒳᕀᐤᑲᵘᐉᐱᔲᐨ	egg hatching month
oskâpêwis	ᐅᕀᐱᐃᐧᐨ	helpers
	ᒳᵘᐱᐨᕀ	Skinny Man, the hard luck spirit
paskohkopâwiyiniwak	ᒳᕀᐪᵘᐪᐸᐧᐊᐧᕀᓯᐊᐧᐄ	the Parklands People
paskwâw mostoswak	ᒳᕀᐱᐧᐤ ᒍᐣᑐᕀᐧᐄ	buffalo
paskwâwiyiniw	ᒳᕀᐱᐃᐧᐊᐧᓯᐤ	the Plains Cree People
pâstâhowin	ᐧᕀᒡᵘᐊᐧᐃᐧᐧ	transgression, breaking of the natural order
pawâmiwin	ᐧᐊᐧᕑᐃᐧᐧ	dream power
pêhonân/pehonan	ᐁᵛᵘᐅᐧᐱᐧ	gathering place

picikwâs	ᐱᒋᑳᐧᐢ	apple
pihtikwe	ᐱᐦᑎᑫᐧ	enter, come in
pimâcihisowin	ᐱᒫᒋᐦᐃᓱᐃᐧᐣ	making one's own living
pimâcihowin	ᐱᒫᒋᐦᐅᐃᐧᐣ	the ability to make a good living
pimâtisiwin	ᐱᒫᑎᓯᐃᐧᐣ	the act of living, life
pipon	ᐱᐳᐣ	winter
sakâwiyiniwak	ᓴᑳᐃᐧᔨᓂᐊᐧᐠ	Northern Plains Cree People
sihci-wâhkohtôwin	ᓯᐦᒋ ᐋᐧᐦᑰᐦᑐᐃᐧᐣ	your own immediate clan, your own bloodline
sîpîwiyiniwak	ᓰᐲᐃᐧᔨᓂᐊᐧᐠ	the River Cree People
tapahtêyimisowin	ᑕᐸᐦᑌᔨᒥᓱᐃᐧᐣ	humility
tipahamitowin	ᑎᐸᐦᐊᒥᑐᐃᐧᐣ	treating each other commensurately
tipêyihcikêwin	ᑎᐯᔨᐦᒋᑫᐃᐧᐣ	ownership, "is viewed as a gift of collective stewardship for Mother Earth, a living being, from The Great Spirit (*Kechi Manitow*)" (Ghostkeeper 2007, 79)
tipiyawêwisowin	ᑎᐱᔭᐁᐧᐃᐧᓱᐃᐧᐣ	self-sufficiency
wâhkohtôwin	ᐋᐧᐦᑰᐦᑐᐃᐧᐣ	the normative principles guiding relationships
wâpanacâhkos	ᐋᐧᐸᓇᒑᐦᑯᐢ	stars, the celestial bodies, the morning star
wâpayôminak	ᐋᐧᐸᔫᒥᓇᐠ	rice
wâskahikaniwiyiniwak	ᐋᐧᐢᑲᐦᐃᑲᓂᐃᐧᔨᓂᐊᐧᐠ	House Cree People/House People of the Plains Cree
wawiyatâcimowina	ᐊᐧᐃᐧᔭᑖᒋᒧᐃᐧᓇ	a genre of funny stories in Cree
wîhkask	ᐄᐧᐦᑲᐢᐠ	sweetgrass
wîhkohtowin	ᐄᐧᐦᑯᐦᑐᐃᐧᐣ	big feast
wihtikow	ᐃᐧᐦᑎᑯᐤ	a greedy person
wîsahkecâhk	ᐄᐧᓵᐦᑫᒑᕽ	the Cree cultural hero who is a principal character in many Cree stories
wîtaskewin	ᐄᐧᑕᐢᑫᐃᐧᐣ	a peace treaty

Notes

Chapter 1: Grounding Methods

1 I have three middle names. Charlotte acknowledges my paternal grandmother and Wuttunee my family name on my maternal side.

2 The proper way to refer to one's mother's brother is nisis ᓂᓯᐢ; however, the fact of my father's death and my uncle's father-like guidance and role in my life makes "little father" a more appropriate description.

3 Zapotec scholar Isabel Altamirano-Jiménez first introduced me to the concept of waterscape.

4 Renée Beausoleil and I came up with this visual as a way to explain concepts like ontology, epistemology, methodology, and methods at a community workshop we were teaching.

5 According to Okimāsis and Wolvengrey (2008, 5):

> One of the overriding principles in the design of the SRO is to have a single symbol for each important sound of the Cree sound system. Using both upper and lower case symbols, leading to two distinct spellings for many if not all words, would defeat the purpose. In an attempt to adhere to the original principle and minimize the number of spelling rules, a very simple solution is possible: no capitalization is ever used in writing in Cree.

The only exception to this is in the title of this book, which conforms to the capitalization guidelines of foreign titles found in the *Chicago Manual of Style*. As a personal note, I do appreciate the capitalization of an Indigenous people as a statement of nationhood.

6 We drew on information in Milloy (1990), including Maps 1 and 2.

7 Grounded theory includes the gathering of information and knowledge (sometimes called "data"), where the analysis and development of theories comes after you have gathered the information – the theory is then "grounded" in the

knowledge itself. For further reading, see Hutchison, L. Johnston, and Breckon (2010).

8 A snowball technique is a method for finding research subjects in which one participant gives the names of other potential participants, who in turn provide more names (Miller and Brewer 2003, 275).

9 The Federation of Sovereign Indigenous Nations was formerly known as the Federation of Saskatchewan Indian Nations.

10 Belcourt (2007, 61) explains some of the medicinal uses of the rose by prairie Indigenous peoples: "The roots can be used as cold and fever remedies, and they also treat diarrhea and liver and stomach problems. They are also good for infections, colds, sore throats, and for cleansing toxins from the body. The petals in the tea are a good heart tonic."

11 I draw from Kiera Ladner's (2003a) use of "AlterNative," understandings of Indigenous peoples based on their own sociopolitical systems.

Chapter 2: Grounding Economic Relationships

1 Cree scholars Gina Starblanket and Dallas Hunt (2020, 105–6) call the logic needed to come to such a decision as "settler reason": in settler colonialism certain bodies, for example, white men, possess reason where other bodies, like Indigenous people, are excluded; if they transgress what is deemed "reasonable," then they will be met with immediate sanctioned violence.

2 I recognize that all people are holders of knowledge. One of the roles of a researcher is to gather specific holders of knowledge related to an inquiry, using the proper ethical process, and present their knowledge in ethical and informative ways.

3 I draw from Robert Nichols's idea of categorizing different modes of settler colonialism. For example, he explains two modes of settler-colonial governmentality as "the strategies of 'ordering-taxonomizing particularity' and 'difference-blind universalizing,'" using the example of enfranchisement of Indigenous peoples and nations as a "political technology of assimilation" (Nichols 2014, 105–7).

4 I use the term "Indigenous" to refer to Métis peoples, Inuit peoples, and First Nations peoples. I use the term "Aboriginal" to refer to the identities and relationships entrenched in Section 35 of the *Constitution Act, 1982*, which defines "Aboriginal" as Métis, Inuit, and Indian. I use "Metis" or "Métis" depending on how the collective to which I am referring spells it. For example, it is Metis Settlements of Alberta, but the Métis Nation of Alberta.

5 Although I see external social indicators as important to demonstrating the uneven development path under capitalism, it is also important to analyze critically the impact of external social indicators such as those related to quality of life. For example, Finley-Brook (2011, 347) argues that "economic parity is an externally defined benchmark that may often require mainstreaming and integration."

6 Frank Tough (2005, 54) writes that economic exploitation preceded political oppression for Indigenous peoples in Canada.

7 In the staples theory, the core (e.g., Britain) dominates the periphery or hinterland (e.g., Canada during the fur-trade era): export of different staples shapes the regional economy's development and its increasing dependency on the core (R.B. Anderson 1998, 36; Innis 1999).

8 I use the term "buffalo" instead of "bison" as this is the commonly used term historically and contemporarily.

9 Moore's (1993) analysis focuses solely on the economic factor, arguing that neither religion, culture, nor ethnicity formed the conflict (15).

10 There are distinct categories of Indigenous lands as defined by the Canadian state (e.g., reserve lands, treaty lands, Aboriginal title lands).

11 Although I connect this literature to CIPE, the scholars referenced might or might not define their work similarly.

12 When I speak of relationships with the land, this is not simply an attachment to land but "a space of ontological relationships among people and between people and their environments" (Altamirano-Jiménez 2013, 43).

13 This is what I heard when I sat in the Battleford courtroom during the trial. This is also corroborated in a CBC News article (Quenneville 2018).

Chapter 3: nehiyawak Peoplehood and Relationality

Parts of this chapter were previously published in Shalene Jobin, "Cree Peoplehood, International Trade, and Diplomacy," *Revue Générale de Droit* 43, 2 (2013): 599–636.

1 nisikos is of the kitchenuhmaykoosib inninuwug. She is closely connected to her culture and is a fluent speaker of anishnabamowin. Laura is committed to the promotion and protection of all sacred living things.

2 I locate this research within the geographic region of the Canadian plains, and for this study I look at the Plains Cree. It is beyond the scope of this chapter to explore how my findings compare with those among Cree people living in other geographic regions.

3 In Robert Innes's innovative book, he shows the complexity of Cree identity on the Plains. His analysis focuses on the Downstream People, specifically the Cowessess First Nation, compared to my analysis related to the Upstream People. Based on his analysis, he shows the multicultural nature of Cowessess – how they included Plains Cree, Saulteaux, Assiniboine, Métis, and other cultural groups (Innes 2013, 7). The importance of kinship responsibilities was paramount, and these non-Cree members of this First Nation helped to solidify alliances. This kinship rationality has continued to assist with relationships and responsibilities to those members disenfranchised as a result of different settler-colonial policies (Innes 2013).

4 I struggle with how to include this in a written format compared to seasonal retelling in oral histories. I let you, the reader, know when I share these stories to give you the oppourtunity to follow this teaching.

5 I use the term "trade," but this is not to be confused with buying in a monetary system.

6 In an interview on August 9, 1934, on Sweetgrass First Nation, Fine Day told Mandelbaum: "One group of ogihtcitau couldn't give the dance of another bunch unless they bought it. A long time ago the Stonies bought the Rattler's tipi from the Cree" (Fine Day 1934).

7 muskwa is spelled "Maskwa" in Mandelbaum's text.

8 This excerpt and wîsahkecâhk story was previously published in Jobin (2016).

Chapter 4: Canada's Genesis Story

1 Frank Tough (2005, 524) writes that economic exploitation preceded political oppression for Indigenous peoples in Canada.

2 Political geographer and Indigenous studies scholar Frank Tough (2018, 2) writes: "In the Rupertsland Order the Crown accepted the surrender of Rupertsland from the HBC and then transferred Rupertsland and the North-Western Territory to the Dominion of Canada ... The Hudson's Bay Company Territory was one of the largest territorial entities in the British Empire and it is equivalent to 63.5 percent of present-day Canada's total land mass."

3 Big Bear was selected as a Chief in 1865. Cree legal and treaty scholar Sharon Venne (1998, 198) writes that initially his following was small, but near the end of his life his camp was one of the largest. Significantly, Big Bear was not invited to the original Treaty Six negotiations. Venne gives numerous reasons for this, including government representatives' fear of Big Bear's influence, as well as the fact that he did not subscribe to the Christian faith and therefore was not being influenced by priests, who were said to have been "active in trying to persuade the Indigenous peoples to accept less in negotiations."

4 "Enfranchisement is a legal process for terminating a person's Indian status and conferring full Canadian citizenship. Enfranchisement was a key feature of the Canadian federal government's assimilation policies regarding Aboriginal peoples" (Crey n.d.).

5 The enforcement of a Euro-representative, democratic, municipal style of government under the *Indian Act* also fundamentally affected Indigenous governing systems. For an early discussion of this, see MacInnes (1946, 392–93).

6 My great-great-grandfather, Old Wuttunee, was our last Chief before the *Indian Act* system came into effect. When reserve life was on the horizon, he asked his brother Red Pheasant to become Chief of our people.

Chapter 5: Δ·"∩dᵒ Warnings of Insatiable Greed

Parts of this chapter were originally published in Jobin (2020).

1 "The Government of Canada's Approach to Implementation of the Inherent Right and the Negotiation of Aboriginal Self-Government" states that "the Government of Canada recognizes the inherent right of self-government as an existing Aboriginal right under section 35 of the Constitution Act, 1982" (Canada n.d.).

2 For example, Status Indians did not have the right to vote until 1960 (*An Act to Amend the Canada Elections Act*, S.C. 1960, c. 7, s. 1.).

3 I have "citizenship" in quotation marks as First Nations were not considered citizens; they were seen as wards of the state.

4 Indigenous legal scholar James (Sákéj) Youngblood Henderson (2000, 425–40) critiques federal citizenship for Aboriginals as ignoring *sui generis* rights. He argues that the offer of citizenship to Aboriginal peoples is another attempt to assuage the colonial conscience, and that it "subverts the constitutional rights of Aboriginal peoples for the interests of the dominant immigrant groups" (416). Different from Canada's hollow offer of citizenship, Indigenous peoples are developing an "alternative pluralism"; treaty citizenship is said to preserve Indigenous

heritage while enabling "authentic options and life choices" (422). According to Youngblood Henderson, treaty citizenship requires constitutional space for public discourse (433).

5 For example, Canada's $200-million *Federal Framework for Aboriginal Economic Development* is an example of this triangulation. The *Framework* report highlights resource development as a major "win" for Indigenous peoples, identifying "over $315 billion in major resource developments" in or near Aboriginal communities. Additionally, in the North, the mining and oil and gas sectors have "proposed developments in the range of $24 billion that will impact Aboriginal communities in the next decade" (Canada 2009, 9).

6 For example, a 2012 federal policy paper states: "Canada's funding of self-government arrangements will be offset by a portion of the capacity of the Aboriginal group to generate its own source revenues. This offset will be phased in over time leading to a gradual reduction of reliance on federal funding and greater self-sufficiency" (Aboriginal Affairs and Northern Development Canada 2012, 6).

7 In Ghostkeeper's book, he uses the spelling Metis instead of Métis.

8 Chapters 5 to 7 provide examples grounded in nehiyâwiwin ᐅᐦᒋᐸᐟᐃᓯ (Creeness).

Chapter 6: Indigenous Women's Land and Bodies

1 For example, *The Final Report of the Truth and Reconciliation Commission of Canada*, Volume 5, is titled *Canada's Residential Schools: The Legacy*. It states, "The closing of residential schools did not bring their story to an end. The legacy of the schools continues to this day. It is reflected in the significant educational, income, and health disparities between Aboriginal people and other Canadians – disparities that condemn many Aboriginal people to shorter, poorer, and more troubled lives. The legacy is also reflected in the intense racism some people harbour against Aboriginal people and the systemic and other forms of discrimination Aboriginal people regularly experience in Canada. Over a century of cultural genocide has left most Aboriginal languages on the verge of extinction. The disproportionate apprehension of Aboriginal children by child welfare agencies and the disproportionate imprisonment and victimization of Aboriginal people are all part of the legacy of the way that Aboriginal children were treated in residential schools" (Truth and Reconciliation Commission 2015, 3).

2 This is not to say that there was not also agency for Indigenous peoples during the fur-trade era.

3 kitatamihin to Dr. Tracy Bear for sharing her thoughts on this disposable logic.

4 For example, "in May 2004, a former British Columbia Provincial Court judge, David William Ramsey, pleaded guilty to buying sex from and assaulting four Indigenous girls, aged 12, 14, 15 and 16, who had appeared before him in court. The crimes were committed between 1992 and 2001. In June, the former judge was sentenced to seven years in prison" (Amnesty International 2004, 24).

5 For Kim Anderson (2000, 18), the reconstruction of Native womanhood will happen through the processes of individual resistance, reclamation, reconstruction, and action.

Chapter 7: Theorizing Cree Economic and Governing Relationships

1 I used the term "archives" in a broad sense, not as items recalled from a physical, designated archive building. I draw from the *Oxford English Dictionary* definition: "a collection of historical documents or records providing information about a place, institution, or group of people."

2 See Shiva (2005) for a discussion of nature's economy, the sustenance economy, and the capitalist economy.

3 For the purpose of this corner of my broader research project, I am using grounded theory with the intent to have the principles and practices emerge from the stories. I therefore do not engage with other scholars' writings on Indigenous economies in this chapter. I engaged with the secondary literature on Indigenous economies and the important work scholars have already completed in Chapters 1–6. Although these chapters come first in the book, they actually occurred after the grounded theory and interviews in the research process.

4 All of the people I interview for this chapter have pseudonyms; this was at the request of two of the Elders, and the rest of the people agreed to this practice. One person interviewed did not want his/her workplace connected with some of the critiques he/she was making of certain economic practices.

5 I could not find this term in the Cree dictionary. Dorothy Thunder explained to me that it is related to the word okwêmêsiw ᐅᖏᒣᓯᐤ, meaning to be named after or to have the same name.

6 I characterize the stories based on a typology of different types of stories, which was part of my coding process. For example, wawiyatâcimowina ᐚᐁᐧᔭᒉᒪᐃᐧᓇ are a genre of funny stories in Cree. By describing this as a "legend," I in no way mean to demean the type of knowledge found in legends. If anything, I am attempting to display its legitimacy on its own terms.

7 I use the spelling as in Ahenakew's (1995b) account.

8 For information on the Indigenous Law Research Unit (ILRU), see https://ilru.ca.

9 In this example, Chief Thunderchild's father did nothing wrong but was asked to bring the peace offering. Ê-pay-as listened and responded in kind.

10 Walter shared an experience with me where his deceased father came to him in his sleep:

> A couple of times when I was driving home from Prince Albert to Saskatoon, which is about 85 miles, it was about 30 below. I was so tired and feeling sick. It was late at night. I was falling asleep as I was driving. I fell asleep two or three times. I turned the heat up in the car and then I'd fall asleep. Dad would come wake me up and he said: "Son, you can't sleep here. You got to get home." "I'm sorry, Dad," I said. I'd try to stay awake. Five minutes later I'd be falling asleep. I'd have to pull over again. On the third time I did that, he drove the car for the last 50 miles, and when I woke up we were just pulling into my house in Saskatoon. I said, "You know, Dad, I'm really sorry that you had to take all that time to drive me all the way home." But he drove me

all the way home, which took about an hour, or maybe 45 minutes out of his time. Maybe an hour out of his time. (Walter 2014a)

11 *Merriam-Webster Dictionary* defines "institution" as "a significant practice, relationship, or organization in a society or culture," https://www.merriam-webster.com/dictionary/institution.

12 Spelled "mite-wiwin" in Mandelbaum's text.

13 This was the name the Plains people gave Welsh when they first met. It meant "the Turned-Up-Nose" (Welsh as told to Weekes 1994, 18).

14 "These tiny people had mysterious powers and often played tricks on the Indians. Hence, every time anything peculiar happened, they attributed it to the May-may-quay-she-wuk" (Brass and Nanooch 1978a).

15 Connie also explained an experience she had with the little people; they came to her after the death of a loved one.

Chapter 8: Colonial Dissonance

1 It is important to also acknowledge the huge loss of life from the global pandemic, ongoing since 2020. There is a need for a socio-political examination of how certain peoples, like Indigenous peoples, are being impacted, and the lack of resources some of these nations are being afforded.

2 In this paragraph I try to use much of the same phrasing as the report in terms of the specific legal principles they name, as their word choice is quite deliberate.

Chapter 9: Principles Guiding Cree Economic Relationships

1 Part of this process is to examine how Cree economic relationships have been and can be more fully reengaged, even within the confines and pressures exerted by nation-states like Canada. Today, Cree economic relationships are often embedded in a landscape in which Canadian state governance and policy reigns.

2 Governance can be described as "a process whereby societies or organizations make their important decisions, determine whom they involve in the process and how they render account" (Graham and Wilson 2004, 2).

3 The quotation marks in this passage are duplicated from the original publication.

4 Person and People are capitalized in the original text.

5 For example, a collection of Cree legends says, "Generosity has always been a traditional value in our culture; it is interpreted as a gesture of love and respect" (Cuthand, Deiter-McArthur, and Federation of Saskatchewan Indian Nations 1987).

6 It is important to note that Chief kah-payuk-wah-skoonum invited Welsh's team to participate and share in the resource, and that it was not expected or taken without consent. Also, often Métis and Cree people share kinship relations.

7 These customary practices are common in other Indigenous societies as well; there are current examples of governance norms around berry harvesting among the Gwich'in (Parlee, Berkes, and Teetł'it Gwich'in Renewable Resources Council 2006).

NOTES TO PAGES 122–62 227

8 Dorothy Myo, leader of the Saskatchewan Indian Cultural Centre, writes that the Plains Indigenous world view "embodies a kinship relationship with all of creation and Mother Earth" (McAdam 2009, xi).

9 This is from the word nâcinêhikêw ᐊᒋᓀᐦᐃᑫᐤ; Arok Wolvengrey's (2011) definition is "s/he gets spiritual help, assistance or counselling (from s.o. [someone]) by offering appropriate gifts or payment" (see also the *Online Cree Dictionary*, www.creedictionary.com/).

10 In his foundational text "The Gift," Marcel Mauss (1967) examines different societies' gifting practices. In terms of gifting, he writes, "In all these instances there is a series of rights and duties about consuming and repaying existing side by side with rights and duties about giving and receiving" (11).

Chapter 10: Renewed Relationships through Resurgent Practices

1 Edward Ahenakew (1995b) writes: "I remembered that in old days an encampment sometimes found itself suffering misfortune and bad luck. The best of the hunters could kill nothing, and the people starved ... Perhaps someone in the camp had offended him directly, or had angered a person in another camp who was under his protection; for [he] does not bring bad luck indiscriminately upon people, though he may turn even upon his favoured one should that person fail to carry out a promise made to him. There is always that element of human vindictiveness in him; and since he has control over game, it could be fool-hardy to anger him or to give offence to one he favoured."

2 "This ceremony was banished by the Indian agents as they felt the Indians were too poor to lose their valuables. They failed to understand that the bearer of gifts always received another gift of the same value. It was a re-distribution of goods" (Cuthand, Federation of Saskatchewan Indian Nations, and Deiter-McArthur 1987, 23).

3 In the ceremonial cycle of the Cree, specific ceremonies happen during each season with certain distinctions occurring even within a season – for example, with the mâhtâhito ᒫᐦᒑᐦᐃᐟ happening in the winter season while there is still snow on the ground.

4 See the Indian Claims Commission's "Primrose Lake Air Weapons Range Report II" (Bellegarde and Prentice 1995).

5 J. Johnston, Biro, and MacKendrick (2009, 513) write that "organic certification institutionalized what was originally intended, for many participants, to be an anti-institutional movement."

6 H. Friedland and I were academic leads on this project, with me holding and administering funds as principal investigator, with administrative support through the Faculty of Native Studies. The university team also included Renée Beausoleil and Tara Kappo. The community team included Ken McDonald (community coordinator); Elders Philomene Moberly, Adelaide McDonald, Mabel Wanyandie, Dorothy Karakuntie, and Russell Wanyandie; and helpers and knowledge holders Robert Wanyandie, Vicky Wanyandie, Yvonne MacPhee, Alice Moberly, Carol Wanyandie, and Danny McDonald. The Community Engagement, Research and Learning grant from the University of Alberta made

this project possible.

7 This project received course-based research ethics approval through our university.

8 Darcy Lindberg, "Brain Tanning and Shut Eye Dancing: Recognizing Legal Resources within Cree Ceremonies" (LAW 502 final paper, University of Victoria, 2016), 2.

9 Corntassel (2012, 98–99) writes:

> Everyday acts of resurgence aren't glamorous or expedient. It might involve a personal vow to only eat food that has been hunted, fished or grown by Indigenous peoples, and/or speaking one's language to family members or in social media groups, or even growing traditional foods in your own backyard... Overall, one sees that grassroots efforts like the ones referenced above don't rely heavily on rights as much as community responsibilities to protect traditional homelands and food systems... Through our everyday acts of resurgence, our ancestors along with future generations will recognize us as Indigenous to the land. And this is how our homelands will recognize us as being Indigenous to that place.

Chapter 11: Upholding Relations

1 I debated whether to share this painting and my beading as I am not (yet) a beader or a painter. Through an ethic of grounded practice and in humbleness, I chose to include it.

References

Abele, Francis. 2001. "Small Nations and Democracy's Prospects." *Inroads Journal* 10: 137–49.

Aboriginal Affairs and Northern Development Canada. 2012. "Results-Based Approach to Treaty and Self-Government Negotiations." Ottawa: AANDC, September 4.

Accessing Justice and Reconciliation Project. 2013a. "Cree Legal Synthesis: Examples of Some Legal Principles Applied to Harms and Conflicts between Individuals within a Group." http://indigenousbar.ca/indigenouslaw/wp-content/uploads/2012/12/Cree-Summary-of-Legal-Principles.pdf.

–. 2013b. "Cree Legal Summary." A Part of: Cree Legal Traditions Report. Community Partner: Aseniwuche Winewak Nation. https://www.indigenousbar.ca/indigenouslaw/wp-content/uploads/2017/10/cree_legal_summary.pdf.

Ahenakew, Beth, Sam Hardlotte, and Norma Jensen. 1973. *Cree Legends*. 2 volumes. Saskatoon, SK: Saskatchewan Indian Cultural College.

Ahenakew, Edward. 1995a. "Old Keyam." In *Voices of the Plains Cree*, edited by Ruth M. Buck, 53–104. Regina, SK: Canadian Plains Research Center, University of Regina.

–. 1995b. *Voices of the Plains Cree*. Edited by Ruth Matheson Buck. Regina, SK: Canadian Plains Research Center, University of Regina.

Alfred, Taiaiake. 2008. *Peace, Power, Righteousness: An Indigenous Manifesto*. 2nd ed. Toronto: Oxford University Press.

Alfred, Taiaiake, and Jeff Corntassel. 2005. "Being Indigenous: Resurgences against Contemporary Colonialism." *Government and Opposition* 40 (4): 597–614.

Alook, Angele, Nicole Hill, and Ian Hussey. 2017. "Seeking 'Good Jobs' in the Oil Patch: How Gender and Race Shape Experiences of Work in Alberta's Extractive Industries." *The Monitor* (November/December): 28–32. https://policyalternatives.ca/sites/default/files/uploads/publications/National%20Office/2017/10/CCPA%20Monitor%20Nov%20Dec%202017%20WEB.pdf.

Alook, Angele, Ian Hussey, and Nicole Hill. 2019. *Indigenous Gendered Experiences of Work in an Oil-Dependent Alberta Community*. Edmonton: Parkland Institute, University of Alberta.

Altamirano-Jiménez, Isabel. 2004. "North American First Peoples: Slipping Up into Market Citizenship?" *Citizenship Studies* 8 (4): 349–65.

–. 2009. "Neoliberal and Social Investment Re-Constructions of Women and Indigeneity." In *Women & Public Policy in Canada: Neo-Liberalism and After?* edited by Alexandra Dobrowolsky, 125–45. Don Mills, ON: Oxford University Press.

–. 2013. *Indigenous Encounters with Neoliberalism: Place, Women, and the Environment in Canada and Mexico*. Vancouver: UBC Press.

Amnesty International. 2004. "Stolen Sisters: A Human Rights Response to Discrimination and Violence against Indigenous Women in Canada." AMR 20/003/2004. London: Amnesty International. https://www.amnesty.ca/sites/amnesty/files/amr200032004enstolensisters.pdf.

–. 2016. "Out of Sight, Out of Mind: Gender, Indigenous Rights, and Energy Development in Northeast British Columbia." AMR 20/4872/2016. London: Amnesty International. https://www.amnesty.org/en/documents/amr20/4872/2016/en/.

Anderson, Kim. 2000. *A Recognition of Being: Reconstructing Native Womanhood*. Women's Issues Publishing Program. Toronto: Sumach Press.

Anderson, Kim, Maria Campbell, and Christi Belcourt, eds. 2018. *Keetsahnak: Our Missing and Murdered Indigenous Sisters*. Edmonton: University of Alberta Press.

Anderson, Robert Brent. 1998. "Economic Development among First Nations: A Contingency Perspective." PhD dissertation, University of Saskatchewan.

Atleo, Clifford. 2015. "Aboriginal Capitalism: Is Resistance Futile or Fertile?" *Journal of Aboriginal Economic Development* 9 (2): 41–51.

Bargh, Maria. 2007. *Resistance: An Indigenous Response to Neoliberalism*. Wellington, NZ: Huia.

Barkwell, Lawrence. 2018. "The Nehiyaw Pwat (Iron Alliance) Encounters with the Dakota." Winnipeg: Louis Riel Institute. http://www.metismuseum.ca/resource.php/149482.

Battiste, Marie. 2000. "Maintaining Aboriginal Identity, Language, and Culture in Modern Society." In *Reclaiming Indigenous Voice and Vision*, edited by Marie Battiste, 192–208. Vancouver: UBC Press.

BearPaw Media and Education. 2016. "Wahkohtowin: Cree Natural Law." Posted June 8, 2016. YouTube video, 23:47. https://www.youtube.com/watch?v=NTXMrn2BZBo.

Beavon, Daniel J.K., and Martin Cooke. 2003. "An Application of the United Nations Human Development Index to Registered Indians in Canada, 1996." In *Aboriginal Conditions: Research as a Foundation for Public Policy*, edited by Jerry P. White, Paul S. Maxim, and Dan Beavon, 201–21. Vancouver: UBC Press.

Belanger, Yale Deron. 2010. *Ways of Knowing: An Introduction to Native Studies in Canada*. Toronto: Nelson Education.

Belcourt, Christi. 2007. *Medicines to Help Us: Traditional Métis Plant Use*. Saskatoon, SK: Gabriel Dumont Institute.

–. 2012. "Christi Belcourt: This Painting Is a Mirror." Resilience, Mentoring Artists for Women's Art (MAWA). https://resilienceproject.ca/en/artists/christi-belcourt.

REFERENCES 231

Bellegarde, Daniel J., and P.E. James Prentice. 1995. "Primrose Lake Air Weapons Range Report II." Ottawa: Indian Claims Commission.

Bennett, Mark. 2005. "'Indigeneity' as Self-Determination." *Indigenous Law Journal* 4 (1): 71–115.

Boldt, Menno. 1993. *Surviving as Indians: The Challenge of Self-Government.* Toronto: University of Toronto Press.

Borrows, John. 2002. *Recovering Canada: The Resurgence of Indigenous Law.* Toronto: University of Toronto Press.

–. 2010. *Canada's Indigenous Constitution.* Toronto: University of Toronto Press.

Brass, Eleanor, and Henry Nanooch. 1978a. "May-May-Quay-She-Wuk." In *Medicine Boy and Other Cree Tales.* Calgary, AB: Glenbow Museum.

–. 1978b. "Musqua and the Greedy Ones." In *Medicine Boy and Other Cree Tales.* Calgary, AB: Glenbow Museum.

–. 1978c. "Saskatoons and the Serpent." In *Medicine Boy and Other Cree Tales.* Calgary, AB: Glenbow Museum.

Brodie, Janine. 2002. "Three Stories of Canadian Citizenship." In *Contesting Canadian Citizenship: Historical Readings,* edited by Robert Adamoski, Dorothy Chunn, and Robert Menzies, 43–66. Peterborough, ON: Broadview Press.

–. 2003. "On Being Canadian." In *Reinventing Canada: Politics of the 21st Century,* edited by Janine Brodie and Linda Trimble, 18–31. Toronto: Pearson Education Canada.

Brown, Ernest. 1927. "Aboriginal Transportation." Provincial Archives of Alberta, Edmonton, AB.

Bryan, Liz. 2005. *The Buffalo People.* Rev. and updated. Surrey, BC: Heritage House.

Brzozowski, Jodi-Anne, Andrea Taylor-Butts, and Sara Johnson. 2006. "Victimization and Offending among the Aboriginal Population in Canada." *Juristat* 26 (3). http://caid.ca/Juristat2006v26n3.pdf.

Buck, Wilfred. 2018. *Tipiskawi Kisik: Night Sky Stories.* Winnipeg: Manitoba First Nations Education Resource Centre.

Campbell, Maria. 2007. "We Need to Return to the Principles of Wahkotowin." *Eagle Feather News* (Saskatchewan). November.

–. 2017. "Keynote Address." Presented at the Reconciliation/Wahkohtowin Conference, Edmonton, AB.

Canada. 1996. *Report of the Royal Commission on Aboriginal Peoples.* 5 vols. Ottawa: The Commission.

–. 2009. "Federal Framework for Aboriginal Economic Development." Minister of Indian Affairs and Northern Development, Ottawa.

–. n.d. "The Government of Canada's Approach to Implementation of the Inherent Right and the Negotiation of Aboriginal Self-Government." Accessed March 4, 2014. https://www.rcaanc-cirnac.gc.ca/eng/1100100031843/1539869205136.

Cardinal, Clifford. 2014. "Cree Syllabics." Presented at the Nehiyaw (Cree) Language Lessons, Centre for Race Relations, Native Healing Centre, Edmonton, AB, March 24.

Cardinal, Harold. 2007. "Nation-Building as Process: Reflections of a Nehiyow (Cree)." In *Natives and Settlers Now and Then: Historical Issues and Current Perspectives on Treaties and Land Claims in Canada,* edited by Paul W. DePasquale, 65–77. Edmonton: University of Alberta Press.

Cardinal, Harold, and Walter Hildebrandt. 2000. *Treaty Elders of Saskatchewan: Our Dream Is That Our Peoples Will One Day Be Clearly Recognized as Nations.* Calgary, AB: University of Calgary Press.

Carter, Sarah. 1993. *Lost Harvests: Prairie Indian Reserve Farmers and Government Policy.* McGill-Queen's Native and Northern Series 3. Montreal/Kingston: McGill-Queen's University Press.

–. 1999. *Aboriginal People and Colonizers of Western Canada to 1900.* Toronto: University of Toronto Press.

Castro-Rea, Julián, and Isabel Altamirano-Jiménez. 2008. "North American First Peoples: Self-Determination or Economic Development?" In *Politics in North America: Redefining Continental Relations,* edited by Yasmeen Abu Laban, Radha Jhappan, and François Rocher, 349–65. Peterborough, ON: Broadview Press.

Chamberlin, Edward, and Peter Vale. 2010. "The Humanities in All of Us." *Mail and Guardian,* December 3, 2010. http://mg.co.za/article/2010-12-03-the-humanities-in-all-of-us.

Chartrand, Paul. 1999. "Aboriginal Peoples in Canada: Aspirations for Distributive Justice as Distinct Peoples. An Interview with Paul Chartrand." In *Indigenous Peoples' Rights in Australia, Canada and New Zealand,* edited by Paul Haveman, 88–107. Auckland, NZ: Oxford University Press.

Chief Red Pheasant. 1881. "Letter from Chief Red Pheasant to Dewdney, Indian Commissioner and Lieutenant-Governor for the North-West Territories, August 31, 1881." M-320-p.1187, Edgar Dewdney fonds, Glenbow Archives, Calgary, AB.

Chief Sweetgrass, Kihewin, The Little Hunter, and Kiskion. 1871. "Letter from the Cree Chiefs of the Plains, Saskatchewan, to His Excellency Governor Archibald, 13 April 1871." In *The Treaties of Canada with The Indians of Manitoba and the North-West Territories,* by Alexander Morris, chap. 9. Electronic Reprint. http://www.gutenberg.org/etext/7126.

Christie, W. 1875. "Letter from W. Christie, Treaty Commissioner (Treaties 4 and 6) Fort Garry to Mr. Hardisty, Edmonton, July 26, 1875." M-477- 678, Series 14-11, Richard C. Hardisty fonds, Glenbow Archives, Calgary, AB.

Connie. 2013. Interview by Shalene Jobin, June 24, 2013, AI transcript.

Cornell, Stephen, and Joseph P. Kalt. 2006. "Two Approaches to Economic Development on American Indian Reservations: One Works, the Other Doesn't." Joint Occasional Paper on Native Affairs No. 2005-02. Tucson, AZ, and Cambridge, MA: Udall Center for Studies in Public Policy and Harvard Project on American Indian Economic Development.

Corntassel, Jeff. 2012. "Re-Envisioning Resurgence: Indigenous Pathways to Decolonization and Sustainable Self-Determination." *Decolonization: Indigeneity, Education & Society* 1 (1): 86–101.

Corntassel, Jeff, and Richard C. Witmer. 2008. *Forced Federalism: Contemporary Challenges to Indigenous Nationhood.* Norman: University of Oklahoma Press.

Coulthard, Glen. 2007. "Subjects of Empire: Indigenous Peoples and the 'Politics of Recognition' in Canada." *Contemporary Political Theory* 6 (4): 437–60.

–. 2014a. *Red Skin, White Masks: Rejecting the Colonial Politics of Recognition.* Minneapolis: University of Minnesota Press.

–. 2014b. "Red Skin, White Masks." Keynote presentation at "Unsettling Conversations, Unmaking Racisms and Colonialisms: 14th Annual Critical Race and Anticolonial Studies Conference," Edmonton, AB, October 19.

Coutu, Phillip. 2004. *Castles to Forts: A True History of Edmonton*. Edmonton, AB: Thunderwoman Ethnographics.

Crane, Brian A., QC, Robert Mainville, and Martin W. Mason. 2008. *First Nations Governance Law*. Markham, ON: LexisNexis Butterworth's.

Crey, Karmen. n.d. "Enfranchisement." *Indigenous Foundations*. First Nations Studies Program, University of British Columbia. https://indigenousfoundations.arts.ubc.ca/enfranchisement/.

Cruikshank, Julie. 1998. *Social Life of Stories: Narrative and Knowledge in the Yukon Territory*. Vancouver: UBC Press.

Cuthand, Stan, Pat Deiter-McArthur, and Federation of Saskatchewan Indian Nations. 1987. "Mâtahitôwin (Gifts Exchanged Are a Blessing)." In *Dances of the Northern Plains*, 20–23. Saskatoon, SK: Saskatchewan Indian Cultural Centre.

Cuthand, Stan, Federation of Saskatchewan Indian Nations, and Pat Deiter-McArthur. 1987. *Dances of the Northern Plains*. Saskatoon, SK: Saskatchewan Indian Cultural Centre.

De Soto, Hernando. 2000. *The Mystery of Capital: Why Capitalism Triumphs in the West and Fails Everywhere Else*. New York: Basic Books.

Dickason, Olive Patricia. 2002. *Canada's First Nations: A History of Founding Peoples from Earliest Times*. Vol. 3. Don Mills, ON: Oxford University Press.

Dion, Joseph F. 1958. "History of Cree Indian 1958–69." M-4373, Joseph Dion fonds, Glenbow Archives, Calgary, AB.

–. 1996. *My Tribe the Crees*. Calgary, AB: Glenbow-Alberta Institute.

–. n.d. "Programme of Dances." Handwritten Scribbler. M-331-30, Joseph Dion fonds, Glenbow Archives, Calgary, AB.

Dora and Connie. 2013. Interview by Shalene Jobin, June 24, 2013, A1/B1 transcript.

Dowling, Christina. 2005. "The Applied Theory of First Nations Economic Development: A Critique." *Journal of Aboriginal Economic Development* 4 (2): 120–28.

Eckford, Clarice, and Jillian Wagg. 2014. "The Peace Project: Gender Based Analysis of Violence against Women and Girls in Fort St. John." Fort St. John, BC: Fort St. John Women's Resource Society. https://thepeaceprojectfsj.files.wordpress.com/2014/03/the_peace_project_gender_based_analysis_amended.pdf.

Encyclopedia Britannica. n.d.-a. "Cognitive Dissonance (Psychology)." Accessed March 7, 2014. http://www.britannica.com/EBchecked/topic/124498/cognitive-dissonance.

–. n.d.-b. "Mercantilism." Accessed March 2, 2020. https://www.britannica.com/topic/mercantilism.

Estes, Nick. 2017. "Fighting for Our Lives: #NoDAPL in Historical Context." *Wicazo Sa Review* 32 (2): 115–22.

–. 2019. *Our History Is the Future: Standing Rock versus the Dakota Access Pipeline, and the Long Tradition of Indigenous Resistance*. London: Verso.

Festinger, L. 1957. *A Theory of Cognitive Dissonance*. Stanford, CA: Stanford University Press.

–. 1962. "Cognitive Dissonance." *Scientific American* 207 (4): 93–107.

Fine Day. 1934. Fine Day #3 Interview by David Goodman Mandelbaum. TAPE NUMBER: IH-DM.87. http://ourspace.uregina.ca/bitstream/handle/10294/1769/IH-DM.42.pdf?sequence=1#page=1&zoom=auto,-74,798.

–. 1935a. FINE DAY #21 Interview by David Goodman Mandelbaum. TAPE NUMBER: IH-DM.64.

–. 1935b. Fine Day #31 Interview by David Goodman Mandelbaum. TAPE NUMBER: IH-DM.87. http://ourspace.uregina.ca/bitstream/handle/10294/1855/IH-DM.87.pdf?sequence=1.

–. 1973a. "Societies." In *My Cree People*, 32–35. Vol. 9. A Tribal Handbook. Calgary, AB: Good Medicine Books.

–. 1973b. "Tipis." In *My Cree People*, 52–57. Vol. 9. A Tribal Handbook. Calgary, AB: Good Medicine Books.

–. 1973c. "Dogs." In *My Cree People*, 5–7. Vol. 9. A Tribal Handbook. Calgary, AB: Good Medicine Books.

Finley-Brook, Mary. 2011. "Inter-Indigenous Development Aid: Markets, Corporations, and Biases." *Canadian Geographer* 55 (3): 334–53.

First Nations Development Institute. 2004. "Asset Building in Native Communities: An Asset Building Framework." Fredricksburg, VA: FNDI.

–. 2009. "Native American Asset Watch: Rethinking Asset-Building in Indian Country." Longmont, CO: FNDI.

–. 2013. "Reclaiming Native Food Systems, Part 1: Indigenous Knowledge and Innovation for Supporting Health and Food Sovereignty." Longmont, CO: FNDI.

Flanagan, Thomas. 2013. "Can Native Sovereignty Coexist with Canadian Sovereignty?" In *Crosscurrents: Contemporary Political Issues*, edited by Mark Charlton and Paul Barkers, 44–54. 7th ed. Toronto: Thomson/Nelson.

Florence. 2014. Interview by Shalene Jobin, January 7, 2014, L1 transcript.

"Flying Dust First Nation." n.d. Accessed July 31, 2014. http://www.flyingdust.net/lands.php.

Flying Dust First Nation and Dalhousie University. 2007. *Flying Dust First Nation Community Plan: Kopahawakenum Mamawicihitowin*. Halifax, NS: Cities and Environment Unit, Faculty of Architecture and Planning, Dalhousie University.

Friedland, Hadley. 2018. *The Wetiko Legal Principles: Cree and Anishinabek Responses to Violence and Victimization*. Toronto: University of Toronto Press.

Friedland, Hadley, and Val Napoleon. 2015. "Gathering the Threads: Developing a Methodology for Researching and Rebuilding Indigenous Legal Traditions." *Lakehead Law Journal* 1 (1): 16–44.

Fulcher, James. 2004. *Capitalism: A Very Short Introduction*. Oxford: Oxford University Press.

Gaudry, Adam. 2016. "Fantasies of Sovereignty: Deconstructing British and Canadian Claims to Ownership of the Historic North-West." *Native American and Indigenous Studies Journal* 3 (1): 46–74.

Ghostkeeper, Elmer. 2007. *Spirit Gifting: The Concept of Spiritual Exchange*. 2nd ed. Raymond, AB: Writing on Stone Press.

Gibson-Graham, J.K. 2006. *A Postcapitalist Politics*. Minneapolis: University of Minnesota Press.

Gillies, Carmen. 2021. "Curriculum Integration and the Forgotten Indigenous Students: Reflecting on Métis Teachers' Experience." *In Education* 26 (2): 3–23.

Goyette, Linda. 2004. *Edmonton in Our Own Words*. Edmonton: University of Alberta Press.

Graham, John, and Jake Wilson. 2004. "Aboriginal Governance in the Decade Ahead: Towards a New Agenda for Change." Ottawa: Institute on Governance. httpp://www.iog.ca/publications/tanaga_framework.pdf.

Green, Joyce. 2001. "Canaries in the Mines of Citizenship: Indian Women in Canada." *Canadian Journal of Political Science* 34: 715–38.

–. 2007. *Making Space for Indigenous Feminism*. Halifax, NS: Fernwood.

Haggarty, Liam. n.d. "Nehiyawak (Plains Cree) Leadership on the Plains." Our Legacy.Accessed August 17, 2014. http://scaa.sk.ca/ourlegacy/exhibit_nehiyawak_leadership.

Hall, Frank. 1969. "Carlton Trail – First Western Highway." *Manitoba Pageant* 14 (3). http://www.mhs.mb.ca/docs/pageant/14/carltontrail.shtml

Harvey, David. 2005. *A Brief History of Neoliberalism*. New York: Oxford University Press.

Helin, Calvin. 2006. *Dances with Dependency: Indigenous Success through Self-Reliance*. Vancouver: Orca Spirit.

Hildebrandt, Walter. 2008. *Views from Fort Battleford*. Electronic resource. Regina, SK: Canadian Plains Research Center, University of Regina Press.

Holm, Tom, J. Diane Pearson, and Ben Chavis. 2003. "Peoplehood: A Model for the Extension of Sovereignty in American Indian Studies." *WICAZO SA Review* 18 (1): 7–24.

Honor the Earth. n.d. *Sustainable Tribal Economies: A Guide to Restoring Energy and Food Sovereignty*. Minneapolis, MN: Honor the Earth.

Hutchison, Andrew, Lynne Johnston, and Jeff Breckon. 2010. "Using QSR-NVivo to Facilitate the Development of a Grounded Theory Project: An Account of a Worked Example." *International Journal of Social Research Methodology* 13 (4): 283–302.

Innes, Robert Alexander. 2013. *Elder Brother and the Law of the People: Contemporary Kinship and Cowessess First Nation*. Critical Studies in Native History. Winnipeg, MB: Canadian Electronic Library.

Innis, Harold Adams. 1999. *The Fur Trade in Canada: An Introduction to Canadian Economic History*. Toronto: University of Toronto Press.

International Work Group for Indigenous Affairs. 1997. *Honour Bound: Onion Lake and the Spirit of Treaty Six. The International Validity of Treaties with Indigenous Peoples*. IWGIA Document no. 84. Copenhagen: IWGIA.

Jackson, Robert J., and Doreen Jackson. 2006. *Politics in Canada: Culture, Institutions, Behaviour and Public Policy*. 6th ed. Toronto: Pearson Prentice Hall.

Jenson, Jane. 1999. "Understanding Politics: Concepts of Identity in Political Science." In *Canadian Politics*, edited by James Bickerton and Alain G. Gagnon, 3rd ed, 39–56. Peterborough, ON: University of Toronto Press, Higher Education Division.

Jenson, Jane, and Susan Phillips. 1996. "Regime Shift: New Citizenship Practices in Canada." *International Journal of Canadian Studies* 14: 111–35.

Jobin, Shalene. 2013. "Cree Peoplehood, International Trade, and Diplomacy." *Revue générale de droit* 43(2): 599–636. https://doi.org/10.7202/1023207ar.

–. 2016. "Double-Consciousness and Nehiyawak Cree Perspectives: Reclaiming Indigenous Women's Knowledge." In *Living on the Land: Indigenous Women's Understanding of Place*, edited by Nathalie Kermoal, Isabel Altamirano-Jiménez, 39–58. Edmonton, AB: Athabasca University Press.

–. 2020. "Market Citizenship and Indigeneity." In *Creating Indigenous Property: Power, Rights, and Relationships*, edited by Angela Cameron, Sari Graben, and Val Napoleon, 94–119. Toronto: ON: University of Toronto Press.

Jobin, Shalene, Hadley Friedland, Renée Beausoleil, and Tara Kappo. 2021. "Wahkohtowin: Philosophy, Process, and Pedagogy." *Canadian Legal Education Annual Review Journal* 8: 51–85.

Jobin, Shalene, and Avery Letendre. 2017. "Indigenous Scholar Summary Report." Prepared for the Government of Alberta. Edmonton: Indigenous Relations, Government of Alberta.

Johnston, Basil. 1995. *The Manitous: The Spiritual World of the Ojibway*. Saint Paul: Minnesota Historical Society Press.

Johnston, Josée, Andrew Biro, and Norah MacKendrick. 2009. "Lost in the Supermarket: The Corporate-Organic Foodscape and the Struggle for Food Democracy." *Antipode* 41 (3): 509–32. https://doi.org/10.1111/j.1467-8330.2009.00685.x.

kâ-kîsikâw-pîhtokêw (Coming Day). 1930. "The Bear-Woman." In *Sacred Stories of the Sweet Grass Cree*, edited by Leonard Bloomfield, 57–61. Ottawa: F.A. Acland.

Kaplan, William. 1992. "Who Belongs? Changing Concepts of Citizenship and Nationality." In *Belonging: The Meaning and Future of Canadian Citizenship*, edited by William Kaplan, 245–64. Montreal/Kingston: McGill-Queen's University Press.

Kappo, Tara Vanessa. 2021. "Mîkistahikâcimo (to Tell a Story through Beadwork)." MA thesis, University of Alberta. https://doi.org/10.7939/r3-h9ke-kw89.

Kovach, Margaret. 2005. "Emerging from the Margins: Indigenous Methodologies." In *Research as Resistance: Critical, Indigenous, and Anti-Oppressive Approaches*, edited by Leslie Brown and Susan Strega, 19–36. Toronto: Canadian Scholars' Press.

–. 2009. *Indigenous Methodologies: Characteristics, Conversations and Contexts*. Toronto: University of Toronto Press.

Knott, Helen. 2018. "Violence and Extraction: Stories from the Oil Fields." In *Keetsahnak: Our Missing and Murdered Indigenous Sisters*, edited by Kim Anderson, Maria Campbell, and Christi Belcourt, 147–59. Edmonton: University of Alberta Press.

Kuokkanen, Rauna. 2006. "Sámi Women, Autonomy, and Decolonization in the Age of Globalization." Keynote presentation at "Rethinking Nordic Colonialism: A Postcolonial Exhibition Project in Five Acts," Arctic Center, University of Lapland, Rovaniemi, June 17. http://www.rethinking-nordic-colonialism.org/files/pdf/ACT4/ESSAYS/Kuokkanen.pdf

–. 2007. "Gift." In *Reshaping the University: Responsibility, Indigenous Epistemes, and the Logic of the Gift*, 23–48. Vancouver: UBC Press.

–. 2008. "Globalization as Racialized, Sexualized Violence." *International Feminist Journal of Politics* 10 (2): 216–33.

–. 2011. "Indigenous Economies, Theories of Subsistence, and Women: Exploring the Social Economy Model for Indigenous Governance." *American Indian Quarterly* 35 (2): 215–40.

–. 2019. *Restructuring Relations: Indigenous Self-Determination, Governance and Gender.* New York: Oxford University Press.

Kymlicka, Will. 2014. "Citizenship, Communities, and Identity in Canada." In *Canadian Politics*, edited by James Bickerton and Alain G. Gagnon, 5th ed., 21–46. Toronto: University of Toronto Press, Higher Education Division.

LaBoucane-Benson, Patti. 2009. "Reconciliation, Repatriation and Reconnection: A Framework for Building Resilience in Canadian Indigenous Families." PhD dissertation, University of Alberta. http://www.collectionscanada.gc.ca/obj/thesescanada/vol2/AEU/TC-AEU-590.pdf.

LaBoucane-Benson, Patti, Ginger Gibson, Allen Benson, and Greg Miller. 2012. "Are We Seeking Pimatisiwin or Creating Pomewin? Implications for Water Policy." *International Indigenous Policy Journal* 3 (3): http://ir.lib.uwo.ca/iipj/vol3/iss3/10/.

Lacombe, Father Albert. 1876. "Letter from Father Albert Lacombe Suggesting New Law to Department of the Interior – Indian Affairs," March 9, 1876. RG 10, Volume 3627, File 6157, Ottawa: National Archives.

Ladner, Kiera. 2003a. "Governing within an Ecological Context: Creating an AlterNative Understanding of Blackfoot Governance." *Studies in Political Economy: A Socialist Review* 70: 125–52.

–. 2003b. "Treaty Federalism: An Indigenous Vision of Canadian Federalisms." In *New Trends in Canadian Federalism*, edited by François Rocher and Miriam Smith, 2nd ed., 167–94. Peterborough, ON: Broadview Press.

LaDuke, Winona. 1999. *All Our Relations: Native Struggles for Land and Life.* Cambridge, MA: South End Press.

Lakusta, Ernie. 2007. *The Intrepid Explorer: James Hector's Explorations in the Canadian Rockies.* Calgary: Fifth House.

Larocque, Emma. 2007. "Métis and Feminist: Ethical Reflections on Feminism, Human Rights and Decolonization." In *Making Space for Indigenous Feminism*, edited by Joyce Green, 53–71. Halifax: Fernwood.

Larner, Wendy. 2000. "Neo-Liberalism: Policy, Ideology, Governmentality." *Studies in Political Economy* 63 (Autumn): 5–25.

LeClaire, Nancy, and George Cardinal. 1998. *Alberta Elders' Cree Dictionary/alperta ohci kehtehayak nehiyaw otwestamâkewasinahikan.* Edmonton: University of Alberta Press.

Leitner, Helga, Jamie Peck, and Eric Sheppard. 2006. *Contesting Neoliberalism: Urban Frontiers.* New York: Guilford Press.

Levy, Bryan. 2011. "Community Proud of Gardening Success." *The Western Producer*, August 11. http://www.producer.com/2011/08/community-proud-of-gardening-success/.

Light, Douglas. 1987. *Footprints in the Dust.* North Battleford, SK: Turner-Warwick Publications.

Lindberg, Darcy. 2019. "Wahkotowin, Corporate Separateness and Potential Futures for Indigenous Laws." Series: Environmental Challenges on Indigenous Lands. Centre for International Governance Innovation. July 4, 2019. https://www.cigionline.org/articles/wahkotowin-corporate-separateness-and-potential-futures-indigenous-laws/.

Little Bear, Leroy. 2000. "Jagged Worldviews Colliding." In *Reclaiming Indigenous Voice and Vision*, edited by Marie Battiste, 77–85. Vancouver: UBC Press.

Lloyd, Christopher, and Jacob Metzer. 2012. "Settler Colonization and Societies in World History: Patterns and Concepts." In *Settler Economies in World History*, edited by Christopher Lloyd, Jacob Metzer, and Richard Sutch, 1–34. Global Economic History Series 9. Leiden: Brill.

MacInnes, T.R.L. 1946. "History of Indian Administration in Canada." *The Canadian Journal of Economics and Political Science/Revue canadienne d'économique et de science politique*, no. 3: 387. https://doi.org/10.2307/137292.

Makokis, Leona. 2001. "Teachings from Cree Elders: A Grounded Study of Indigenous Elders." EdD, University of San Diego.

–. 2009. *Leadership Teachings from Cree Elders: A Grounded Theory Study*. Cologne, Germany: Lambert Academic.

Mallery, Garrick. n.d. "Hand Talk: American Indian Sign." Accessed December 13, 2012. http://sunsite.utk.edu/pisl/site.html.

Mandelbaum, David Goodman. 2001. *The Plains Cree: An Ethnographic, Historical and Comparative Study*. Regina, SK: Canadian Plains Research Center.

Maskwacîs Dictionary of Cree Words/Nêhiyaw Pîkiskwêwinisa. 2009. Maskwacis, AB: Maskwachees Cultural College.

Mauss, Marcel. 1967. *The Gift: Forms and Functions of Exchange in Archaic Societies*. New York: W.W. Norton.

McAdam, Sylvia. 2009. *Cultural Teachings: First Nations Protocols and Methodologies*. Saskatoon, SK: Saskatchewan Indian Cultural Centre.

–. 2015. *Nationhood Interrupted: Revitalizing Nêhiyaw Legal Systems*. Saskatoon, SK: Purich Publishing.

McCullough, Alan. 2013. "Peyasiw-Awasis (Thunderchild)." *Dictionary of Canadian Biography*. University of Toronto/Université Laval. http://www.biographi.ca/en/bio/peyasiw_awasis_15E.html.

McLeod, Neal. 2000. "Plains Cree Identity: Borderlands, Ambiguous Genealogies and Narrative Irony." *Canadian Journal of Native Studies* 20 (2): 437–54.

–. 2007. *Cree Narrative Memory: From Treaties to Contemporary Times*. Saskatoon, SK: Purich.

Merasty, Susan, Gladys Cardinal, and Len Sawatsky. 2013. Interview by Shalene Jobin, August 27, 2013, N1 Transcript.

Miller, Robert L., and John D. Brewer. 2003. *The A-Z of Social Research: A Dictionary of Key Social Science Research Concepts*. London: Sage.

Milloy, John S. 1990. *The Plains Cree: Trade, Diplomacy and War, 1790 to 1870*. Winnipeg: University of Manitoba Press.

–. 2008. "Indian Act Colonialism: A Century of Dishonour, 1869–1969." Vancouver: National Centre for First Nations Governance.

Moore, John H. 1993. *The Political Economy of North American Indians*. Electronic resource. Norman: University of Oklahoma Press.

Morris, Alexander. 1875. "Government Letter from Alexander Morris, Lieutenant-Governor, to George McDougall, Methodist Minister, August 9, 1875." Series

1-a, M-729-2a, George and John McDougall Family fonds, Glenbow Archives, Calgary, AB.

—. 1880. *The Treaties of Canada with the Indians of Manitoba and the North-West Territories, Including the Negotiations on Which They Were Based, and Other Information Relating Thereto.* Toronto: Belfords. http://www.canadiana.org/ECO/mtq?doc=30387.

Napoleon, Val. 2009. "Ayook: Gitksan Legal Order, Law, and Legal Theory." PhD dissertation, University of Victoria.

Napoleon, Val, and Hadley Friedland. 2016. "An Inside Job: Engaging with Indigenous Legal Traditions through Stories." *McGill Law Journal* 61 (4): 725–54.

National Inquiry into Missing and Murdered Indigenous Women and Girls. 2019. *Reclaiming Power and Place: Final Report of the National Inquiry into Missing and Murdered Indigenous Women and Girls.* 2 volumes. https://www.mmiwg-ffada.ca/final-report/

Newhouse, David. 2004. "The Challenges of Aboriginal Economic Development in the Shadow of the Borg." *Journal of Aboriginal Economic Development* 4 (1): 34–42.

Newton, Brandi. 2017. "Saskatchewan River." *The Canadian Encyclopedia.* Historica Canada. Retrieved from https://www.thecanadianencyclopedia.ca/en/article/saskatchewan-river

Nichols, Robert. 2014. "Contract and Usurpation: Enfranchisement and Racial Governance in Settler-Colonial Contexts." In *Theorizing Native Studies*, edited by Audra Simpson and Andrea Smith, 99–121. Durham, NC: Duke University Press.

—. 2020. *Theft Is Property! Dispossession and Critical Theory.* Durham, NC: Duke University Press.

Okimāsis, Jean, and Arok Wolvengrey. 2008. "How to Spell It in Cree: The Standard Roman Orthography." Saskatoon, SK: Houghton Boston, *misāskwatōminihk.*

Paget, Amelia M. 2004. *The People of the Plains.* Regina, SK: Canadian Plains Research Center.

—. 2009. *The People of the Plains.* Charleston, SC: BiblioLife.

Parlee, Brenda, Fikret Berkes, and Teetl'it Gwich'in Renewable Resources Council. 2006. "Indigenous Knowledge of Ecological Variability and Commons Management: A Case Study on Berry Harvesting from Northern Canada." *Human Ecology* 34: 515–28.

Pasternak, Shiri, and Hayden King. 2019. "Land Back: A Yellowhead Institute Red Paper." Yellowhead Institute. http://redpaper.yellowheadinstitute.org.

Petrow, Erin. 2017. "Food Bank Receives Two Tonne Donation from Flying Dust First Nation." *Saskatoon Star Phoenix*, February 22. http://thestarphoenix.com/news/local-news/food-bank-receives-two-tonne-donation-from-flying-dust-first-nation.

Petty, Thomas. 1962. "Trails of Alberta." A Glenbow Foundation Project. Trails of the Prairie Provinces Research Project Collection. Glenbow Archives, Calgary, AB.

"Plains Cree Elders Quotes," n.d. Saskatchewan Indian Cultural College. Accessed May 4, 2014. http://www.sicc.sk.ca/plains-cree-elders-quotes.html.

Price, Richard, ed. 1987. *The Spirit of the Alberta Indian Treaties.* 2nd ed. Edmonton: University of Alberta Press.

Quenneville, Guy. 2018. "What Happened on Gerald Stanley's Farm the Day Colten Boushie Was Shot, as Told by Witnesses." *CBC News*, February 12.

Reeves, Brian. 1990. "How Old Is the Old North Trail?" *Archaeology in Montana* 31 (2): 1–18.

Rob. 2013. Interview by Shalene Jobin, August 26, 2013, F1 transcript.

Russell, Ralph Clifford. 1840. "Dr. Russell's Carlton Trail, Handwritten Notes." Saskatchewan Archives Board.

–. 1955. "Dr. Russell's Historical Notes, Typed Notes." Saskatchewan Archives Board.

Saskatchewan Archives Board. 1890. *Cree Boatmen on a Cree Flat Boat on the Montreal River, Saskatchewan.* Photo. 26030, S-B2869, Saskatchewan Archives Board Photo Collection. Saskatchewan Archives Board.

Saskatchewan Indian Cultural Centre. 2011. *Saskatchewan Indian Cultural Centre Cultural Awareness Training Handbook.* Saskatoon, SK: SICC.

Saskatchewan Indian Cultural College. 1976. *Treaty Six: "... for as Long as the Sun Shines, the Grass Grows, and the Rivers Flow ... ; Saskatchewan and Alberta, 100 Years, 1876–1976.* Saskatoon, SK: Saskatchewan Indian Cultural College.

Savigny, Heather. 2007. "Citizenship." In *Encyclopedia of Governance*, edited by Mark Bevir, 81–83. Thousand Oaks, CA: Sage.

Schild, Veronica. 2000. "Neo-Liberalism's New Gendered Market Citizens: The Civilizing Dimension of Social Programmes in Chile." *Citizenship Studies* 4 (3): 275–305.

Scott, Major General Hugh. 1930. "Indian Sign Language Council of 1930 – YouTube." http://www.youtube.com/watch?v=bfT2a5SGDFA&feature=player_detailpage.

Settee, Priscilla. 2011. "Indigenous Perspectives on Building the Social Economy of Saskatchewan." In *New Directions in Saskatchewan Public Policy*, edited by David P. McGrane, 73–90. Regina, SK: Canadian Plains Research Center Press.

Shiva, Vandana. 2005. *Earth Democracy: Justice, Sustainability, and Peace.* Cambridge, MA: South End.

Sikka, Anette. 2009. "Addressing the Trafficking of Aboriginal Girls: Child Welfare and Criminal Justice Responsibilities." Policy Brief. Aboriginal Policy Research Series. Institute on Governance.

Simon, Steve. 1995. *Healing Waters: The Pilgrimage to Lac Ste. Anne.* Edmonton: University of Alberta Press.

Simpson, Audra. 2014. *Mohawk Interruptus: Political Life across the Borders of Settler States.* Durham, NC: Duke University Press.

Simpson, Audra, and Dale A. Turner. 2008. "Indigenous Leadership in a Flat World." Vancouver: National Centre for First Nations Governance.

Slattery, Brian. 2015. "The Royal Proclamation of 1763 and the Aboriginal Constitution." In *Keeping Promises: The Royal Proclamation of 1763, Aboriginal Rights, and Treaties in Canada*, edited by Terry Fenge and Jim Aldridge, 14–32. Montreal/Kingston: McGill-Queen's University Press.

Slowey, Gabrielle A. 2008. *Navigating Neoliberalism: Self-Determination and the Mikisew Cree First Nation.* Vancouver: UBC Press.

Smallboy, Bob. 2012. "A Treaty Six Workshop." Day of teachings presented at the University of Alberta, March 31.

Smith, Linda Tuhiwai. 2005. "On Tricky Ground: Researching the Native in the Age of Uncertainty." In *The SAGE Handbook of Qualitative Research*, edited by Norman K. Denzin and Yvonna S. Lincoln, 3rd ed., 85–107. Thousand Oaks, CA: Sage.

Smith, Nicola. 2007. "Neoliberalism." In *Encyclopedia of Governance*, edited by Mark Bevir, 597–98. Thousand Oaks, CA: Sage.

Soagie, Joan. n.d. "Mistaseni Rock." Accessed December 13, 2012. http://www.virtualsk.com/current_issue/mistaseni.html.

Starblanket, Gina, and Dallas Hunt. 2020. *Storying Violence: Unravelling Colonial Narratives in the Stanley Trial*. Winnipeg: ARP Books.

Stasiulis, Daiva, and Yasmeen Abu Laban. 2003. "Unequal Relations and the Struggle for Equality: Race and Ethnicity in Canadian Politics." In *Canadian Politics in the 21st Century*, edited by Michael Whittington and Glen Williams. Toronto: Nelson College Indigenous.

Sunney. 2014a. Interview by Shalene Jobin, January 30, 2014, K2 transcript.

—. 2014b. Interview by Shalene Jobin, March 9, 2014, K3 transcript.

Talbot, Robert J. 2009. *Negotiating the Numbered Treaties: An Intellectual and Political Biography of Alexander Morris*. Saskatoon, SK: Purich.

Thomas, Robert. 1990. "The Tap Roots of Peoplehood." In *Getting to the Heart of the Matter: Collected Letters and Papers*. Vancouver: Native Ministries Consortium. http://works.bepress.com/robert_thomas/50/.

Thomas, Robina. 2005. "Honouring the Oral Traditions of My Ancestors through Storytelling." In *Research as Resistance Critical, Indigenous and Anti-Oppressive Approaches*, edited by Leslie Allison Brown and Susan Strega, 237–54. Toronto: Canadian Scholars' Press.

Thompson, Christian. n.d. "Flying Dust First Nation." *The Encyclopedia of Saskatchewan*. Accessed August 2, 2014. http://esask.uregina.ca/entry/flying_dust_first_nation.html.

Tough, Frank. 1992. "Aboriginal Rights versus the Deed of Surrender: The Legal Rights of Native Peoples and Canada's Acquisition of the Hudson's Bay Company Territory." *Prairie Forum* 17 (2): 225–50.

—. 2005. "From the 'Original Affluent Society' to the 'Unjust Society': A Review Essay on Native Economic History in Canada." *Journal of Aboriginal Economic Development* 4 (2): 30–70.

—. 2018. "Financializing a Junk Charter? British Capital and the Survival of the Mercantilist." Presentation at Economic History Society Annual Conference, Keele University, Newcastle, UK, April. https://files.ehs.org.uk/wp-content/uploads/2020/11/29060838/ToughFullPaper.pdf

Trudeau, Pierre Elliott. 1994. "Values in a Just Society." In *Crosscurrents: Contemporary Political Issues*, edited by Mark Charlton and Paul Barker, 2nd ed., 84–90. Scarborough, ON: Nelson College Indigenous.

Truth and Reconciliation Commission. 2015. *The Final Report of the Truth and Reconciliation Commission of Canada*. Volume 5: *Canada's Residential Schools: The Legacy*. Montreal/Kingston: McGill-Queen's University Press, for the Truth and Reconciliation Commission.

Turner, Dale A. 2006. *This Is Not a Peace Pipe: Towards a Critical Indigenous Philosophy*. Toronto: University of Toronto Press.

Vandall, Peter. 1987. "A Fast Learner." In *Wâskahikaniwiyiniw-âcimowina = Stories of the House People*, edited by Freda Ahenakew, 64–69. Winnipeg: University of Manitoba Press.

Venne, Sharon. 1998. "Understanding Treaty 6: An Indigenous Perspective." In *Aboriginal and Treaty Rights in Canada: Essays on Law, Equality, and Respect for Difference*, edited by Michael Asch, 173–207. Vancouver: UBC Press.

Ventura, Patricia. 2012. *Neoliberal Culture: Living with American Neoliberalism*. Farnham, UK: Ashgate Publishing.

Wallace, Anthony. 1970. *Culture and Personality*. 2nd ed. New York: Random House.

Walter. 2014a. Interview by Shalene Jobin, February 10, 2014, M1 transcript.

–. 2014b. Interview by Shalene Jobin, February 11, 2014, M2 transcript.

Welch, Stephen. 2013. *The Theory of Political Culture*. Oxford: Oxford University Press.

Welsh, Norbert, as told to Mary Weekes. 1994. *The Last Buffalo Hunter*. Saskatoon, SK: Fifth House.

Wolfe, Patrick. 1999. *Settler Colonialism and the Transformation of Anthropology: The Politics and Poetics of an Ethnographic Event*. Writing Past Colonialism Series. London: Cassell.

Wolvengrey, Arok. 2011. *Cree: Words*. 2 vols. Bilingual edition. Regina, SK: University of Regina Press.

Wolvengrey, Arok, and Freda Ahenakew. 2013. *Nēhiyawēwin: Itwēwina/Cree: Words*. Regina, SK: University of Regina Press.

Women's Earth Alliance and the Native Youth Sexual Health Network. 2016. *Violence on the Land, Violence on Our Bodies: Building an Indigenous Response to Environmental Violence*. Berkeley, CA: Women's Earth Alliance/Toronto: Native Youth Sexual Health Network.

Woodruff, Christopher. 2001. "Review of de Soto's *The Mystery of Capital*." *Journal of Economic Literature* 39: 1215–23.

Wuttunee, Lillian. 1993. Interview by Loretta Jobin. Dictated by Lillian Wuttunee on February 27, 1993, to Loretta Jobin, Edmonton, Alberta.

Wuttunee, Wanda A. 2004. *Living Rhythms: Lessons in Aboriginal Economic Resilience and Vision*. Montreal/Kingston: McGill-Queen's University Press.

Wuttunee, Winston. 2003. Interview by Shalene Jobin.

Youngblood Henderson, James (Sákéj). 2000. "Postcolonial Ghost Dancing." In *Reclaiming Indigenous Voice and Vision*, edited by Marie Battiste, 77–85. Vancouver: UBC Press.

Index

Note: "(f)" after a page number indicates a figure.

Aboriginal. *See entries beginning with* Indigenous

Accessing Justice and Reconciliation Project (AJR), 117–18, 148, 159

agency, 73, 99, 103, 129, 131, 138, 151, 157, 194, 206, 210; collective, 181; of Indigenous women, 103; natural, 153

agriculture, 75, 77–79, 99, 189–90, 198

Ahenakew, Edward, 116, 121, 147, 157–59, 228n1

Ahenakew, Freda, 155

Alberta, 8–9, 12, 23, 49, 94, 99, 141, 143, 213, 222n4, 228n6

all my relations, 39, 42, 105, 180

alliances, 44, 50–51, 223n3; formal, 50; military, 10

Alook, Angele, 105

Altamirano-Jiménez, Isabel, 37, 64, 87, 221n3

Amnesty International, 102, 104, 105

ancestors, 49, 59, 93, 189, 229n9

Anderson, Kim, 105, 225n5

Anderson, Robert, 34

animacy, 44, 84

Anishinaabe (people), 11, 125

Arapaho, 51

archaeology, 52–53, 55

Archibald, Adams George, 62, 68

archival research, 19, 51, 63, 178; documents, 73; sources, 62, 133

archives, 27, 108, 226n1

Arrow Top (Cree man), 54

Aseniwiche Winewak Nation (AWN), 16, 201

Assiniboine (people), 10, 50–51, 56, 223n3

autonomy, 35, 65, 87; economic, 81

avoidance, 118, 149

balance, 31, 34, 39, 81, 90, 92, 127, 131, 145–46; ecological, 30; economic, 106

bands, 47, 49, 57, 75, 101, 117, 122, 162, 170

Bargh, Maria, 36, 91

Battiste, Marie, 138

Battle River, 9, 108

Battleford, 22–23; Industrial School, 22

beading, 16–17, 152, 192, 229n1

Bear, Tracy, 42, 107

Beausoleil, Renée, 221n4, 228n6

Beauval Residential School, 188

244

Beaver Hills (or Mountain) House (Edmonton): 9(f), 164, 203, 214
Beaver Hills (West) Cree People: 8–9, 12, 47, 48(f), 58, 111, 114, 119, 170, 183, 186
behaviour, 95, 97, 100, 139–40, 142, 145, 154–55; criminal, 103; economic, 27
beings: human, 39–40, 133, 144, 167, 178, 199; living, 17–18, 40–43, 46, 83, 86, 88–89, 129, 134, 136, 171, 181; nonhuman, 5, 17, 20, 37–38, 84, 86, 109, 111, 114, 116, 122, 124–25, 141–42, 143, 145, 162, 198–99, 209–10; spirit, 17, 20, 114, 121–22, 124–25, 133, 136–37, 152, 209–10; spiritual, 43, 109, 118, 134, 157, 168
Belanger, Yale Deron, 30–31
Belcourt, Christi, 16, 21, 222n10
beliefs, 30, 33, 93, 96–97, 99, 101, 137, 144, 182, 192, 202
Bennett, Mark, 83
Bernie (interviewed by L. Makokis), 162, 181
berries, 4, 52, 116, 147–48, 156, 161, 163, 171, 191, 193; patches, 147, 161; picking, 116, 148, 163
Big Bear (Chief), 75–76, 224n3
Big River First Nation, 144
Big Rock, 49
Bill, Jacob, 86
birds, 42, 46, 60, 76, 212
bison, 49, 52, 57, 65, 67, 69–70, 74, 122, 126, 145, 223n8
Blackfoot (people), 51, 53–54, 68–69, 117
Blackfoot Tracks (Old North Trail), 53–54, 164–65
Blackguard (Cree messenger), 57, 122
blood quantum, 44, 50
bodies, 20, 63, 81, 89, 94–96, 98–101, 104–5, 127, 138–39, 170, 222n1; celestial, 113
Boldt, Menno, 33, 78
Bono (Paul Hewson), 150
Borrows, John, 11, 143–45, 173, 177
Boushie, Colten, 22, 39–40
Brertton, George, 42
Brings-Down-The-Sun (Cree spiritual leader), 53

Britain, 28, 98, 222n7
Brodie, Janine, 85
Buck, Wilfred, 13
buffalo, 28, 49, 57, 70, 121–23, 126–27, 134, 145–47, 159–61, 163, 223n8; hunt, 57, 122, 127, 146; meat, 131, 147; population, 146
Buffalo Bill (Samuel Cody), 147
Buffalo Mountain, 182, 211
Bush Cree, 45

Calling Badger, 45
Calmwind, Laura, 41, 168
camp, 10, 47, 48(f), 94, 126, 148, 159–61, 165–66, 183–84, 201, 224n3, 228n1
Campbell, Maria, 106, 210
Campiou, Fred, 144
Canada: Dominion of, 62, 67, 224n2; genesis story of, 63, 79; as settler state, 28
Canadian: economic development, 28, 33, 78; flag, 97–98; government, 19, 28–30, 88, 126; society, 40, 67, 212; state, 18–19, 28, 34, 37, 67, 77, 98, 103, 223n10; state policy, 78, 88, 189, 227n1
Canadians, 26, 62, 65, 203, 225n1
capitalism: 17–18, 28, 36, 38, 39, 81–82, 200, 203–4, 208, 213; birth of, 28, 36; and exploitation of Indigenous peoples and land, 27, 28–29, 38, 62–63, 66–67, 78, 81–82, 92; vs. Indigenous economic systems (subsistence/trade/communal), 25, 33, 66, 92, 193, 209; and neoliberalism, 30, 33–34; as tool for Indigenous self-determination, 34; white (wild rose as symbol of), 213
Cardinal, Clifford, 45
Cardinal, Douglas, 211
Cardinal, Gladys (FDFN, interviewee), 191, 193–94, 199, 204, 206, 210
Cardinal, Harold, 47, 86, 140, 155
Carlton Trail, 54
Carter, Sarah, 78, 99, 189
ceremonies: 14–15, 19, 46–48, 52–53, 56, 57, 72, 74, 91, 112–13, 122–25, 156–57, 164–66, 183–87, 208–10, 228n2, 228n3;

INDEX 245

ceremonial bundles, 129, 131; ceremonial cycles, 7, 26, 43–44, 46, 119–20, 182, 189, 207–9, 228n3; ceremonial practices, 52, 158, 191, 206, 208–9; Cree, 119–20; religious, 49; seasonal, 209; spiritual, 49, 73, 112, 145

Chamberlin, Edward, 11

Cheyennes, 54

Chō-ka-se (Nakoda man), 160

Christie, W.J., 68, 70–73

CIPE (critical Indigenous political economy), 19, 36, 38, 223n11

citizens, 34, 45, 50, 84–87, 189, 224n3; ideal, 34, 85; second class, 24, 84

citizenship, 19, 37, 43–44, 50, 82, 84–87, 224n3; Canadian, 84, 224n4; Cree, 82, 86, 89; differentiated, 85; Indigenous, 37, 85–86; market, 20, 82, 87–89, 92, 200; treaty, 224n4; understanding of, 85

civility, 160, 162, 164, 167, 192

codes, 12, 91, 140, 155–56; of behaviour, 139, 155

Cody, Samuel (Buffalo Bill), 147

colonialism, 20–22, 27, 29, 63, 98, 101–2, 106, 136, 138, 141–42, 208, 210; Anglo settler, 37–38; British settler, 64, 70, 98; Canadian, 40, 77, 98, 100, 101–2; capitalist, 25; colonial domination of Indigenous peoples, 27, 36, 82; logics of, 20, 27, 29, 33, 63, 82, 92, 199; policies of, 27, 140, 188; systems of, 49, 96. *See also* settler colonialism

colonialists/colonizers, 64, 97, 103, 136–37, 138, 144

colonization, 24, 36–37, 87, 91, 102–3, 109, 112, 140, 166

Coming Day (Plains Cree man), 160–61

commodity, 30, 85, 90–91, 103

communities: Cree, 91, 186, 201; engagement, 196; gardens, 190–91, 193–95, 198, 200; Indigenous, 7, 11, 13, 26, 29–30, 32, 34–36, 87, 90, 115, 118, 205, 208; life, 15, 28

Comprehensive Land Claim, 29

conflicts, 109, 117–18, 137, 142, 145, 148–49, 154, 181, 199, 223n9; economic, 33, 66

Connie (Beaver Hills Cree, interviewee), 119–20, 132, 145, 185–86, 206, 210, 227n15

conquest, 90, 102

contact, European, 53, 55, 57, 164, 189

control, bureaucratic, 20, 34, 64, 82, 199

Cornell, Stephen, 35

Corntassel, Jeff, 7

corporations, 29, 34, 62, 65, 68, 92, 99, 166, 196

Coulthard, Glen, 36, 200, 209

Coutu, Philip, 165

Cowessess First Nation, 223n3

creation, 31, 43, 49, 63, 106, 122, 152, 162, 170–71, 188, 192

Creator, 46, 48, 70, 73, 112, 119, 129, 137, 144, 146, 165, 168, 170–71; laws of, 111, 144

Creator's Lake (Lake of the Spirit), 13, 164

Cree: concepts, 51, 139–41, 155, 158, 201; economic relationships, 21, 109, 110(f), 208; economy, 88, 122, 139, 141, 193; epistemology, 88, 142; governance, 46, 209; identity, 20, 137, 168, 223n3; knowledge, 5, 21, 86, 207; knowledge holders, 6, 12, 14, 20–21, 108–9, 114, 136, 154–55, 178, 181, 183; language, 5, 7, 14, 43–44, 51, 69–70, 73, 84, 88, 99, 108, 215–20; law, 117, 145, 148, 201, 203; Nation, 69–70, 73, 75, 79; peoplehood, 19, 42, 45, 47–48, 58, 63, 73, 134, 189, 223; peoples, 44, 59, 64, 82, 130, 137, 205; personhood, 20, 83, 86, 137–38, 184, 189; perspectives, 86, 181; practices, 38, 110, 122, 209; principles, 15, 110, 118, 181, 204, 206; society, 15, 18, 44–45, 119, 122, 134, 141, 144, 148, 155–56, 181, 183–84; syllabics, xi(f), 44–45, 215–20; teachings, 70, 120, 143, 194, 196; warriors, 22, 149; world view, 85–87, 110–11, 113, 138

246 INDEX

Creeness, 39, 225*n*8
critical Indigenous political economy.
 See CIPE
Crown, British, 8, 65, 67–68, 73, 76,
 224*n*2
culture, 14–15, 35, 45, 64, 90, 97, 168,
 189, 203, 223*n*9, 227*n*5; political, 20,
 94, 96–99, 101
customs, 38, 45, 74, 83, 154
cycle, lunar, 13–14

Dakota (people), 52, 56, 125
dancers, 117, 149, 157
dances, 46, 106; Bear, 46; Bee, 47;
 Buffalo, 46, 52, 56, 125; Calumet, 46;
 Ghost, 46, 120; Giveaway, 57, 184;
 Horse, 46, 120; Rattlers,' 52; Round,
 120, 211–12; Skunk, 47; Sun, 47, 120–
 21, 157, 164; Tea, 46, 120; Thirst, 47
de Soto, Hernando, 34
decisions, economic, 17, 66
decolonization, 10–11, 105, 154, 181,
 207
Deer Lodge, 54
Dënesųłıné (people), 8
dependency, 31–32, 37, 66, 98, 200,
 222*n*7; economic, 99; financial, 34
development: industrial resource extraction, 188; people-centred, 35; programs,
 29, 82
Dewdney, Edgar, 79
Dickason, Olive, 55
Dion, Joseph, 45–47
diplomacy, 42, 50, 55–59
discourse, 20, 36, 39, 106; discriminatory,
 97; public, 100–3, 224*n*4
discrimination, 96, 99–102, 225*n*1; systemic gendered, 102
dispossession, 32, 37–38
dissonance, 136–37, 140, 150, 152–53,
 204–6; cognitive, 137–38, 141, 143, 150,
 152; colonial, 20–21, 135–38, 140–43,
 150–53, 181, 191, 199, 201, 204–6, 208–
 9, 213
diversity, 91, 122, 124, 165; cognitive, 141

doctrines, traditional First Nations, 15,
 139
Dora (Plains Cree knowledge holder,
 interviewee), 119–20, 132, 145, 185–87,
 204, 206, 210
dreams, 15, 41–42, 45, 59, 120–21, 156,
 158, 173; guidance, 121
duties, 23, 47, 57, 67, 77, 106, 122,
 228*n*10; reciprocal, 140

Eagle Hills, 9, 22, 24
economic development, 6, 18, 26, 28–30,
 34–35, 38, 81, 87; discourse of, 35; initiatives, 26, 30; literature, 35
economic functions, 39, 105, 122, 171,
 183, 208
economic model: liberal, 86; livelihood,
 15–18, 16(f), 86, 109, 206(f)
economic relationships, 12, 15, 17–18,
 20–21, 25–27, 108–10, 113, 134–35, 145,
 147, 154–55, 181–82, 204, 207–9, 227*n*1;
 accepted, 149; appropriate, 149; contemporary, 109; good, 152
economies: Indigenous, 17–18, 29, 31–32,
 35, 64, 67, 200, 226*n*3; living, 18, 21;
 neoliberal, 81–82; settler, 32, 64, 181
economy, 24, 26, 28, 31–33, 35, 37, 39, 64,
 94, 103, 105–6, 163, 182; market, 64,
 199; nature's, 18, 39, 109, 226*n*2;
 regional, 52, 98; social, 15, 39, 105;
 sustenance, 39, 109, 226*n*2
Edmonton (Beaver Hills or Mountain
 House), 9, 49, 52–54, 129, 164–65, 203
education, 43, 76, 200
Elders, 11–12, 14–16, 51, 83, 86, 132, 139–
 41, 144–45, 169, 171–72, 185–86, 188–
 89, 191–92, 196–98, 201–2, 210; Cree,
 13, 18, 64, 69–70, 76, 83, 114–15, 140,
 142, 144, 162, 167
Elk Tongue (Cree man), 54
emotions, 89, 107, 139, 151
enfranchisement, 77, 222*n*3, 224*n*4
environment, 26, 28, 42, 49, 64, 83, 87,
 99, 102, 142–44, 146, 193–94; degradation of, 35

INDEX 247

Ê-pay-as (Cree man), 117–18, 226n9
epistemologies, 6, 207, 221n4
Estes, Nick, 37
ethics, 14, 92, 229n1; general, 13; self-reflective, 14
eulachon (candlefish), 55, 127
Europeans, 66, 70, 142, 165; settlement of, 51–52, 69, 83, 127; traders, 33, 65
Eustergerling, Amy, 4
exclusion, 82, 84, 106
exploitation, 18–20, 29, 63, 66, 79, 95–96, 98–100, 102–4, 139, 205; capitalist, 20, 27–28; economic, 18–21, 25–30, 33, 38, 62–66, 68, 78, 81–82, 92, 98, 137, 181–82, 199, 205, 207–8; of Indigenous lands, 63, 99; of Indigenous peoples, 24, 63, 66, 79; of Indigenous women, 104; of lands and bodies, 20, 95, 99, 101; settler, 21, 92; sexual, 101; and women, 20, 96
exports, 33, 52, 222n7
extraction, 32, 104; industry, 104, 141, 143

famine, 70, 75–76, 146, 190
FDFN (Flying Dust First Nation), 187–90, 190(f), 193, 195–96, 198–200
feast, 45, 123, 130–31, 153, 164, 186; memorial, 123; Smoke, 46
Federal Framework for Aboriginal Economic Development, 87, 225n5
Federation of Sovereign Indigenous Nations (FSIN), 14, 188, 222n9
Fine Day (Plains Cree leader), 44–45, 47, 130, 134, 149–50, 159, 163, 170, 223n6
Finley-Brook, Mary, 222n5
First Nations, 8, 10, 28–29, 34, 44, 47, 77–78, 83, 85, 88, 137, 186, 188, 195, 223n3, 224n3
First Nations Development Institute (FNDI), 32, 196
fish/fishing, 29, 46, 52, 55, 76, 94, 128, 145, 181, 196
Flanagan, Tom, 33
Florence (River Cree, interviewee), 174–77, 210

Florence (Saddle Lake Cree, interviewed by L. Makokis), 167, 181
Flying Dust First Nation. *See* FDFN
FNDI (First Nationals Development Institute), 32, 196
food: 52, 131, 172, 191–92, 194, 200; healthy, 189, 194; sovereignty, 15, 49, 189; systems, 25, 229n9
forests, 6, 53, 93, 108, 133, 210'
Fort Carlton, 54, 71, 75, 77
Fort de la Corne, 55
Fort Edmonton, 54
Fort Ellice, 54
Fort Garry, 68
Fort Pitt, 54, 71
Friedland, Hadley, 11, 81, 92, 154
Frog Lake uprising, 22
FSIN (Federation of Sovereign Indigenous Nations), 14, 188, 222n9

Gail (Elder, interviewee), 13–14, 130, 210
gardens, 189, 191–200
gas, 28–29, 32, 97–98, 100, 104, 131; industry, 97, 143, 225n5
Gaudry, Adam, 67
General Enfranchisement Act, 77
generosity, 75, 86, 111, 160–61, 173–74, 184, 227n5; acts of, 39, 175
George III (British monarch), 65
Ghostkeeper, Elmer, 17, 82, 88–91, 99, 193–94
gift paradigm, 38, 105
gift-giving, 57, 113–14, 115–16, 118, 123–25, 133, 167–68, 171–72, 173, 175–78, 184–86, 193, 198; practices, 123, 125, 198, 228n10; spirit, 88–89, 91, 99, 193
giveaway, 57, 109, 120, 122–24, 132, 134, 137, 183, 187, 198–99, 208; ceremony, 91, 110, 122, 124, 171, 178, 183–84, 209; harvest, 199; memorial, 123, 183; practice, 183–84; Round-Dance, 183
Glenbow Archives, 78
good life, 24, 40, 52, 59, 105–6, 111, 152, 155, 182, 204–5

good relationships, 18, 24, 26, 86, 111, 113, 116, 119–20, 126, 132, 137, 142–43

governance, 8, 10, 30, 33, 36, 43, 69, 109, 199, 201, 203, 205, 208; options, 19, 59; policy and practices, 199; principles, 149, 158, 200–1; systems, 8–9, 79, 136

government, 23, 50, 70–71, 74–75, 77, 97, 100, 224n3; federal, 29, 87, 188; settler, 19, 32, 137, 190

Great Dogs (ceremony), 47

Great Spirit, 47, 50, 71, 89, 99

Greyeyes, Connie, 100, 104

Hardisty, Richard, 70

harmony, 10, 111, 139, 142, 167

Harvard Project on American Indian Economic Development, 35

harvesting, 5, 29, 89, 161, 163, 166–67, 188, 192–93, 195, 198, 200; collective, 161; techniques, 193

Haudenosaunee, 10, 112–13

HBC (Hudson's Bay Company), 19, 29, 55, 62, 65–68, 70, 71, 98, 147, 224n2

healing, 40, 149, 164, 168, 191, 201, 214

hegemony, 36, 43, 81, 213

Helin, Calvin, 34

Henderson, James (Sákéj) Youngblood, 138, 224n4

herbs, 4, 133, 165, 191, 195

Hewson, Paul (Bono), 150

hides, 121, 131, 134, 146–47, 163, 192–93, 201–3; home-tanned, 16; tanning, 193, 201, 203

Hildebrandt, Walter, 33, 86, 140, 155

history, 3, 6, 10, 49–50, 98, 100, 103–4, 140–41, 181, 187, 189; collective, 66; colonial, 82; economic, 33, 66, 98; of Indigenous economies, 31–32; living, 7, 18, 43–46, 48, 182, 189, 207–9; oral, 5, 10, 14, 19–20, 27, 109, 133, 155, 178, 223n4; sacred, 45–46

Holm, Tom, 45

homesteading, 23–24

Horse Wars, 51

horses, 52, 55, 57, 75, 78, 117–18, 125–26, 130, 150, 159–60, 184

House Cree, 8–9, 12, 47, 117, 128

Hudson's Bay Company. *See* HBC

Hunt, Dallas, 39–40, 222n1

hunting, 49, 75–76, 91, 145, 161, 172, 183–84, 198, 228n1

identity, 3, 5, 9, 19–20, 44, 82–85, 92, 101–2, 119, 193, 202–3; collective, 20; Indigenous notions of, 19, 82; personal, 137

ideologies, neoliberal, 35–36

immigrants, 24, 40, 138

imperialism, cognitive, 138

independence, 30, 139; economic, 26

Indian Act, 10, 28, 43, 77, 79, 85, 97, 101, 199, 208, 224n5, 224n6; pass system in, 78, 99

Indian Laws, 117, 159

Indian nationhood, nations, 73, 77

Indigeneity, 37, 81–84

Indigenous Law Research Unit, 117, 226n8

Indigenous peoples, 10, 17–20, 24–28, 31–40, 43, 51–52, 63–69, 81–85, 87, 90–92, 97, 99–100, 105–6, 138, 141–42, 181–82, 196, 207–9; and Canada, 19, 33, 35–37, 63, 66, 79, 165, 222n6, 224n1; Plains, 56, 67, 70, 78, 125, 145, 160, 164, 189; removing, 33, 78; on Turtle Island, 136, 170

Indigenous Peoples' Global Consultation, 189

Indigenous perspectives, 11, 24, 77, 82, 99; on citizenship, 82

Indigenous political economy (IPE), 19, 30–31, 36, 38

Indigenous societies, 21, 27, 29, 32, 39, 65, 99, 105, 115, 205, 207–9; pre-contact, 30–31

Indigenous world view, 6, 10, 20, 24, 26, 38–40, 46, 88–92, 99, 105, 182

Innes, Robert, 10, 223n3

Innis, Harold, 28, 98

INDEX 249

interconnections, 7, 15, 17, 109, 207

interdependence, 149, 167, 180, 207

Inuit, 83, 222n4

IPE (Indigenous political economy), 19, 30–31, 36, 38

Iron Alliance/Iron Confederacy, 10, 51

Johnston, Basil, 80, 82, 92

Kahnawake, 112–13

Kalt, Joseph, 35

Kappo, Tara, 228n6

Karakuntie, Dorothy, 228n6

Kay, Julie, 101

Kechi Manitow (Great Spirit), 99. *See also* Great Spirit

King, Hayden, 38

kinship: 10, 43, 106, 214, 223n3; norms, 140–41; practices, 10, 208; relations, 165, 227n6, 227n8; structures, 45

Kit Foxes (ceremony), 47

Knott, Helen, 104

knowledge: ancient, 15; ceremonial, 12; holders/keepers, 5, 12–13, 40, 74, 100, 111, 167, 169, 207, 210, 222n2; Indigenous, 7, 35, 39, 61, 91, 106, 207; sharing, 129, 194; systems, 26

Konsmo, Erin Marie, 94, 95(f)

Kovach, Margaret, 86, 141

Kuokkanen, Rauna, 17, 36, 38–39, 102–3, 105

LaBoucane-Benson, Patti, 111, 141

labour, 30, 34, 66–67, 89; wage, 25

Lac Ste Anne, 164–65, 167

Lacombe, Albert, 70

Ladner, Kiera, 75

LaDuke, Winona, 145

land: communal, 76; Indigenous, 20, 27–29, 32, 39, 43, 63–65, 67–68, 94, 98–99, 104–5, 208; nurturing, 162, 181; reserve, 199, 223n10; stolen, 19

landscape, 5–6, 40, 145, 204, 209, 212, 227n1 (chap. 9)

language, 7, 11, 26–27, 43–44, 46, 48, 50, 57–58, 83–84, 86, 106, 207, 209;

English, 88, 178; hybrid, 57; Indigenous, 7, 43, 69, 86, 181, 208; sign, 57–58, 58(f); written, xi(f), 44

Larner, Wendy, 36

LaRocque, Emma, 105

laws: customary, 77, 97, 144; sacred, 143–44

LeClaire, Nancy, 111

legends, 12, 14, 59, 61, 108, 113–14, 133, 154, 157, 161–62, 226n6; Cree, 147, 161, 227n5

lessons, 46, 88, 124, 158, 162

Lightfoot, T.J., 104

Lindberg, Darcy, 145, 203

Little Bear, Leroy, 141, 154

livelihood, 15–16, 18, 49, 51, 69, 89, 109, 141, 146–47, 200, 204–5; economy, 152, 207; model, 16(f), 16–17, 206(f); practices, 188

Lloyd, Christopher, 64

lodges, 57, 74, 120, 125, 129, 158, 160; holders, 111, 140

logics, 20, 26–27, 30, 39–40, 63, 82, 87, 99–100, 199, 209, 222n1; of exploitation, 100; internal, 63; legal, 67; settler, 20, 26, 62–63, 81

Macdonald, Sir John A., 77

MacKendrick, Norah, 196, 228n5

MacPhee, Yvonne, 228n6

Makokis, Leona, 83, 114, 162, 167, 183

Mandan (people), 51, 56

Mandelbaum, David, 57, 170

Manitou Lake, 165–66

Manitou Stone, 146

Māori (people), 36–37

market, 30, 33, 37, 53, 66, 87; forces, 27, 92; interests, 20, 86–87

marketization, 34, 37, 87

Martin, Vera, 105

Marx, Karl, 36

Mauss, Marcel, 228n10

McAdam, Sylvia, 74, 106, 134, 144, 168, 180, 210

McClintock, Walter, 53

McDonald, Adelaide, 228n6

250 INDEX

McDonald, Danny, 228*n6*
McDonald, Ken, 228*n6*
McDougall, George, 71–72, 146
media, 94, 103; bias, 102; popular, 97
medicines, 4, 57, 61, 125, 129, 153, 156, 158, 164–65, 167, 170, 189, 191–92
Merasty, Susan, 189–94, 196–99, 204, 206, 210
methodologies, 6–8, 6(f), 10, 168, 170, 207, 221*n4*; resurgent, 7, 207–8
Métis (Metis), 10, 51, 57, 70, 83, 122, 163, 165, 222*n4*, 223*n3*, 225*n7*, 227*n6*
Meyer, David, 55
Milloy, John, 50
missing and murdered Indigenous women, girls, and Two-Spirit + persons (MMIWG+), 20, 100–4
Mis-ta-wa-sis (Chief), 73, 117–18
MMIWG+ (missing and murdered Indigenous women, girls, and Two-Spirit + persons), 20, 100–4
Moberly, Alice, 228*n6*
Moberly, Philomene, 228*n6*
Montana, 53, 58, 127, 146
Moore, John H., 33
Morris, Alexander, 69, 71–76, 72(f), 190
Mother Earth, 89, 93, 98–99, 130, 141, 165, 167–68, 170, 181, 192, 227*n8*
Murray, Anne Campbell, 163
Myo, Dorothy, 227*n8*

Nakoda (people), 8, 10, 50–51, 53, 160
Napoleon, Val, 11, 109, 154
narratives, 109, 116; old, 103; oral, 27; written, 125
nations, Indigenous, 29, 53, 65, 82–83, 88, 127
nation-states, 38, 43, 50, 56, 85, 227*n1* (chap. 9)
nature, 7, 31–32, 39, 45, 60, 119, 125, 136, 156–58, 163, 167; natural world 39, 61, 105, 144, 150
nehiyawak, 5, 7, 15, 17, 26–27, 80, 83, 86, 127, 134, 204, 206; governance, 74, 106; peoplehood methodology, 5, 7, 8(f), 108, 207

neoliberalism, 19–20, 30, 34, 36–37, 81, 87, 91, 196, 199; governmentality, 199–200; instruments of capitalism, 36, 90; trajectory, 37, 81, 87
networks, 31, 53, 55, 164, 204
New Zealand, 36, 63–64
Newhouse, David, 35
Nichols, Robert (Plains Cree, interviewee), 37, 133–34, 161–62, 210, 222*n3*
norms, 46, 56, 91, 140–43, 154, 159–62, 179, 198, 207
North Saskatchewan River, 3, 9, 165, 210, 214

Oakes, Gordon, 76
offerings, 167–68, 170, 179
oil, 28–29, 32, 55, 94, 97–98, 100, 104, 127, 143, 225*n5*
Old North Trail, 53–54, 164–65
Old Wuttunee (Chief), 224*n6*
One Arrow (Chief), 160
ontology, 6, 11, 109, 221*n5*; Indigenous, 27, 202
oolichan. *See* eulachon
oppression, political, 33, 66, 222*n6*, 224*n1*
orders, legal, 11, 63–64, 143, 154

Paget, Amelia McLean, 46, 163
Parklands Cree, 8–9, 12, 47
Pasternak, Shiri, 38
Paul (Elder, interviewee), 13, 130, 156, 210
Pemmican (Cree man), 54
peoplehood, 7, 20, 38, 43–44, 50, 137–39, 181–83, 207, 209; model, 7, 17
Peoplehood Matrix, 43, 50
personhood, 137, 139
perspectives, 21, 34, 39, 42, 73, 75, 84–85, 88, 133, 139, 141; collective, 159, 161; cultural, 88; interlocking, 5
philosophy, 10, 17, 44, 89, 154, 167, 174
pipe, 60–61, 72, 112–13, 119, 123, 158, 170–72, 183; carrier, 123; ceremony, 71, 73; stem, 71–72, 125
Plains Ojibway, 57, 125

INDEX   251

policies, 79, 85, 87, 97, 99, 101, 103, 136–37, 144, 188–89, 199; provincial, 38, 87; settler-colonial, 138, 223n3

political economy, 45, 50, 108–9, 200; Canadian, 98

porcupine quills, 131, 133

Poundmaker (Chief), 50, 116

poverty, 106, 141, 162

power, 29, 33, 37–38, 45, 93, 97, 129, 133, 152, 166, 172; political, 98–99; real, 33, 66

powwows, 120, 183

practice: economic, 15, 109–10, 122, 125, 134, 154, 182, 184, 200, 204, 208–9; grounded, 187, 207, 229n1; historical, 27, 124, 188, 198, 204; international trade, 51, 58–59; normative, 65, 154; political, 152, 209

Prairie Chicken Dance Society, 46–47

prayer, 71, 88–89, 113, 116, 119, 123–25, 129–30, 146, 152, 157–58, 165, 168, 170, 192–93

Primrose Lake Air Weapons range, 188

principles: economic, 109, 116, 122, 154, 204, 208; legal, 81, 149, 155, 227n2 (chap. 8)

production, 31, 36, 66, 89–90, 196; agricultural, 189; communal modes of, 33, 66; of goods, 39, 213; sustainable, 189, 200

profit, 28, 36, 67–68, 93, 100, 167

property, 38, 56, 63, 68

prophecies, 45, 145–46

protocol, 13, 56–58, 115, 116, 122–23, 125–26, 131, 167–69, 185, 187, 192, 198

racism, 20, 99, 102–3, 225n1; cultural, 138; in discourse, 104

Ramsey, David William, 225n4

Rattlers Society, 47

RCAP (Royal Commission on Aboriginal Peoples), 31–32, 34, 77

reciprocity, 12–13, 24, 39, 86, 105, 145, 162, 167, 176–79, 181, 186; principle of, 12, 149, 176, 184

reclamation, 5, 18, 38, 213–14, 225n5

Red Pheasant (Chief), 79, 224n6

Red Pheasant Cree First Nation, 3, 8, 22, 78

Red River, 54, 57, 68–69

reflexivity, collective, 82, 90, 92, 205–6

relationality, 17, 40, 42, 61; economic, 213–14

relations: economic, 6, 11, 18, 39, 106, 109, 122, 124–25, 184, 192, 204–5; non-human, 18, 162, 186, 201; social, 39, 81, 105, 109

relationships: active, 39, 105; animal, 145–46, 160; Cree, 79, 108–9, 122, 136; dissolving, 79, 136; enduring, 25, 182, 205; establishing, 124, 195; governing, 21, 26, 108–10, 136–37; Indigenous, 37, 83; ontological, 19, 43, 223n12; reciprocal, 5, 19, 82, 86, 89–90, 92, 109, 119, 170; renewed, 21, 188, 191, 194, 207; restoring, 109, 123–25, 134, 154, 187, 189, 198, 204, 206, 209; ruptured, 142, 199, 209; symbiotic, 49, 168; treaty, 69, 88

renewal, 46, 63, 187, 200, 201, 203, 208, 210; acts of, 40, 119; practices of, 47, 201

reserve, 4, 28, 34, 42, 74–76, 78, 190–91; boundaries, 79, 137; status, 188; system, 33, 78

resistance, 5, 10, 21, 26, 37–38, 151, 153, 191, 200, 203–4, 206, 209–10; acts of, 191, 209; creative, 204, 206; Indigenous, 26, 37; individual, 225n5; modes of, 210; practices of, 200, 204, 206

resource(s): development, 29, 87, 92, 225n5; extraction, 20, 25, 29, 34, 82, 96–99, 104–5, 143; extractive, 94–95; intellectual, 138, 207; natural, 32, 34–35, 64

responsibilities: collective, 39, 105, 149, 159; reciprocal, 49, 70, 85

restitution, 117–18, 149

restoration, 90, 122, 124, 142, 152, 184–86

resurgence, 5, 7, 21, 38, 183, 206–8, 229n9; acts of, 38, 204, 206; economic, 18–19, 59, 109; Indigenous, 7, 17, 203, 208

252   INDEX

revitalization, 26, 90, 92, 115, 155, 194, 198, 208

rhetoric, 37, 62, 87

Riel Rebellion, 128, 146

rights, 11, 37–38, 43, 73, 83–85, 93, 101, 150, 178, 224n4, 228n10, 229n9; Indigenous, 87–88, 96; private property, 34, 64

ritual, 61, 89

River Cree (people), 3, 8–9, 12, 47, 108, 115, 119, 130, 160, 174, 210

Riverside Market Garden, 193–94

Roan, Lazarus, 77

Rocky Mountains, 3, 50, 53–55, 201

Royal Alberta Museum, 146

Royal Commission on Aboriginal Peoples (RCAP), 31–32, 34, 77

Rupertsland, 224n2

ruptures, 136, 141, 152–53, 209

Saddle Lake, 127, 146, 167, 181

Saddle Lake Cree Nation, 114, 183

Saskatchewan, 3–4, 9, 12, 15, 22–23, 46, 49, 51, 55, 71, 74–75

Saskatchewan River, 54–55, 108

Saulteaux (people), 10, 51, 57, 125, 223n3

Sawatzsky, Len (interviewee), 195–98

schools, residential, 97, 137, 199, 225n1

self-determination, 5, 17–18, 21, 32, 34–35, 37, 43–44, 81, 83, 85, 87, 104–5, 109, 111, 204–5; act of, 28, 44, 189; economic, 25

self-government, 20, 27, 29–30, 34–35, 37, 81, 85, 87, 90, 199, 224n1, 225n6

Settee, Priscilla, 15, 106

settler colonialism, 25, 27–28, 33, 36–38, 40, 63–64, 66, 81, 84, 137–39, 181–82, 199, 208, 222n1; analysis of, 37; contexts, 17, 36, 43; logic, 28–29, 199; states, 28, 62, 152

settlers, 26, 31, 38–39, 54, 57, 64, 66, 70, 77–78, 189, 196; societies, 27, 82, 142, 205

Shaking Tent (ceremony), 46

Sharlene (knowledge holder, interviewee), 14, 130, 210

Shash-apew (Chief), 57, 65, 122–23

shells, 52, 127; abalone, 127; mussel, 52

Shiva, Vandana, 39

Shoal Lake, 54

Simpson, Audra, 83, 85

Sioux (people), 54

Skinny Man, 183–84

Skywoman (Cree knowledge keeper), 114, 167–68

Slattery, Brian, 65

Slowey, Gabrielle, 34

Smallboy, Bob, 42

sovereignty, 19, 65, 67, 76, 140

spirituality, 46, 49, 163

Spread Sitter, 122

St. Denis, Verna, 97

Stanley, Gerald, 22, 39–40

Starblanket (Chief), 57, 126

Starblanket, Gina, 39–40, 222n1

state: control, 37, 81; domination, 27, 63, 82, 92

Stoney (people), 52, 223n6

stories: archival, 20, 129; creation, 12, 144; Cree, 5, 12, 20, 167, 179, 181; Indigenous, 11, 27; oral, 14, 136, 152, 204, 206; sacred, 12, 108, 160

storytelling, 10–11, 19

Strike-Him-On-the-Back (Cree man), 45, 71

subsistence, 25, 31, 82, 106, 200; lifestyle, 25–26, 29–30, 67, 89, 194; practices, 67, 87, 92

Sunney (Beaver Hills Cree knowledge keeper, interviewee), 111–15, 124, 126–27, 129–31, 140–44, 146, 152–53, 156, 158–59, 162, 165, 167–69, 171–72, 179–80, 201, 210; teachings, 167, 169, 180

survival, economic, 16, 51, 88, 139

Sweetgrass (Chief), 62, 68–69

Sweetgrass First Nation, 46, 223n6

symbiosis, 112, 168, 179–81, 201

system: economic, 33, 39, 66, 90, 204; fur-trade, 33, 66–67; legal, 17, 148; pass, 78–79, 99, 136–37; settler road, 53, 164; trade, 50, 59

INDEX 253

tanning, 163–64; brain, 163, 201. *See also* hides

teaching wheel, 158–59

territory: Cree, 8, 48, 79, 137, 188; Indigenous, 6, 18, 28, 30, 34, 37, 43, 62, 87, 98, 105; settled, 63; traditional, 34, 63, 76; of Upstream People, 9(f)

theory, grounded, 11–12, 221n7, 226n3

Thomas, Robert, 17, 43, 45

Thunderbird, 157

Thunderchild (Chief), 117–18, 121–22, 134, 159–60, 226n9

TLE (Treaty Land Entitlement), 188, 199

tobacco, 57, 60, 89, 113–15, 123, 126, 130, 165–66, 168–72, 192, 198; giving, 115, 170; law of, 171–72

Tough, Frank, 33, 66–67, 222n6, 224n1, 224n2

trade, 29, 31, 42, 51–59, 68, 115, 124–34, 192, 194, 196, 204; fur, 19, 28–29, 31, 33, 53–55, 63–67, 79, 98, 126, 164, 222n7, 225n2; international, 19, 50–51, 56–58; languages, 50, 57–58, 131; networks, 50, 53, 55, 65, 127, 164; practices, 52, 65, 124–25, 193; protocol, 127, 132; relationships, 52, 126–27, 129, 131, 134

traders, 57, 122, 126, 130, 146–47; fur, 54, 57; non-Indigenous, 129

traditions, 20, 83, 166, 168, 171; legal, 11, 117–18, 148; oral, 6, 11, 26–27

trail systems, 51, 53–56, 116, 119, 127, 134, 164

treaties, 19, 31, 39, 50–51, 65, 67, 69–71, 74–75, 77, 79, 147; first, 42, 59, 79, 168; negotiations, 70–71, 73, 189

Treaty Land Entitlement (TLE), 188, 199

Treaty Six, 3, 8–9, 12, 18, 19, 28, 65, 69–71, 73, 75, 76, 79, 111, 119, 140, 190, 201, 210; Confederacy, 28; Elders, 88; and FDFN, 187–88; negotiations 8, 62, 76, 189, 224n3; and TLE, 188

Truth and Reconciliation Commission of Canada, 100, 225n1

Turner, Dale, 83

Turtle Island, 51, 53, 56, 65, 112, 113, 115, 127, 136, 164, 168, 170, 179

2SLGBTQQIA people, 20, 98

Two-Spirit + persons, 20, 98, 100, 103

United States, 35, 37, 63, 115, 128

Upper Canada, 70

Upper Fort Garry, 54

Upstream Cree, 8–9, 9(f), 12, 47, 108, 223n3

Vale, Peter, 11

values, 35, 37, 82, 88–89, 126, 129–31, 137–39, 153–54, 172, 178, 184; collective, 97; liberal-democratic, 85; traditional, 227n5

Vandall, Peter, 128–29

Venne, Sharon, 74, 224n3

victimization, 103, 151, 225n1

violence, 63, 95, 98–105; domestic, 20; gender-based, 101; settler, 39–40; sexual, 104

wâhkohtôwin, 17, 20–21, 26, 108–13, 131, 134, 136–37, 140–42, 152–54, 201, 204, 206, 209; norms, 43, 146–47; practices, 141; restoring, 21, 153

Wallace, Anthony, 90–91

Walter (River Cree Elder, interviewee), 86, 115–16, 118–21, 123–24, 127, 141–42, 153, 156–58, 162–63, 172–77, 210, 226n10

Wanyandie, Carol, 228n6

Wanyandie, Mabel, 228n6

Wanyandie, Robert, 228n6

Wanyandie, Russell, 228n6

Wanyandie, Vicky, 228n6

Wapiti Society, 46

warriors, 47, 150, 159–60; Dakota, 125; societies, 149, 159, 170

Waskahat, Peter, 86

wealth, 28, 31, 33, 66, 91, 93, 98, 123, 138, 184

weendigo, 80–81, 92–93; and economic exploitation, 92; modern, 93

254 INDEX

Welsh, Norbert, 57, 122–23, 126, 146, 160, 184, 227*n*13, 229*n*6
western Canada, 23, 50, 94, 96
Western economic practices, 17, 92
Western institutions, 87, 119
Western scientific knowledge, 91
wisdom, 26, 45–46, 108, 167–68, 178, 192
Wolf Tracks (Old North Trail), 53–54, 164–65
Wolfe, Patrick (63-64), 63
Wolvengrey, Arok, 155, 228*n*9
women: bodies, 20, 94, 96, 99; Cree, 4, 14, 106, 133–34, 200, 206; Indigenous, 20, 94, 96, 99–105, 134;
Woods Cree (people), 51
Wuttunee, Elsie (daughter of Lillian), 4
Wuttunee, Gavin (grand uncle of author), 25(f)
Wuttunee, Gilbert (grandfather of author), 3, 22–23, 25(f), 116
Wuttunee, James (great grandfather of author), 25(f)
Wuttunee, Lillian (grandmother of author), 3–5, 4(f), 16, 59, 61, 116
Wuttunee, Loretta (mother of author, daughter of Lillian), 4, 116
Wuttunee, Mary (daughter of Lillian), 4
Wuttunee, Wanda A. (niece of Lillian), 35
Wuttunee, Winston (uncle of author), 5, 86
Wuttunee, Yvonne (daughter of Lillian), 4